Electronic Funds Transfers and Payments: The Public Policy Issues

Electronic Funds Transfers and Payments: The Public Policy Issues

edited by

Elinor Harris Solomon
The George Washington University

Kluwer•Nijhoff Publishing
a member of the Kluwer Academic Publishers Group
Boston / Dordrecht / Lancaster

Distributors

for the United States and Canada: Kluwer Academic Publishers, 101 Philip Drive, Assinippi Park, Norwell, MA 02061, USA

for the UK and Ireland: Kluwer Academic Publishers, MTP Press Limited, Falcon House, Queen Square, Lancaster LA1 1RN, UK

for all other countries: Kluwer Academic Publishers Group, Distribution Centre, P.O. Box 322, 3300 AH Dordrecht, The Netherlands

Library of Congress Cataloging-in-Publication Data

Electronic funds transfers and payments
Includes bibliographies and index.
1. Electronic funds transfers. 2. Electronic funds transfers—Government policy. I. Solomon, Elinor Harris.
HG1710.E45 1986 332.1'028 86-10416
ISBN 0-89838-179-7

PRINTED IN THE UNITED STATES.

Contents

Contributing Authors

Allen B. Frankel,
Chief, International Banking Section,
Division of International Finance,
Board of Governors of the Federal Reserve System,
Washington, D.C. 20551

Henry Geller,
Director, Washington Center for Public Policy Research (Duke University),
1776 K Street, N.W. (Suite 900),
Washington, D.C. 20006

Thomas M. Havrilesky,
Professor of Economics, Duke University,
Department of Economics,
Durham, North Carolina 27706

Paul B. Henderson, Jr.,
Operations Consultant; Senior Vice President for Operations, Federal Reserve Bank of New York (1978–84),
Box 4589
525 Spencer Way
Incline Village
Nevada, 89450

David Burras Humphrey,
Vice President and Payments System Advisor,
Federal Reserve Bank of Richmond,
P.O. Box 27622,
Richmond, Virginia 23261

Jeffrey C. Marquardt,
Economist, Bank for International Settlements (Basle, Switzerland) and Division of International Finance;
Board of Governors of the Federal Reserve System,
Washington, D.C. 20551

Linda K. S. Moore,
Editor-in-Chief, Electronic Banking Abroad,
Research Company of America,
654 Madison Avenue,
New York, New York 10021

Almarin Phillips,
Hower Professor of Public Policy and Professor of Economics and Law,
University of Pennsylvania,
Philadelphia, Pennsylvania 19104

Elinor Harris Solomon,
Professor of Economics, The Department of Economics,
The George Washington University,
Washington, D.C. 20052

James Tobin,
Sterling Professor of Economics, Yale University,
P.O. Box 2125 Yale Station,
New Haven, Connecticut 06520-2125

Preface

The developing new financial technology is changing our concepts of money, banks, and the payments media. The 1980–1982 legislation enables financial institutions to take advantage of the electronic funds transfer (EFT) opportunities. Other legislation is being considered by Congress and the states. However, important public policy questions remain.

Their identification demands a multidisciplinary synthesis. This the book attempts to accomplish by drawing on unique skills of distinguished academic and Federal Reserve economists, lawyers, and other experts in the new financial technology. It is hoped that our combined efforts in the chapters that follow will help identify potential directions of change and illuminate some major public policy issues for further investigation and resolution.

The areas we explore from diverse backgrounds are fourfold. First, part I examines the updated character of money, the transformed processes of money transmission around the world. Part II looks at the evolving payments and settlement arrangements, both national and international, and the risks that are beginning to surface. Part III addresses the monetary policy issues and the kinds of rethinking which macroeconomic theory and modeling may require in this brave new world. Part IV, finally, analyzes the role of the market, deregulation, and antitrust policy in EFT development. Consumer issues and trade-offs come here also to the forefront.

How to use this book. We have attempted to provide coverage of many issues. We have also sought diversity of viewpoints and skills. This book is designed for use, therefore, by all practitioners of the new money technology, be they banks, financial institutions, nonbank suppliers, or legislators.

Emphasis is on international as well as national questions. We have also pitched the volume for researchers in the new money technology, the economists, lawyers, and operational engineers who can put their best skills to use jointly in developing practical solutions.

This book is planned for classroom use as well. In order to aid the professor, the introduction sets forth the format of the book and the recurrent themes one finds throughout the individual chapter discussions. It also presents questions toward which the individual chapters have been directed. In addition, each of the four parts is preceded by background discussion and integration of the individual papers.

Money and Banking students can most profitably study parts I and II for an updated view of money and payments mechanisms, now and future. Monetary Theory and Macroeconomics classes may focus on part III, then supplement the macro theory with earlier operational and descriptive portions of the book according to interest. Students of antitrust and industrial organization economics may find part IV useful for microeconomic and legal analysis. Consumer users and students of banking law should also start with part IV, then turn to the operational realities highlighted in earlier papers.

This volume is, however, not a textbook in any standard sense of the term. It is designed for all of us since all are users of the new payments technology and its elusive supermoney. Each part meshes with the chapters preceding and adds fuller coloration to the story. The book is designed to elicit discussion; research into new, uncharted areas; a rethinking of our traditional central banking concepts; and, yes, controversy.

Acknowledgments. I wish to express appreciation to the distinguished and dedicated contributors for their penetrating original analyses of the many complex issues. I also admire very much their courage in expressing openly their reservations as well as praise for the new technology. They have patiently and skillfully answered my many questions and provided, for me surely, an intellectually exciting and often consuming experience. I owe a debt of gratitude to Professors Robert Goldfarb, John Kwoka, Michael Bradley, Robert Dunn, James Barth, Lisa Pittman, and other Economics Department colleagues and students at The George Washington University. I wish also to thank Stephen Rhoades, Steven Felgran, Robert Gemmill, Penelope Hartland-Thunberg, Eleanor Hadley, Phillip Ruppell, Spencer Nilson, William Curran, and Federal Reserve Board Governor Henry Wallich for valuable suggestions and help. The vast expertise of the Electronic Banking Economist Society (THEBES) has been much appreciated. Catherine Forman has provided outstanding secretarial assistance in preparation of my portions of this volume. Zachary Rolnik and David Marshall have been supportive in every way in guiding this project to completion, and I am especially grateful for Kluwer-Nijhoff's strong encouragement and enthusiasm.

Finally, I thank my wonderful husband and family for moral and tangible support, criticisms, and comments. They, like my students, have been willing to listen patiently to the day-to-day rundown on an amazing story of technology change which promises to revolutionize money and payments modes throughout the world.

INTRODUCTION

The questions confronting policy makers grow broader, questions which this volume seeks to explore. For example, what is modern money going to look like in the years 1990–2000? What will be the features and characteristics of money in the new technology? How soon is electronics likely to become fully acceptable as a means of payment? Who—or what—will create money then, and make the transfer to payee? What direct or indirect role will the Federal Reserve System play in the creation, clearing, and control of this futuristic money?

The mode of money delivery, or clearing, is changing. The paths between transactions initiators and money recipients now can take many forms, old-fashioned paper delivery (checks), magnetic tape transfer of ownership, or on-line electronic delivery of money assets. What will be the considerations affecting transactions path selection and configurations? What factors affect the shifting mix from paper and tape to electronics by users at different stages of the delivery, clearing, and settlement process? Will the current trend toward deregulation, and more open use of the electronic networks, permit an efficient money deliveries path to develop throughout the payments system? What still needs to be done to achieve this optimal vision of the future?[1]

Part I., Money, Now and Future, begins to answer these questions. From a multidisciplinary vantage, the authors examine the critical questions of what money looks like these days, how we can recognize money when we see it. They describe the possible substitutes in future years for paper clearing and the old-style physical delivery of pieces of paper, money, or checks that one could touch or hold.

In chapter 1 the distinguished Dr. Paul Henderson, now in private practice but for many years Senior Vice President for Operations of the New York Federal Reserve Bank, provides an in-depth look at the new money. Money gradually is being transformed from a physical phenomenon that comes to rest at end of day into an ethereal nonphysical and computer-generated flow. Money components of that flow, which are acceptable as a medium of exchange, can be created and destroyed within a day or less. Henderson vividly portrays the new process, and the behavioral as well as economic factors altering future money makeup and use through the end of the century. He points up the policy-making errors that may result from continued perception of all money as an end-of-day measurable stock. Henderson compares the European giro (or credit-based system) and the United States paper clearing (or debit-based) system. He concludes that the more efficient credit-based clearing system will probably emerge eventually, although our present clearing mechanisms favor and subsidize the bank depositor.

In the new money mode, involving short-lived phantom electronic impulses, we see the gradual transformation of old-line clearing paths and choices. That change affects regulatory policy, user and vendor benefits, and the code of banking laws in rather dramatic ways. Even the terminology sounds different to our ears. Linda Moore, Editor, *Electronic Banking Abroad*, translates the old-style clearing concepts into technology-based payments deliveries concepts in chapter 2. Based on extensive experience as Special Assistant for Operations at the Federal Reserve Bank of New York, the author highlights the myriad new choices, and new problems. In the old prerevolution days payments users faced more limited choices. They had to decide whether to clear through the Fed banks, their correspondent banks (which probably also cleared through the Fed), or private clearing houses. Now the decisions are far more complex. Money can be "zapped" either directly or in circuitous routes from payor to payee, or money recipient.

Moore looks in-depth at all the many trade-offs users face in making up their minds about whether to go for the new or stick with the old paper clearing mode. Indeed, for some purposes, a blend (or "discontinuous transactions" system) may work out best. Moore's innovative decision-making model provides almost unlimited user possibilities. Moore also highlights, as does Henderson, the bank and nonbank vendor and user's benefits, constraints, and social policy questions. She shows that banks have wonderful new opportunities but also potential problems wherever wholesale financial activities are met on both ends by computer networks. Given a nonhuman computer interface, consumers too face new varieties of error or fraud unless the legal or regulatory rules of the game are altered in such a way as to reflect the new way in which the business of payments delivery is in reality conducted.

Henry Geller's imaginative legal and social analysis of the telecommunications links is presented in chapter 3. Now Director of Duke University's Washington Center, Geller's expert knowledge of the new money delivery potential also reflects his experience as General Counsel of the Federal Communications Commission and Assistant Secretary for Telecommunications (U.S. Department of Commerce). Geller focuses specifically on the critical telecommunications links between vendors and users, the way the new technology supplants the physical clearing of pieces of paper through trucks or planes. He provides insights into the market opportunities for nonbank vendors, and interprets the regulatory process. For example, Geller discusses what the Federal Communications Commission (FCC), which regulates telecommunications, and the Justice Department's Antitrust Division, which safeguards competition, can do and have done to keep the money transmission paths both open and optimal.

Geller looks at new delivery modes involving small-user earth stations and satellite, then relates the role of international institutions such as INTELSAT and EUROSAT. Their cooperation facilitates money and information deliveries worldwide and helps link up national money delivery systems. Geller also highlights the policy issues including some potential conflicts of interest between international and private vendors selling essentially the same services worldwide.

Part II., Electronic Payments Systems Links and Risks, describes the United States institutional payments framework and international linkages. The new payments patterns, including high-speed money flows, bring to center stage the central bank's historical role as settlement agent and lender of last resort. Major systemic risk questions also surface. Given the system's sharply rising money transactions gross, relative to backup settlement reserves, one bank's failure to meet its payment obligations can spread rapidly throughout the private wire system. Dr. David B. Humphrey, now Vice President and Payments System Advisor of the Federal Reserve Bank of Richmond, in chapter 4 analyzes both the issues and the feasible solutions. Humphrey also provides a lucid background explanation of the new wholesale payments modes and their interrelationships.

The within-day process of money creation and destruction, described earlier by Henderson, is fueled by very short-term financial system loans, given electronic transactions speeds. Some of these loans are contractual—

for example, based on takedowns from lender lines of credit—while others are system generated (daylight credits and overdrafts). Under present payments codes, the Fed must provide immediate and final ("good") funds to the payee when the payor transmits payment over Fedwire. However, Fed regulations do not require that payor funds be available for Federal Reserve account deduction until end of day. Hence the Fedwire procedures permit the creation of "daylight credits," prior to end-of-day debits from the payor's reserve account. Similarly, the private CHIPS wire provides the payor bank with interbank "daylight overdrafts," available for brief use prior to end-of-day CHIPS system "net net settlement" in Fed funds. Then, any funds deficiencies at end of day often can be met by overnight borrowing in the Federal ("Fed") funds market.

Astute banks and corporate managers may take advantage of the new daylight credits generated within the system, wherever lags exist between virtually immediate wire payments funds availability and end-of-day Fed funds settlement. Proceeds can be invested for fractions of a day prior to settlement. Very short-term reserves and money are created during the day, then destroyed at time of final reserve settlement debiting (Fedwire) or net net settlement (CHIPS). In both cases, the new money forms are providing the wherewithal for purchase of goods or financial assets for very short periods of time. In addition, payments "churning" can arise from same-day rapid turnover of financial assets, whether or not any new money and credits are created. As shown by Humphrey, the result has been a sharply rising gross level of daily average wire transfers relative to funds available for final settlement.

Among other things, Humphrey looks at the chances of the ultimate payments disaster: the so-called "unwind" potentially affecting one-third the payments obligations of CHIPS network members (close to $100 billion in average daily payments volume). The Fed, of course, stands ready to avert a chain-reaction payments disaster, through discount window loans or other means of exercising its traditional function as "lender of last resort." Private steps to internalize the risks can remove the likelihood that that last-resort Fed action will become necessary. Humphrey stresses also the legal and institutional changes in both Fed and private payments arrangements that may defuse the present systems risk problems.

Dr. Allen Frankel (Chief, International Banking) and Dr. Jeffrey Marquardt, Federal Reserve Board of Governors and Bank for International Settlements, provide insights into international payments mechanisms and links in chapter 5. They view the multilateral currency arrangements from user and supplier point of view. This chapter presents a timely look at what is happening right now to change worldwide money and reserve base concepts. Their analysis views the dynamics of international clearing and deliveries modes, including the British CHAPS and the ECU (European Currency Unit) schemes. Frankel and Marquardt examine the implications of new European arrangements for payments users worldwide, and the relative importance as a clearing base of gold, the dollar, and the new international clearing currencies.

Part III, Macroeconomic Policy Updated, makes the leap, next, from the operational realities (parts I and II) to macroeconomic issues. Consider the future, the years 1985–2000 described by Henderson, as a period in which electronic money increasingly will enter the payments stream. Will EFT and the redesigned network architecture discussed by Moore and Geller reduce the central bank's effectiveness in controlling money supply at that time? Analysis in part III is devoted to resolving this question. Practically all the elements involved in Fed/money supply links seem certain to change in a rising EFT payments mode.

The reader should bear in mind that the familiar linkages work as follows. The Fed, through open-market operations or loans to member banks at the discount window, can create (or destroy) member bank deposits and reserves at the Reserve banks. When the Fed creates new reserves, for example through open-market purchases, the banks can create new money in multiple amounts depending upon the average reserve requirements against deposits (or money multiplier).

However, some new electronic money forms (e.g., money market deposit accounts) now bear no reserve requirements, putting these types of money creation beyond the reach of the Fed's general credit control. We saw also (parts I and II) that other money forms are created and extinguished electronically before they can be entered into end-of-day reservable accounts subject to Fed control. The new phantom money can be spent or reinvested within fractions of a day, even, theoretically, milliseconds. With rapid turnaround, such money, although used as payment for goods and services, will not necessarily show up in the end-of-day money supply data upon which the Fed hangs its policy hat.

The official money velocity data will not reflect all this money churning either. Fueled by the new phantom or "virtual" money (to coin a phrase from particle physics), the same financial instrument can turn over many times during a single day rather than being used once for funding or asset portfolio purposes.[2] Meanwhile, lower asset conversion costs, due to EFT economies, reduce the public's money holdings as a medium of exchange relative to income or transactions. The rate of use of the public's shrunken transactions money holdings, or M1 velocity, will likely rise. Economists are only just now beginning to ask how these new unknowns will affect monetary and public policy. Part III addresses these difficult questions of attenuated policy links to money and real income creation and growth.

In chapter 6 the distinguished Nobel Laureate James Tobin redefines, for the upcoming payments era, the macroeconomic model of real goods and money market equilibrium. Professor Tobin's portfolio model examines altered interest rate relationships and customer behavior in interest-deregulated customer, depositor, and money markets, and the factors that now motivate portfolio decisions.

Professor Thomas Havrilesky, of Duke University, develops (chapter 7) a different macro model but one, like Professor Tobin's, lucid and attuned to the new money technology. Havrilesky also provides the reader with extensive discussion and review of prior economic work on these new issues. After careful analysis of a macro world moving toward zero transactions balances (perhaps leaving intact the cash which Havrilesky, like Henderson, believes will always be in demand), Havrilesky's innovative analysis concludes that monetary policy can best be implemented through rules. Given the future shrinking characteristic of narrow transactions money, these rules, he believes, must target the monetary (reserve) base rather than money per se. Society will also benefit if the Federal Reserve promptly makes available all its raw data to market participants and refrains from engaging in deliberate policy "surprises." A stable monetary policy environment is very much to be desired, one free of bureaucratic or politically motivated shifts in policy rules or self-seeking goals.

Professor Tobin (chapter 6) argues for a much different policy emphasis. In contrast to Havrilesky, Tobin continues strongly to favor discretion over rules. The new technology and the deregulation of bank interest rates does not alter this classic position, rather they enhance the arguments for Federal Reserve discretion to target the real sector such as gross national product. A "super monetarist" policy, or one designed to maintain constant money growth rates despite money demand volatility, will only exacerbate real sector instability. In addition, Tobin urges the changeover of reserve requirements from a liability-based system (deposits) to an asset-based system, including money and capital markets instruments held by banks as well as customer loans. In this manner, the asset creation made possible by the exotic new lending and money creation modes described in parts I and II will be subject, still, to Federal Reserve influence. Given this changed policy emphasis, Professor Tobin believes the central bank will exercise effective control and the payments system will be more efficient and convenient.

The microeconomic world for banks and consumers seems greatly altered. These changes are mostly, but not always necessarily, for the better. It all depends on how one happens to view the gains and losses, or tradeoffs. In part IV, Microeconomic Issues: Banks and Consumers, both contributors agree that the competitive development of retail EFT systems has been impressive. The wholesale operational problems of market failure described in part II are downplayed here, at retail. We believe the retail small-dollar EFT markets have functioned pretty much as microeconomic theory suggests they ought to behave. Nonetheless, disputes remain these days especially with regard to the role of government. To what extent, if any, does the Fed's role as payments guardian (discussed in part II) conflict with its legislative mandate under the 1980 Monetary Control Act to promote private competition within the payments system? Where payment technology broadens from paper to electronics, the private sector, including many nonbank firms, is able to take over more payments functions from the Fed. What is the present function of the regulator or antitrust enforcer, given these new entry possibilities today? Has vigorous retail competition managed to evolve because of the continued (albeit diminished) presence of government here, or despite it?

Part IV begins (chapter 8) with the work of a pioneering and distinguished scholar, Professor Almarin Phillips, Professor of Law and Public Policy at the University of Pennsylvania. Now that we have so much new entry from nonbanks into formerly sheltered local markets, what is the nature and potential of the new competition? Do banks no longer deserve their tainted reputation of past years? With a broad and important historical emphasis, Phillips views the shift from the frequent monopoly banking positions of the olden days to the new competition made possible both by deregulation and the new technology. Phillips analyzes in depth the post-sixties banking legislation and its beneficial economic impact on markets, given the opportunities made possible by the new technology. Phillips urges a reevaluation of legal and economic concepts appropriate to the dynamic new payments environment. The author's microeconomic analysis of joint ventures questions points the way for altered antitrust perspectives.

Chapter 9 (Solomon) analyzes some issues of special consumer interest, including the ways in which the retail credit and debit card systems have evolved in waves since their early introduction in the sixties. Market competition has shaped the development of these systems in major and often unexpected ways. Like Phillips, this writer views the current trend toward greater price as well as nonprice competition between system members as very encouraging and by all odds likely to continue. However, the policy goals here can be contradictory. Perhaps, in regulatory and antitrust deliberations we have not sufficiently considered the natural conflicts between players with different stakes in the new technology development. Perhaps the consumer has been underrepresented in those deliberations, in part because of confusion about how the interaction of complex markets affects the consumer at the bottom line. The questions anent intertemporal sector subsidy also produce particular controversy. The differing points of view cannot, and should not, go away but they can be better understood by market participants. Some thorny trade-offs between efficiency, competition, sector distribution of benefits, and risk deserve, I believe, much future careful study.

Common themes of this volume. Each author presents his specific public policy conclusions. It would seem both presumptuous and unnecessary to repeat them all here. I do set forth, however, some recurrent themes that are repeated and developed quite independently by the lawyers, hands-on operations people and engineers, microeconomists, and distinguished academic theorists contributing to this volume.

Paul Henderson suggests in chapter 1 that replacement of the familiar paper money by the new money may take place more slowly than earlier thought. Most probably it will be the year 2000 or later before electronic money becomes fully as important as old-style paper money as an accepted medium of exchange. The volume's contributors unanimously note that universal access, service, and acceptance will be necessary before the new money fully displaces the old. A revision of consumer attitudes and especially the present subsidy to check writers in the form of float and other incentives will be a necessary part of that change. The banking legal code requires a thorough overhaul appropriate to the esoteric new concepts of money creation we still can barely understand. Also, Fed and other government regulations relevant to payments transfers require careful updating to eliminate problems not foreseen when such regulations first were drawn up many years ago.

Thus, contributors all in all take an up-beat view of the new opportunities in store for us. However, there is some consensus in this volume that a gradual phasing in of the new money may not be out of line after all. Much remains to be done to assure reliability of the new payments modes, as well as safety for society and payments efficiency. There are engineering, regulatory, and political obstacles to be overcome.

The adjustments or corrections may take some time. For example, we need some social and political consensus concerning the appropriate money and payments concepts. A new codified body of public law applicable to the new technology is thought to be necessary. A judicial commission may consider questions. Congress and state and local governments may wish jointly to develop legal standards appropriate to the technology.

Private vendors of the new payments modes have their job cut out for them too. The replacement of paper-appropriate private legal arrangements for ones more suitable to the present payments environment seems mandated. Joint venture formats for supplying the technology will need more generally to assure that users can access the most low-cost and useful money transmission formats (Henderson, Moore, Phillips, Solomon). Also, present safety and eligibility standards may be inadequate, and private suppliers will want jointly to redefine them appropriately. The help of specialized engineers is necessary. The development of workable standards to permit entry of the now nonregulated entities, capable of participation in the new payments systems, will take considerable multidisciplinary thought. These themes appear in the work of Henderson, Moore, Humphrey, and Geller. It is the consensus of most contributors to this volume that some sort of screening of private payments participants is necessary prior to entry, if not by government regulators then at least by private institutional mechanisms. The authors (Henderson, Geller, Humphrey, Frankel and Marquardt) stress the desirability of international cooperation and consultation as well, in order to iron out present conflicts and barriers to universal worldwide access and use of the new payments media.

The problems of settlement risk seem especially important and worthy of the detailed attention Humphrey so strongly urges in chapter 4. The Federal Reserve already has voluntary programs in place designed to limit (or place a "cap" on) interbank daylight overdrafts, which Humphrey explains. Bilateral credit limits are in place and may be usefully extended also. In order to internalize to the private sector any risks on large-dollar private-wire nets, such as CHIPS, Humphrey suggests private insurance or collateralization plans similar to those already in use in private commodity and stock exchanges. Moore, too, advocates changes in the legal and institutional structure, including industry self-policing, and the introduction of better back up telecommunications systems and risk management arrangements. Moore notes the fraud and other consumer difficulties, which systems must address and correct in order to gain acceptance.

Geller applauds the new freedom given to AT&T to compete in financial and information systems technology. Geller urges also the further deregulation of the Bell Operating Companies, in order to "clone" AT&T's capabilities and permit still more new entry, cost reduction, and innovation in this dynamic new field of payments telecommunications transfer. Phillips commends the erasure of product and geographic market barriers thus far, and points out the way the Congress and states still must move. Phillips stresses also the need for appropriate market, joint venture, and antitrust standards in order not to impede development of the new technology.

The appeal for continued deregulation, therefore, is a recurring theme throughout the volume. Not only will erasure of entry and pricing barriers promote competition, as part IV strongly suggests, but interstate branching may also help resolve the settlement risk problems explicitly described by Humphrey (part II, chapter 4). At the same time, most papers also urge that the regulatory wraps not be removed altogether, lest society develop new and, at least as of this writing, uncharted risks or ills. Most papers stress the important, indeed upgraded, Fed role as lender of last resort to avert settlement chain-reaction failure, the "unwind." But Havrilesky views this development of increasing federal government intervention to avert crises as threatening the present progress toward deregulation. The subsidy issue can also be troublesome and is touched on consistently throughout this volume by Henderson, Moore, Geller, Phillips, and Solomon.

The elusive nature of the new and greatly expanded money flows is a common theme of parts I and II. When money can be created and extinguished electronically in milliseconds, the staggering gross payments flows potential was thought by those most familiar with our payments operations to mandate some major changes in conceptual focus. Paul Henderson urges that careful analysis be devoted to placing the new concept of money flows in proper perspective. The theoretical part III of this volume restates that same theme. Once again the emphasis is on gross money flows, not net money at end-of-day rest. Tobin, like Humphrey and Henderson, notes the effects of rapid money transformation on market arbitrage, speculation, and portfolio shifts. Humphrey (chapter 4) describes the market "churning" and a money flows gross many times the at-rest money backup. In part III Tobin and Havrilesky analyze the economic effects of this phenomenon on real goods spending and capital markets activity. Both distinguished scholars present very different policy prescriptions but are satisfied that open-market operations can continue to work well, given some needed targeting changes. Both believe that money and monetary policy will continue to matter in this brave new world.

Notes

1. Solomon earlier presented these and other questions before the Electronic Banking Economist Society in New York City on February 7, 1985—reprinted as "EFT and Money Supply," *The Bankers' Magazine*, July–August 1985, 77–81. The Society's (THEBES) enthu-

siasm in seeking answers was a driving force in our desire to produce this synthesized volume.

2. The notion that a cloud of phantom "virtual particles" surrounds elementary matter was developed by Nobel prize winning physicist Richard Feynman in the seventies. Triggered by a "Heisenberg uncertainty" loan of energy, "virtual" protons and electrons meet to form real matter for a brief time, which is destroyed when the loan of energy is repaid some time later, usually within milliseconds. In the quantum world of subatomic physics, matter is thus continually being created and destroyed. See Richard Feynman, *The Character of Physical Law*, Cambridge, MA: MIT Press, 1982; and Paul Davies, *Superforce*, New York: Simon and Schuster, 1984.

I MONEY, NOW AND FUTURE

Money has been a source of both utility and curiosity to human beings since prehistoric times. It has existed primarily as a medium of exchange, and in early times was always something tangible, like wampum, cows, or precious metals. The shining metal, gold, still fascinates despite the fact that paper and accounting money, or deposits, have gradually replaced the precious metals as a medium of exchange. Now another equally drastic money revolution is in place. It promises gradually to replace the accounting money with something new but also acceptable as a means of payment, intangible electronic bits of information.

In addition to being nonphysical in nature, the new supermoney has other unique characteristics which set it apart from the traditional money one could touch and feel. The new electronic money can be constantly on the move. Fueled by new-tech loans, it is in continual process of creation and destruction, for time periods so short that the "phantom money" can escape detection altogether.

This uncomfortably modern nature of the new money can present monetary policy difficulties. The theoretical links between money, the reserve base, and the macroeconomy become disturbed and weakened. Electronic money may partially escape the official money measures. Money concepts were designed long ago to measure physical money *inventories*, or money stock which comes to rest at end of day. Given the electronic money of today and the future, Dr. Henderson's flow concept is an important one for policy makers and theorists to contemplate. Perhaps a gross transactions flow measure can better capture supermoney gross—which is fueled by electronic "float" but then can vanish, all in the course of a single day.

Now that the nature of money is evolving from physical to computer information bits, its manner of delivery becomes both faster and more specialized. The old-style feature of universal payments access and universal service has been of special importance for satisfactory payments performance. Trucks and airlines carry physical pieces of paper from payor to payee, via the usual private and Federal Reserve clearing mechanisms in place. Everyone has universal access to these time-honored clearing modes, that is, all users can "get into the act." However, now the money payment is likely to consist increasingly of direct payments, or transactions flows, "zapped" directly from sender to money recipients. Henderson points out the difficulties when systems are specialized but not interconnected, so that service is not universal. The transactions or deliveries paths can take any one of a number of directions, restricted to specific system members or some specific use or place.

Linda Moore carries the analysis forward from new-style money to new-style clearing options. The choices often can be very mind boggling. Moore's innovative chapter (chapter 2) portrays the myriad user choices in this new payments environment. No doubt, money payments and pieces of paper will continue to be delivered for a long time into the future through familiar mechanisms and the well-known clearing rules of the game. But money payments also can be made through blends of the old clearing modes and the new, depending upon special participant needs. Moore tells us about the nature and possibilities of these linkages. Moore's matrix analysis serves to capture the new way of user decision making, the process of continuous and discontinuous interaction in transactions nets both complex and simple.

Moore discusses the challenge to banks in this payments environment where they may often play second fiddle as an intermediate link between computer-controlled nets. She describes the great opportunities for both depository institutions and other competent payments participants. Like Henderson, Moore stresses, however, the importance of developing regulatory and legal institutions relevant to the modern payments structure. Moore analyzes constraints on user and vendor access to the nets, and is concerned (as are papers in part IV of this volume) about system rules for participation and membership. She sets forth the consumer fraud and error problems and suggests some simplified noncourt procedures for problem resolution by local public groups.

Henry Geller, in chapter 3, discusses telecommunications policy, and the means of enabling the open access and least-cost payments deliveries modes both Henderson and Moore describe as optimal. Geller translates his intimate knowledge of the technical telecommunications issues into questions important to financial people. The author discusses many issues of special concern to both business and consumer users of the modern money, including access to small ground-earth stations (SBS) and home banking videotex. Geller shares with the reader the actions the FCC could take to permit videotex TV add-ons, and hence to speed up a now disappointingly slow trend toward home banking. He examines the break-up of American Telephone & Telegraph and the implications for fuller financial institution competition in the new technology, both long lines and local. Finally, Geller analyzes the international ramifications for financial suppliers, and the role of INTELSAT and the private U.S. and foreign satellite and cable companies. In order to enhance competition in the financial services, Geller argues for still more deregulation of telecommunications. Geller argues also, however, for safeguards of a type noted by Moore and Henderson to assure open access and the attainment of lowest-cost configurations.

I suggest the reader digest these chapters together. They reevaluate the concepts, in money language of the future and the engineering range for money deliveries and clearing. They develop the complex decisions and payments choices facing users. They analyze the deliveries process in an electronic payments milieu. They examine the role in that world of banking agencies, the Federal Communications Commission, and the international agencies, including potential conflicts and problems.

1 MODERN MONEY

Paul B. Henderson, Jr.

The experiences of different countries under varying conditions provide a crucial test for the understanding of economic concepts and for the validation of economic theories. But the understanding of money and the validation of payment processes are flawed when experiences are misperceived

Experience is critically context-dependent. Money and payment processes are frequently derived from decisions on monetary policy and the banking structure. They are seen only as incidental processes or in a narrow focus of self-interest or competitive position.

Experience is critically time-dependent. When the pace of change is just brisk enough to accommodate the interdependencies of money and payments with other aspects of the society, a relative sense of stability-with-change comes to be accepted as the norm. When the pace of change reaches or exceeds the level of confidence and comfort, there is a tendency to resist further change and to cling ever more firmly to whatever aspects of money seem relatively stable. Thus, especially in the United States, money and payment processes have come to be misperceived under the pressure of changes in technology, in legislation, and in international competition.

Money in economic theory, reflecting historical practices, is expressed in an ever-changing array of "M" definitions substantially bound to physical attributes. Thus money, in theory, remains an inventory. Money in operational use, reflecting its antecedents in barter, is perceived in physical terms. But money includes forms that are substantially free of physical limitations for virtually all national economies and especially in the developed countries. Paced by electronic-based transfers, money is becoming a flow and a process.

The preoccupation with the statics of an inventory rather than the dynamics of a flow has affected the oft-predicted electronic displacement of paper-based systems. As the displacement continues, the predominantly physical concept of money will begin to obscure rather than illuminate the economic concepts and to confound rather than validate payment processes.

Background

Money and payment processes are vital to any national economy that advances beyond barter. While money is always given close attention—most often as a government monopoly—payment processes are often allowed to evolve freely until there is a crisis in confidence, in security, or in international relations.

Some monetary and payment crises have been resolved with notable success by institutional changes—as in the creation of the Federal Reserve System in the United States. In countries that have a limited number of banking institutions and a tradition of cooperation in planning with the Central Bank, as in Belgium, it has been possible to establish broad agreement on a plan for automation of the payment processes. Where periodic evaluation and redefinition of the payment process are required by law, as in Canada, there is a regular attempt to address the long-range needs and opportunities. More commonly, the crisis is not resolved but suppressed by redefining the money supply or the measures of economic activity or the relationships among the participants.

Neither all the best nor all the worst features in payment processes are found in any one country. The experiences of other countries—both successes and failures—offer new ideas and confirm or refute the validity of some old ones. Some techniques can readily be copied; check technology, in several different versions, is being introduced in many developing countries. Other successful innovations resist adaptation; electronic-based systems that function well in other countries—bank and postal giros for example—have not been accepted in the United States. The public policy issues that challenge the United States have not been fully resolved elsewhere and partial solutions should not be copied without thought or change. But there is merit in comparative studies. Partial answers may be available in past experience and from other settings.

The pervasive need for payments for goods and services assures that the payment process will continue to evolve even when it is not formally addressed. From time to time, issues of public policy will be recognized and explored. Thus a rather slow evolution of the payment mechanism accommodates but does not fully satisfy governmental policies, competitive initiatives, and user choices. In consequence, a national payment capability develops as a dynamic balance of the three basic types of systems:

Cash-based systems—especially coin and currency—which use instruments of payments that are treated as valuables,

Paper-based systems—especially checks and giros—which depend on physical objects as evidence of a claim to value,

Electronic-based systems—especially funds transfer—that effect changes in the recorded ownership of value by an interchange of signals.

National payment processes, even in developing economies, are pervasive and, at the least, intricate and thus appear to be rather complex. Numerous variations and combinations, derived from technology, cultural traditions, chance, and competitive innovations tend to obscure the simple elegance of the three basic payment systems. The balance among the payment systems evolves as the earlier systems are supplemented—never eliminated—and variations flourish. In most developed nations, paper is as important as cash; several countries transfer more value electronically than by paper and cash combined; no country has yet reached the point that the number of electronic transactions equals the number of cash transactions.

Cash-based systems use metal and paper objects to store and convey value. Historically, objects of intrinsic value were used to introduce a money economy as a supplement to barter. Cash became the foundation system for national payment processes as intrinsic value objects were replaced with coins, tokens, stamps, coupons, and currency whose value was established by fiat. Cash-based transactions are the most numerous, and in developed countries convey the least value of all means of payment. But, there are not reliable data on either the number or value of coin-based transactions and relatively little on currency. The long history of use of coin and currency and the presumption that small-value payments are not good candidates for displacement by electronics may account for the absence of reliable data and a lack of concern that such statistics be collected.

It is likely that there are more coin than currency transactions in most countries. Since the average value of coin transactions is very low, the transfer value is a small or insignificant portion of the total. Currency serves a more significant portion of the payments process. The number and value of transactions employing paper currency can be estimated from the number of notes in circulation, their useful life and the average number of notes required in a single transaction to tender payment and receive change. In the United States, for example, the usage of Federal Reserve notes implies that there are about 65 billion currency transactions per year. Given an average value of currency transactions of less than $15.00, estimated from the distribution of denominations in active use, currency accounts for no more than $1 trillion in payments each year—less than 1% of the total transaction value, but a significant fraction of the payments for nonfinancial goods and services.

Paper-based systems use physical objects to represent ownership and to direct the transfer of value. The notable features of these systems are the physical transportation of payment instruments and related documents and the reliance on human recognition of the authenticity of the documents and the validity and intent of the transaction and participants. Paper documents characterize the process but both credit transfers (giros) and debit transfers (checks) are often supplemented by plastic cards and magnetic tape. Manual operations characterize the processing although paper-based systems typically involve a substantial degree of mechanization or automation.

The use of checks and giros is reasonably well defined, measured, and studied in the developed economies. In the United States the annual transaction volume has been estimated at about 35 to 40 billion checks in the early 1980s. Value was estimated at about $20 trillion per year.

Electronic-based systems use electrical, magnetic, and optical signals to process, store, and transmit data about transactions. Neither paper nor other physical items are essential to the electronic system concept, but they may be—and usually are—used for incidental and supplemental records. The electronic ideal, when attainable, provides a very effective, convenient, and efficient system. It was attained in the major funds transfer systems in the United States which, since 1980, have come to dominate large-value transfers. The Society for Worldwide Interbank Financial Telecommunications (SWIFT) is bringing into focus a comparable pattern of change for internationally related payments.

The data on electronic funds transfers in the United States are impressive but incomplete.[1] In the mid-1980s the major transfer services handled about 100 million transactions worth about $150 trillion. Transaction volumes and dollar values for regional and local services and for individual institutions are not made public. There are probably several billion electronic or partly electronic transactions each year processed within internal systems of banks and other businesses and in local and regional networks.

The statistics on current payment practices, although fragmentary, provide an overall perspective of current transaction volumes and values and reveal the limited changes that are occurring.[2] The scale of the United States payment mechanism and the number of participants are so great that the future is sure to be strongly influenced by the pattern and momentum that now prevails. The public policy issues that arise from money and payment processes reflect the reality that prevailed in past decades. Money is conceived, defined, and measured in physical terms; and payment processes are visualized, regulated, and evaluated in the physical terms that were dominant in past decades.

Money as a store of value was of paramount concern when cash was the principal payment system. Until very recently economic processes, especially payments, involved more data than could conveniently be processed; it was easier to count and value a physical inventory than to identify and record the sequence of transactions in a flow. Thus, money came to be defined and measured when it came to rest at the close of the business day. This preoccupation with inventories is less appropriate to paper-based systems and is notably ineffective with electronic based systems. Transaction velocity is appropriately a derivative measure when money is inventoried, it must become a primary measure when the process of payment—a flow concept—begins to be recognized as unmanageable as an inventory. For the future, money as a unit of account will be of paramount concern.

The foundation for the inventory view of money and for the acceptance of the traditional measures of money is threatened by the ability to create money as it is needed and to extinguish it before it must be counted as a deposit and by the trend toward worldwide flows that are becoming possible with electronic-based systems. The threat is not yet critical—flow transactions are based on repetitive counting of the same money value and are thus overstated in relation to end-of-day inventories—but the impact will be magnified if the erosion of that foundation is too long ignored.

Prevailing Trends in U.S. Payment Processes

The total value of payment transactions in the United States in 1984 was about $185 trillion as shown in figure 1-1: $160 trillion in electronics, $24 trillion in paper-based systems, $1 trillion in currency, and a negligible amount in coin transactions. Figure 1-1 also reflects an estimate of the

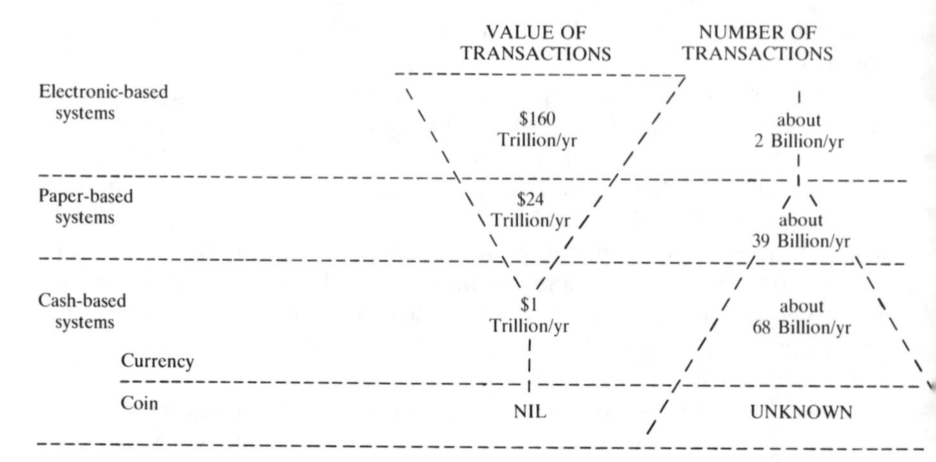

Figure 1-1. The Shape of the United States Payment Mechanism—1984

aggregate number of payment transactions—excluding coin transactions because no data are available—at about 109 billion per year: 2 billion in electronics, 39 billion in checks, and 68 billion in currency.

The distribution of the number of transactions by the three types of payment processes has changed slowly over the past half century. When checks were displacing other means of payment, annual growth rates were in the range of seven percent. In recent years, the rate declined to a level closer to the aggregate rate of growth—perhaps four percent—for all payment transactions. The growth rate for electronic-based transaction is not known but is assumed to be in excess of 10% annually. If the growth rate remains high—as it did for checks for four decades—the electronic share will become significant but not dominant before the turn of the century.

The distribution of dollar values among cash, paper, and electronics has changed dramatically. The electronic share has increased rapidly—in large part because of multiple counting—and is already over 85% of the total.

Interpretations of the meaning of transaction value and of the number of transactions are suspect. Data about cash transactions are very scanty although there is a reasonably close link between a transaction and an actual payment for goods and services. Check and giro transactions are rather well documented even to estimates of the number of intermediate steps in a completed payment; it is possible to obtain consistent estimates of the underlying economic activities with a lag of a few years. Electronic transfers, although expressed in the same terms of value and number of transactions, are not comparable to either cash or paper transfers. The very nature of the transfer arrangement yields separate measures of value and count for each step in the process—a single payment generates a series of transfers and the anticipated end-of-day balances that result can induce a secondary flurry of investment transactions. There is no provision for even a simple classification of the transfers into meaningful economic activities.

Most observers would agree that the dominant position of electronic funds transfer systems in terms of dollar value will not be reversed; a notable change in the overall pattern can occur only if there is a significant increase in the share of the number of transactions served electronically and some identification of the different purposes of electronic transfers. Thus, despite the sense of electronic displacement of other means of payment, there is only a gentle squeeze by electronics and currency on the share of checks in the number of transactions in the U.S. payments systems as illustrated in figure 1-2.

The available statistics confirm that electronic funds transfers, card-originated transactions, and currency transactions are being used as substitutes for checks. But the net growth rate of checks is probably still in excess of 3% per year. The annual increase in the number of checks is comparable to—and possibly still greater than—the total number of electronic transactions.

With respect to electronics, very-large-value individual transactions were converted from checks at a rapid rate beginning about 1970. The conversion has continued with an intensity proportional to the transaction value. Most payments in excess of $100,000 have already been moved to funds transfer systems. The preference for EFT in large-value transfers is not based so much on speed as it is on the certainty of the process; the assurance that an extra day of interest will not be lost to processing problems.

The cutover value, at which the conversion to electronics is as likely as retention of check payments, reflects the behavioral response to the probability that the check may be delayed by one day, the value of one day's interest, and the comparative cost of the alternative services. Even at $10,000, there will be little impact on the number of remaining checks; substantially less than 1% of all checks are written for $10,000 or more. The effect on total check value would be notable, however, since about 50% of the value is carried by such large-value transactions; the conversion of the remaining 1% of checks for $10,000 and more to funds transfers would decrease the average check value from $600 to about $300.

Currency is also displacing checks under the influence of the automated teller machine (ATM) programs, float reduction efforts, and increasing fee charges and reduced subsidization of check and credit card services. A

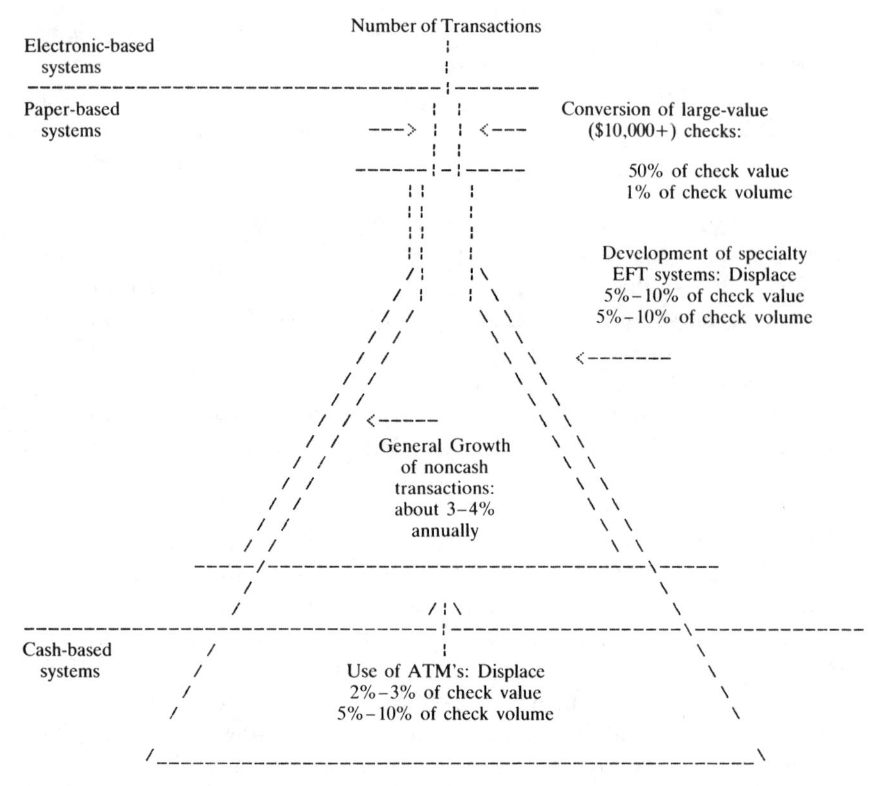

Figure 1-2. The Gentle Squeeze on Checks 1980–1990

significant fraction of the four billion checks written for "cash" may be displaced by cash dispenser transactions in the major ATM introduction period of the 1980s. Currency will be used instead of checks in a comparable number of transactions as it becomes more conveniently available. For the decade, that will mean a loss of one or two percentage points from the prevailing annual growth rate of checks.

Future Money

For the past few decades, it has been widely predicted that electronic fund transfer systems (EFTS) would soon supplant cash and paper. The billions of paper checks in the United States were the most obvious target for conversion to EFT; they have proved to be an elusive target. When the "checkless" society was not attained during the 1960s, the predictions were revised to suggest a "less-checks" society. Now, with continued growth in the number of checks, there are very few predictions of either the extent or the timing of the conversion. The prevailing attitude is that the number of checks might stop increasing in the next decade and might begin to decrease some years later.

That sense of failed prediction is only valid in terms of the number of checks and the underlying payment transactions. The impression of failure is misleading in that it obscures the notable success in substituting electronics for paper in terms of the dollar value of those transactions. It is, at least, arguable that the massive conversion of dollar value is more significant than the failure to convert the more numerous, smaller-value transactions.

The substantially different growth rates for cash-, paper-, and electronic-based systems indicate that existing market shares are moving toward a new balance. Since the total number of nonelectronic payments is very great the long-term underlying trend is one of substantial stability. There is not even a consistent direction of change; ATM's have, for the moment, reversed the preference for checks over cash that prevailed for several decades.

The misperception of the prospects for growth in electronic transactions sufficient to stop the growth of checks and then to attain equality with the number of checks can be resolved; consider the implication of initial distribution volumes, rates of growth, and the period of time needed to accomplish such a conversion. If the number of transactions for 1984 are approximately correct:

Cash-based (excluding coin) = 68 billion/yr
Paper-based = 39 billion/yr
Electronic-based = 2 billion/yr

And the uncertainty in the rates of growth can be accomodated by a range of values:

For the annual increase in total transactions: 2% to 4%
For the annual increase in electronic transactions: 10% to 20%

Since any displacement of cash transactions by electronic transactions will reduce the impact on checks, a conservative assumption is that cash transactions change at the same rate as the overall number of transactions and that checks take all of the residual future growth.

As shown in table 1-1a, with overall growth at 2% and a 10% growth in electronics volume, it will be 2007 before check growth is stopped and 2015

Table 1-1a. Projection of Number of Payment Transactions in the United States: Assumed Aggregate Growth Rate 2%

Year	*Total Number Transactions (billions) 2%*	*Cash Transactions (billions) 2%*	*Electronic Transactions (billions) 10%*	*Paper Transactions (billions) Residual*
1984	109	68	2	39
1985	111	69	2	40
1986	113	71	2	40
1987	116	72	3	41
1988	118	74	3	41
1989	120	75	3	42
1990	123	77	4	43
1991	125	78	4	43
1992	128	80	4	44
1993	130	81	5	44
1994	133	83	5	45
1995	136	85	6	45
1996	138	86	6	46
1997	141	88	7	46
1998	144	90	8	47
1999	147	92	8	47
2000	150	93	9	47
2001	153	95	10	47
2002	156	97	11	47
2003	159	99	12	47
2004	162	101	13	47
2005	165	103	15	47
2006	169	105	16	47
2007	172	107	18	47
2008	175	109	20	46
2009	179	112	22	46
2010	182	114	24	45
2011	186	116	26	44
2012	190	118	29	43
2013	194	121	32	41
2014	197	123	35	39
2015	201	126	38	37

Table 1-1b. Projection of Number of Payment Transactions in the United States: Assumed Aggregate Growth Rate 2%

Year	*Total Number Transactions (billions) 2%*	*Cash Transactions (billions) 2%*	*Electronic Transactions (billions) 20%*	*Paper Transactions (billions) Residual*
1984	109	68	2	39
1985	111	69	2	39
1986	113	71	3	40
1987	116	72	3	40
1988	118	74	4	40
1989	120	75	5	40
1990	123	77	6	40
1991	125	78	7	40
1992	128	80	9	39
1993	130	81	10	39
1994	133	83	12	38
1995	136	85	15	36
1996	138	86	18	34
1997	141	88	21	32
1998	144	90	26	28
1999	147	92	31	24

before electronic volume equals check volume. Table 1-1b shows that, with a 20% aggregate growth rate for electronics, check volume would peak in 1991 (at 40 billion) and would be exceeded by electronic volume in 1999.

If the aggregate growth rate is 4% (table 1-2), the electronic growth must be more than 20% to reach equality by the turn of the century; check growth would peak out at 48 billion checks in 1996.

It is obvious that a crucial variable in the projection is the initial volume of electronic transactions. With only 2 billion of the 40 billion noncash transactions, the shift is very slow—even at a 20% rate of growth. When the electronic volume reaches a critical level (20–25%) of the noncash total, the shift will become notable since the annual increase in electronic-based transactions can exceed the aggregate increase in the total number of transactions at modest growth rates.

It is appropriate to consider why checks have been and are such a persistent choice and what might be done to induce a transition that features growth strong enough to establish that "critical mass" of

Table 1-2. Projection of Number of Payment Transactions in the United States: Assumed Aggregate Growth Rate 4%

Year	*Total Number Transactions (billions) 4%*	*Cash Transactions (billions) 4%*	*Electronic Transactions (billions) 20%*	*Paper Transactions (billions) Residual*
1984	109	68	2	39
1985	113	71	2	40
1986	118	74	3	41
1987	123	76	3	43
1988	128	80	4	44
1989	133	83	5	45
1990	138	86	6	46
1991	143	89	7	47
1992	149	93	9	48
1993	155	97	10	48
1994	161	101	12	48
1995	168	105	15	48
1996	175	109	18	48
1997	181	113	21	47
1998	189	118	26	45
1999	196	122	31	43
2000	204	127	37	40
2001	212	132	44	35

electronic volume of 10–15 billion per year. The reasons why the transition has not occurred as quickly as predicted are best understood by comparing the characteristics of check and electronic systems and their effects on business relationships and behavioral incentives.

The Conditions for Displacement of Paper

There are four reasons why checks should be and are favored over existing electronic systems.

First, the check system provides universal service. The check collection process accomodates checks and other payment instruments (e.g., Credit Union Share Drafts), for any purpose, in any amount, over any distance, and at any time. The electronic systems, on the other hand, serve particular and very limited classes of payments. Each system is conceptually and operationally isolated: distinguished by the dollar value of the transaction, by the location or the device used to create the message, by the means and timing of settlement, or by the code or the piece of plastic used to identify the select participants.

No electronic-based system available today and no combination of existing systems is a credible alternative to the range of services provided by the check system.

Second, the check system provides universal access. That universality is important to social equity as well as to operational reality. In equity, there should be an assured but permissive means of access by all customers—some will choose to avoid written records, others will continue to prefer to deal exclusively in cash. Operationally, there must be an assured means of access to any financial intermediary identified in the transaction. A financial intermediary incurs a significant responsibility in handling a payment—the cost of failure far exceeds the fees earned for correct and timely handling. It is essential that there be an assured means to collect every debit and to deliver every credit.

In the check collection system, each intermediary establishes and sustains preferential relationships with a limited number of other institutions and associations; beyond that number there is a serious risk of loss of operational control and unacceptable liability. It is, however, organizationally feasible to impose interchange standards on subsidiaries, branches, and affiliates. It is operationally feasible to abide by the negotiated standards in a few cooperative arrangements each containing up to several hundred institutions. Thus, an institution can expect to sustain operational relationships of preference with as many as one thousand other financial intermediaries. Since one-third to one-half of all transactions are "on-us" and the preferred relationships can be chosen to cover the more important and heavier "on-others" traffic links, most—but not all—of the transaction value and volume can be accommodated without resort to any general "all-others" service. The more complete conversion to electronics that has been reported in other countries especially in Europe is due, in part, to the small number of financial institutions and the absence of an "all-others" problem; to cover the remaining portion of the 19,000 check issuers, in the United States the Federal Reserve Banks provide an "all-others" service and handle about one-third of the "on-others" checks.

With specialized electronic-based systems there is no means to universal access either by customers or to other intermediaries; and thus there is no possibility of consumer choice. For high-volume, low-cost operations—in checks or in any electronic candidate to displace checks—it is operationally infeasible to examine each transaction in order to refuse those for which there are no established accounting and delivery arrangments. Instead, the existing electronic systems are limited to well-defined and easily recognized classes of transactions among specified participants. For transactions not in the acceptable class, it is common to suggest that a check be used.

No electronic system available today and no combination of existing systems is a credible alternative to the generality of access provided by the check system.

Third, there is a notable imbalance in favor of check writers in the prevailing United States payment processes.

The check system was not designed in its own right so much as it was an incidental by-product of the development of the banking structure. The long-standing banking focus on deposits and loans induced a preference for practices that serve depositors as borrowers and in making payments rather than in receiving them. Since the check was particularly advantageous to the payor it was and still is the preferred choice unless the payee is able and willing to influence the choice of the method of payment. Business interest is probably stronger than individual interest in redefining the terms of payment. Equity may be established by allowing either a few days extra time or a discount of a few percent of the value of nonpaper transactions; both methods are under trial. Further, the present U.S. convention that a check in the mail is final payment although good funds are not available to the payee until sometime—usually several days—later gives the payor the benefit of float and revocation. The payee has little opportunity to express any unwillingness to accept a check; with a check in hand it is arguably better to deposit it for collection than to reject it and ask for another means of payment.

Another consequence of that payor preference in the United States is the use of debit transfers (checks) in which the order-to-pay is given by the payor to the payee and then passed back through the processing chain to the designated paying institution.

A credit transfer is the basis for most electronic and fund transfer systems and for the giro payment systems commonly used in Europe. In a credit transfer the order-to-pay is given by the payor directly to the paying institution. If good funds or credits are available, they are taken from the payor and transferred to the payee. Since the uncertainty of finality and of possible dishonor are not resolved until action is taken by the paying institution, the credit transfer—if it can be used—is inherently more efficient than the debit transfer. It is unfortunate that the vocabulary of debit and credit transfers contradicts the terminology applied to the transaction. For example, a credit card transaction usually results in a debit transfer while a debit card transaction leads to a credit transfer.

The processing chain is short if the payor and payee use the same institution and long if several intermediaries are required to complete the presentment. In the United States the check processing chain has tended to be long—an average of about 2.4 institutions—and intensively used because the very large number of check issuing institutions meant that many checks were "on-others" at the institution of first deposit.

No electronic-based system can begin to displace the check system until the payor bias is reduced and the choice of the means of payment becomes a normal part of business relationships.

Fourth, the behavorial incentives—especially economic incentives—still favor checks over electronics.

The check system was given a sense of universality seventy years ago. From that foundation and the refinements perfected in high-volume operations, the check system has become a complementary aggregation of 19,000 systems. Collectively, and even individually, the processing systems at 19,000 check issuers have attained the equivalence of large scale and the economies that accrue to scale.

Explicit preferences and cost subsidies for checks are being reduced and will eventually be eliminated. A credible offering of a universal electronic alternative and equitable rules for payment finality will be needed to eliminate the more subtle preferences and subsidies.

The more fundamental problem is that existing electronic systems do not exploit either the economies that are well developed in the check system or the even more significant economies that are potentially available through the inherent generality of machinable data. In isolated systems, there is no realization of a general cost reduction to be shared until the transition process is well advanced. Without credible evidence that the transition has begun and can be expected to persist, there is no basis for an expectation of general cost reduction.

For electronic-based systems, the opportunities to establish customer loyalty by way of product differentiation and superior service have seemed to be very limited. The opportunities to compete on price have been rare indeed. With only a few exceptions, the alternative choice has been to differentiate the system itself. The idea was to lock in the customer with a little technology that also locked out competitors: the effect has been to sacrifice the operational characteristics that, through standardization and commonality and complementarity, would permit service and costs competitive with checks.

For the great number of modest-value transactions, existing electronic transfer systems are better than needed in terms of delivery and attention to individual transactions. Those features need to be traded off to gain universal service and access and to attain competitive unit costs.

The Prospects for Electronics as the Dominant Payment System and for a Flow Concept of Money

Some means of accommodation of virtually all classes of payments and all types of payors and payees will be needed if electronic-based systems are to displace a significant portion of the checks. New systems, a broader spectrum of services, the interchange of messages among systems, and standardization of telecommunications protocols and message formats can all contribute to universality of service. Above all, there must be a recognition that electronic systems can provide service that is strongly competitive with checks only when they function in a complementary way.

The aggregate customer population in the United States includes almost 100 million households, several million businesses, and almost one million retail stores. Universal electronic access by customers is a formidable challenge, although no more than a few percent of each of those populations are related to any one financial institution. In contrast, every financial intermediary must have the means to link to every other active intermediary. "All-others" access, in some form at least as universal as checks, will be needed if electronic-based systems are to displace more than a small fraction of the checks. The difference between the two systems, and the more stringent requirement in electronic systems, is inherent in their nature.

The handling of objects—cash, checks, or giros—is inevitably a one-way flow with relatively slow processes for passing the objects and the responsibility to the next party in the processing chain. Since both parties operate under manual controls, there is little benefit and little concern for standardizing and automating the process except at the interface.

The processing of data in machinable form—electronic value transfer—is not at all limited to one-way flow; the same resources can, for example, transmit invoices as well as payments. The interface processes, however, must operate at an electronic not human pace; they must be thoroughly standardized and precisely—automatically—controlled. If the benefits of processing data rather than objects are to be retained, identical operational controls are desirable; compatibility, at least sufficient to permit automatic transformation, is a necessity.

It has been relatively easy to establish complementarity in check processing. The demands are greater and more difficult to meet with electronic systems; only a few institutions have developed automated interfaces. Although there is some effort to detail standards for funds transfers, there is no sense of agreement on the necessity, or the means, to exploit the commonalities, which are potentially so much greater among electronic signals than among physical artifacts. Each user that experiments with electronic service faces a dual cost while deciding whether to stay primarily with checks or shift to substantially complete reliance on electronics. The hope rather than the reality of cost reduction must suffice until the electronic alternative becomes acceptable for most of the transaction needs and the paper handling arrangements can be dismantled.

For most financial intermediaries, there is no prospect for virtually complete conversion for many years. Some customers will choose to stay with checks and most will retain a minimal capability to issue checks when the electronic system is unavailable for any reason. Close attention to service needs and preferences and to cost realities and prospects may yet reveal near-term benefits and the means to allocate them in a constructive and equitable way among the participants.

A mix of payment processes rather than a single system prevails in all except the most primative economies. Barter is displaced—but never eliminated—with the introduction and refinement of a money economy. Cash is supplemental—but remains as a major system alternative—to check and giros. Cash and paper will be supplemented—but not eliminated—if electronic-based systems become perceptibly more effective, more convenient, and more efficient.

The final balance will include a full spectrum of systems to effect payment as well as an array of processes to avoid the need for payment. Subway tokens, commutation passes, postage stamps, and credit card sales accommodate many transactions with a single payment. A more efficient means of payment may restore some sets of transactions to individual payments and thus increase the total number of payments rather than supplant existing systems. For example, extensive use of debit cards could produce that effect since the single monthly check payment covers several transactions in the credit card balance-due.

Thus, electronic-based payments are not limited to direct displacement of checks in the competition for dominance. Cash payments and multiple transactions that are aggregated for periodic remittance both offer rich opportunities for growth without the necessity to displace a check.

Nonetheless, the underlying reality remains: electronic-based systems are not broadly competitive with checks and will not soon reach partity in the number of noncash payments. Even more, the data suggest that cash payments far outnumber paper-based payments and, in the broadest sense, cash remains dominant.

If there is to be a different path of development, the technical capabilities—a full spectrum of customer terminals, secure and controlled on-line access to well-integrated applications, and assured linkage among all financial service intermediaries—must lead and motivate the other changes.

The Future Alternatives

Of the four broad possibilities for the path of future development of the United States payment mechanism, the two extreme cases can be eliminated. It is now abundantly clear that cash and the paper check are not going to disappear. Neither the "cashless" nor the "checkless" society are in prospect and, in reality, never were. Major payment systems are not eliminated by new technology; they coexist and each serves the segment of transaction needs for which it offers comparative advantage. It is also clear that electronics will persist; the "all-cash" or "all-check" society will not return and—unless it be optics—there is no credible image of a technology beyond electronics.

The final resolution between the two mixed alternatives—the "same-check" and "less-check" cases—is not yet predictable. What must be accomplished to influence the outcome is expressed in the four preconditions to electronic displacement of checks. The unpredictability arises because it is not clear whether or when the preconditions will be addressed or how well they will be fulfilled. If there is no major change in the national approach to payment processes, even the "same-check" case is unlikely to be attained in this century. From the base statistics estimated for 1983, a cumulative growth rate of electronic transactions in excess of 10% is needed to stop the growth of checks by 2000. There is no evidence that such a high aggregate rate now prevails. There are strong indications that the period of rapid growth in isolated electronic funds transfer systems will last for less than a decade. The major EFT systems in the United States are now growing at rates notably lower than in the late 1970s. Fedwire and CHIPS have now been extended to serve most of the busier eligible participants, and growth is dependent on displacement of alternative systems until the means to complementarity become available.

In the existing environment, individual electronic-based systems flourish on their own merits and grow and mature on their own schedule. Some systems succeed, but disappear because there is no infrastructure to serve the interdependencies; others mature while still small and cease to grow unless they are restructured or combined.

Simply stated, existing electronic-based systems do not complement each other in the features that contribute to mutual growth and foster the development of services and costs strongly competitive with checks. Thus, the number of checks will continue to increase until they reach a level of 40–45 billion per year and will then stabilize at that level into the next century.

One of the most critical elements in establishing a complementary infrastructure will be the accommodation of electronic systems that now exist. The whole spectrum of terminal devices—from the central processors in major companies to the home computer—is being redefined to exploit microprocessor technology. The provisions for security—even in value-transfer—are only marginally adequate. Reliable operations and confident control of data and messages comes from experience and there are only a few opportunities—ACH is one—to establish that reality at modest risk. Communication protocols and message formats are standardized but there are too many standards and there is too little compatibility. Many financial intermediaries are working to rationalize their internal applications and to integrate their networks; only a few have found adequate solutions; even fewer have implemented them successfully.

To fulfill the preconditions and thereby trigger a transition to the "less-check" case there must come to be an understandable concept of a universal electronic transaction service and a change in the gathering and reporting of money and of flows of funds. In the absence of such a concept, it is unlikely that the complex of new relationships and processes necessary to the transition can be foreseen in the legislative process or negotiated in new business relationships. The subtle resistance to change that is embodied in the concept of money as an inventory will sustain the bias toward debit transfers and paper checks.

The Universal Product Code (UPC) has demonstrated that bringing a sense of feasibility and common purpose to thousands of individuals and institutions is a long, slow process. The automated clearing house has emphasized the difficulty of learning to establish and sustain the degree of control and reliability essential to a common system that is not dependent on human intervention and is not limited to the human pace.

The essential feature of the triggering concept will be a means to add participants to existing networks and to interconnect existing networks despite the differences in equipment. The UPC for EFT will make it possible to use switched telecommunications with certainty of the identity and intent of the unseen party at the other end of the communication. It is feasible to classify every electronic transfer in terms meaningful to monetary and economic analysis. It would even be relatively easy to begin the process. A few systems—CHIPS, Bankwire, and, especially, Fedwire—represent a major portion of the activity and most of the dollar value.

It should be expected that a classification analysis would reveal the extent to which money is created when needed and extinguished or made to flow around the world just before the inventory is taken. Such analysis should also be expected to show that electronics serve a small segment of the demand for payments for nonfinancial goods and services but a major part of the demand for financial flows. Volatile markets and a capability to collect and disperse funds very quickly mean that one or two basis-points advantage will induce major money movements. Efforts to control "day-light" overdrafts will encourage interest charges for a fraction of a day and hasten the development of flow systems to further avoid the costs of holding deposits. But transfer classification will not solve the problems of obtaining collected balances or of bridging the New York to Tokyo time gap that impedes continuous money flows. It would, however, provide a more direct measurement of monetary and economic processes and a better guide to development of a new balance between payors and payees; between credit and debit transfers, and among cash, paper, and electronics.

The normal progression from physical objects to logical signals means that monetary policies and practices have been perfected in terms of physical concepts. That preoccupation is useful and appropriate when cash-based and paper-based systems are predominant. It will be less useful and increasingly inappropriate when electronic-based systems are dominant in both dollar value and number of transactions.

Velocity is clearly a derivative and dependent variable when the stock of money is essentially a physical inventory. Apparent instability in the measure of velocity, readily dismissed as a statistical aberration, may also reflect real variations in money transactions quite unrelated to basic economic activity. Only in the mindset of physical goods delivery is a payment linked to the national accounts; the dollar totals experienced in the major transfer systems—although more precisely measurable than any M—are not yet significant elements of monetary policy.

The proper time for a transition from a physical to a logical conception of money is an important public policy issue. Since electronic-based systems are already dominant in terms of dollar value it is arguable that the policy debate should begin.

Notes

1. CHIPS, operated by the New York Clearing House Association, concentrates on internationally related payments and maintains a strong New York focus. It serves several hundred members and affiliates with transfers that feature same-day settlement. Fedwire, operated by the Federal Reserve banks, serves several thousand depository financial institutions. Fedwire transfers feature immediate final settlement and the system is used to settle the end-of-day positions in both CHIPS and BANKWIRE. SWIFT, operated by the Society for Worldwide Interbank Financial Telecommunication, is the largest financial message service in the world, but does not yet include a settlement service.

2. The payment processes in the United States are summarized along with systems in other major countries in "Payment Systems in Eleven Developed Countries," The Bank for

International Settlements and Bank Administration Institute, 1980. The most complete recent analysis of the check system is presented in a "Quantitative Description of the Check Collection System," Federal Reserve Bank of Atlanta, 1981. A useful general perspective and an outline of the important unresolved issues is presented in "Report on the Payments System," Association of Reserve City Bankers, 1982.

2 PAYMENTS AND THE ECONOMIC TRANSACTION CHAIN

Linda K.S. Moore

The payment mechanism in place in the United States works. Payments and transfers are made on a timely basis and with reasonable accuracy throughout the nation. Coin and currency circulate easily. Checks written in Portland, Oregon on an account held in Portland, Maine will work their way through the check collection system for presentment and payment. Social Security and other direct deposits are delivered on magnetic tape for crediting to bank accounts. Corporations and banks move hundreds of millions of dollars among their accounts daily through electronic funds transfers. These are the four major payment media: cash, paper, tape, and electronic transactions. In terms of the number, not the value of transactions, cash predominates. Checks account for an estimated third of all transactions. Only a few percentage points of transactions are performed electronically.

The methods and procedures set up to handle check and credit transactions dominate the operation of the U.S. payment system. This system works effectively now; it can be made to work more efficiently by increased use of new payment media made possible by computerization and electronic delivery methods. The means to improve efficiency include but are not limited to using electronic transfer systems to displace, replace, or improve upon the paper-based system.

Many of the barriers to introducing electronic transactions are not technical but structural. The existing and potential benefits of electronic funds transfer systems have been identified but have largely not been measured or quantified. The costs of technology are readily quantifiable; the social costs of adapting electronic payment methods are often qualitative and must be identified and defined through political processes rather than market forces.

At issue are the costs and benefits associated with different forms of technology, the manner in which new technology will be implemented, ownership of the technology, and the social structure of the organizations that will manage the new technology. It is already evident that the full benefits of new technology are not realized when it is grafted onto existing operating procedures. Implementing new technology requires a modification of behavior not only on the part of users but also on the part of suppliers who must rethink their organization charts and personnel requirements.

The purpose of this chapter is to review the importance of the payment process in the economic transaction chain, to explore the role of the banking system in the payment process, to establish criteria for selecting transaction media, and to identify some of the economic and political issues related to developing electronic transaction networks.

Economic Transactions

A simple model of supply and demand is the basis for describing the banking system as part of a transaction chain. When the demand for goods and services is met by a supplier, a financial transaction usually occurs as part of the exchange. The facilitator, whose role is to make the exchange more efficient, participates in the payment for goods and services. The payment process has two principal components: the method of delivery and the transaction agent. (See figure 2-1.)

The method of delivery in the payment process entails the choice of a transaction medium and a transaction configuration. The choices are usually made by the facilitator who is acting as the link between the provider of goods and services and the consumer. A merchant, for example, can decide whether or not to accept checks as a transaction medium, whether to accept checks only at a certain checkout counter, whether to accept checks only when banks are closed, etc. There is a tacit agreement between the merchant and his customers that goods will be exchanged for value and that a check is an accepted medium for transferring the value. The transaction configuration chosen by the merchant includes a delivery mechanism, location, and time based on his assessment of the market situation.

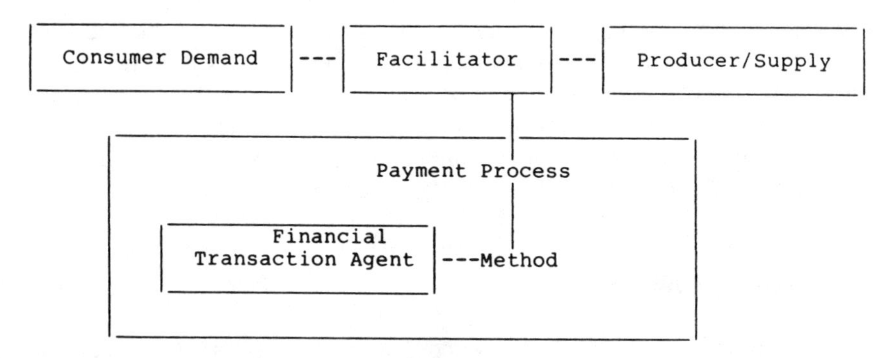

Figure 2-1. Exchange with Financial Transaction

By deciding to accept checks, the merchant is bringing the banks that issue those checks into his transaction process. The merchant becomes an intermediary and the merchant's bank becomes a financial transaction agent in accepting the checks for collection. If the merchant only accepted cash, the bank would not be a financial transaction agent since its direct participation would not be necessary for the payment process to be completed.

Another example of a facilitator would be the payroll department of a corporation. In this case, the company is a consumer of the services of its employees. The payroll department may decide to initiate a direct deposit program as the method of paying employees for the labor they supply. The chosen medium in this case is magnetic tape or similar computer output; the delivery mechanism is probably a combination of physical delivery of tapes and electronic transmission; the location is the specified bank accounts of employees to be paid; and the time when the money becomes available is agreed upon by the payroll department and the bank it chooses as financial transaction agent.

Depository financial institutions are also facilitators. Commercial banks, wholesale banks, community banks, savings banks, and credit unions are some of the types of facilitators that a consumer may choose to supply needs for financial services. Depository financial institutions, like other facilitators, choose the transaction media and configurations they will use in the payment process. A major impact of technology on the role of financial institutions as service providers has been to increase the alternatives for transaction configurations. As an example, automated teller machines have expanded the time and location choices for cash withdrawals.

Although depository financial institutions are only one of many types of facilitators participating in financial transactions, they are almost always present as a transaction agent. Depository financial institutions play a dominate role in the payment process because of their priviliged position in the banking system as agents for distributing coin and currency, collecting checks, buying and selling government financial instruments, and other activities in conjunction with the Federal Reserve System.

The Banking System

The operation of the banking system meets the needs of its users by providing management of both monetary value and information about monetary value. Needs for services that measure, store, transfer, control, enhance, preserve, protect, exchange, sell, or increase the value that has been captured by participants in the economy are met by the banking system and the financial services industry.

The main participants in the banking system are depository financial institutions and agencies, such as the New York Clearing House, which are permitted direct access to services operated by the Federal Reserve. Other types of financial service organizations are indirect participants acting as facilitators to meet the needs of the consumer for financial services in areas such as credit, investment, and insurance. Depository financial institutions and financial service organizations are supported by ancillary service groups, such as data processing centers. Although the banking system supports the financial services industry, only depository financial institutions—and a few financial service organizations and service groups—are permitted direct access to the system.

The banking system receives payments being processed by depository financial institutions acting as transaction agents. The banking system also passes transactions to and receives transactions through bank networks (figure 2-2). Consumers, suppliers, and facilitators are not always customers of the same transaction agent. Each bank, therefore, needs ways to complete a payment process for which it serves as an agent. It does this by participating in a network that increases the number of endpoints available for the execution of its business. A network, for the purpose of this analysis, is any system that takes transactions from more than one financial institution and combines them, exchanges them, or in some other way alters the nature of the transaction to obtain improved efficiency or enhanced value. A network can be as simple as two banks exchanging paper items or as complex as a global, multilocation electronic funds transfer system.

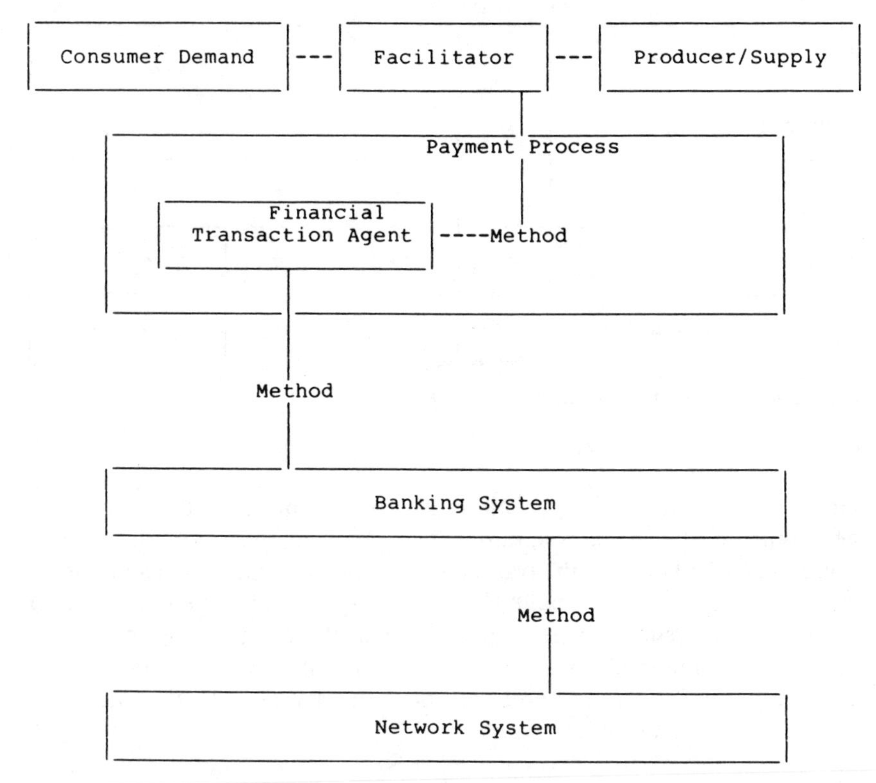

Figure 2-2. Banking System and the Payment Process

Transaction Media

Transactions are received in one of four major payment media: cash (coin and currency), paper, tape (magnetic tape, encoded disk or similar), or electronic transmission (figure 2-3). Before a particular payment process is completed, a transaction could require the use of all four media, or a single medium, and it could involve the transfer back and forth between media as the transaction makes its way along the financial transaction chain (figure 2-4).

Cash typically is used only in dealing face-to-face with the financial services user. It is not used to pass value or information through the banking system. An ever-increasing share of the transactions between bank agents and the network system is done on an electronic basis. The

Used for \ Media	Cash	Paper	Tape	Electronic
Payment Process	•	•	•	•
Banking Transactions	•	•	•	•
Network Transactions		•	•	•

Figure 2-3. Transactions Media

larger a network, the more likely it is to be automated and to use either electronic or tape media for transactions. Although much of the information transfer and most of the transactions involving either small amounts or minor participants in the banking system are still performed using paper or tape-based systems, in general it can be said that cash drops out of the banking system at the point where it interacts with the consumer and that electronic transfers are the preferred medium among network systems for transfering information and value. (See figure 2-4.)

Transaction Configuration Selection

The banks choose a transaction configuration that will continue the payment process from the financial transaction agent through the banking system. The major considerations in selecting a transaction configuration are: (1) cost and characteristics of alternative media, and (2) mix and volume of different types of transactions.

Cost and Characteristics of Alternate Media. The three media used by the banking system to complete a payment are those that can be used in network transactions: paper, tape, and electronic transmission.

Paper. The characteristic of paper that makes it attractive for transactions, even in an environment where float is reduced to near zero, is that it offers variability. The labor needed for handling paper can be purchased in small, discrete quantities over a very large range of volume, while the

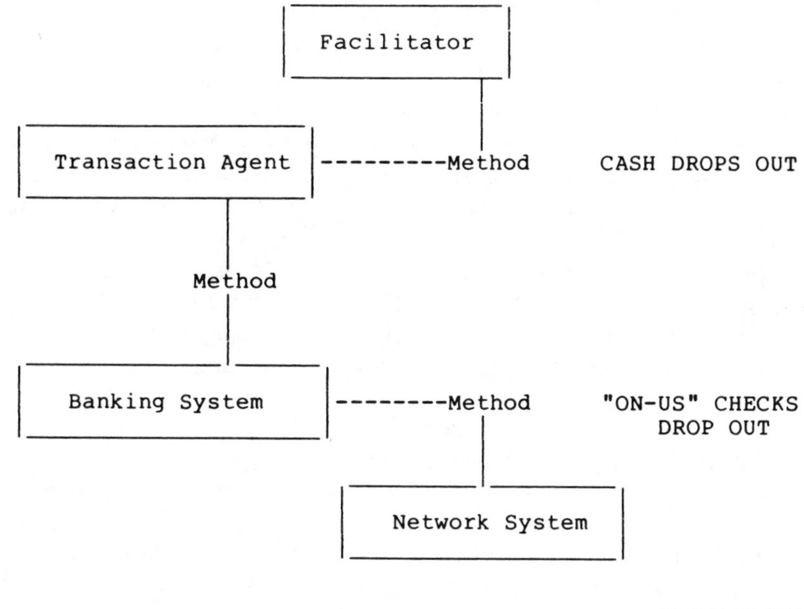

Figure 2-4. The Financial Transaction Path

capital equipment required can be rented as easily as bought. Furthermore, the trade-offs between capital and labor are straightforward, so that the decision to use increments of labor can be cost-justified over a fairly long period of changing transaction volumes before the decision needs to be made to expand capital.

Tape. Tape provides the operational characteristics of predictability, in that a transaction initiator can predict with reasonable certainty when a transaction will enter the network system and be completed. Tape transactions also require predictability; the initiator of a transaction has to have previous knowledge that need for the transaction will occur within a specified timespan. The banking system agents capturing the transaction have to anticipate that they will receive other, similar transactions in the same predetermined timespan. The essence of cost effectiveness for tape transactions is that there must be enough of them within a reasonably short period of time if the consumer or the banking system is to capture any of the value of immediacy offered by the network system.

Electronic Transmission. Electronic transactions are capital intensive, with a high fixed cost which must be spread over a large range of volume. The decision to invest capital in computer hardware, software, and telecommunications for a funds transfer system is predicated on achieving enough transaction volume to equate the cost of electronic transactions with the value of the immediacy such transactions provide. Since different institutions (with different customer needs) place differing values on immediacy, the decision to choose an electronic medium over other media is not the same for all institutions, even when costs are the same.

There are characteristics intrinsic to the three media which influence the decision-making process and which may outweigh the considerations of unit cost. The next diagram suggests the trade-offs among the three media. It identifies the chief characteristic of each payment medium and specifies the timing of the entry of a command (to perform a transaction) into the banking system and the execution of the transaction.

In choosing a transaction configuration, the advantages of a particular medium are weighed against the cost of using it. If no benefits have been identified in the choice of one medium over another, the objective will be to minimize cost, choosing the medium with the lowest unit cost. But, where a payment process participant places value on payment medium

Media / Implementation	Paper	Tape	Electronic
Command to Transaction Agent	Delayed	Delayed	Immediate
Processing by Banking System	Delayed for low value/ immediate for high	Delayed	Delayed for low value/ immediate for high
Execution in Network	Delayed	Immediate	Immediate
MEDIA CHARACTERISTIC:	Variability	Predictability	Certainty

Figure 2-5. Media Trade-Offs

characteristics, the objective will be to maximize benefit, subject to volume and cost constraints.

The Mix and Volume of Transactions. One of the critical differences among the financial transaction media are the differing amounts of volume needed to make the unit cost of a transaction using a particular medium competitive with the unit cost of other available payment means.

To reduce the complexity of their operations, many participants in the banking system have chosen to specialize by meeting sets of needs for financial services. Typically, these specialists offer their customers a range of other financial services to provide additional benefits to valued customers, to attract market share, or for other strategic reasons. The result is that the typical depository financial institution handles a wide variety of items every day; but, across the range of possible transactions at a financial institution, some will be in large quantities and some in rather small quantities, except for those very large institutions that are major providers of all types of financial services. When the volume or the value of a particular type of transaction reaches a certain share of all transactional volume or value, an institution will search for the most cost effective way to handle that type of transaction.

The volume of specific types of transactions flowing through a banking institution in a given time span then becomes a major consideration in planning transaction paths. The operational decisions of the bank entail lumping some types of transactions together to make them look similar and identifying specific types of transactions which merit a dedicated transaction configuration. A small savings bank, for example, might elect to install state-of-the-art teller stations for passbook transactions while handing off all of its paper to a correspondent bank for processing. The correspondent bank that receives the savings bank paper will treat checks, securities coupons, and other items as separate transaction types. Checks will be further separated and batched by criteria such as the location of the bank on which it is drawn (on-us, local, foreign, etc.) and its value (high dollar amounts).

One of the characteristics of the banking system in a largely paper-based operating environment is the need to separate types of transactions into manageable sizes that can be handled cost effectively. With paper, economies of scale come from creating specialized systems to handle different types of transactions. In an electronic environment, on the contrary, the volume of transactions needed for profitable operation is typically high and economies of scale come from homogenization.

Transaction Path Selection

Part of the evaluation process for identifying optimal transaction paths requires evaluating transaction types for common characteristics. The savings bank example has only two types of transactions: mechanism transactions (passbook transactions which can involve all four media) and media transactions (the paper handed off to the correspondent bank).

The savings bank and the correspondent bank represent the two basic approaches to transaction processing: making everything look the same for a single processing method or differentiating transactions in order to specialize the processing methods. These two approaches are referred to here as *continuous* and *discrete* transaction paths because the concepts can be represented mathematically as continuous and discrete functions.

The selection of a transaction path requires that the payment process (medium and configuration) be considered, individually and collectively, at each point where intervention takes place. The transactions are handled either by making them look the same—using one medium from beginning to end—or by differentiating the steps so that intervention and changes of media can occur. By definition, the medium chosen for entry in a continuous transaction path must be the medium for exit. In a discrete financial transaction path (figure 2-6), not only is it possible to enter the transaction path by one medium and exit by another but it is also possible for the intervention process to include more than one transaction configuration and multiple conversions among media.

Discontinuous transaction paths modify the payment media to accommodate the environment in which the transaction is being performed. Continuous transaction paths (figure 2-7) often require the modification of location and time as well as choice of medium and delivery method. The benefits of using a unified medium for a transaction path must combine with the savings generated from eliminating the intervention process so as to outweigh the costs of converting the transaction environment.

New technology provides the means to unify and standardize transaction and information processing. Standardization of paper transactions and information has made it possible to use checks as a single-payment medium to pass value through the financial transaction paths. The possibilities for improving check processing in order to gain significant new economies are diminishing. Magnetic tape transactions, while increasing processing speed, require physical handling and a conversion of the transaction environment, which is only cost effective for large operations. Electronic technology, however, offers opportunities for significant gains in information capture and processing speed. To capture the economies of scale,

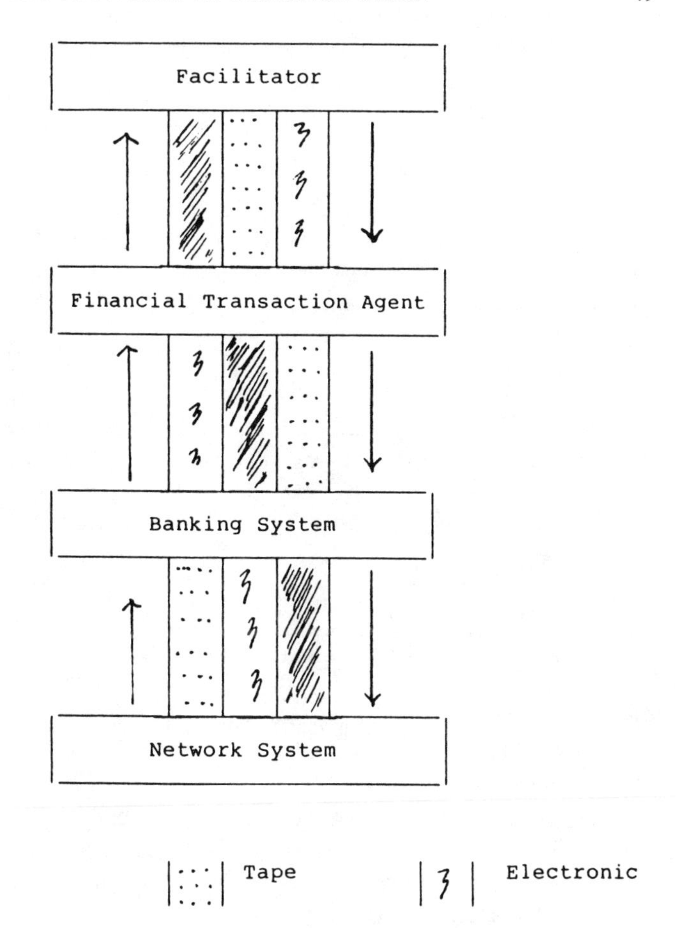

Figure 2-6. Discrete Transaction Paths with Discontinuous Interaction

banks increasingly use networks for receiving and sending electronic transactions. The banking system is at present attempting to enlarge these existing networks in order to include more financial transaction agents and facilitators in an electronic payment loop.

The Trend Toward Networks

As the number and complexity of transactions increase, network management becomes a major operational concern for a financial service

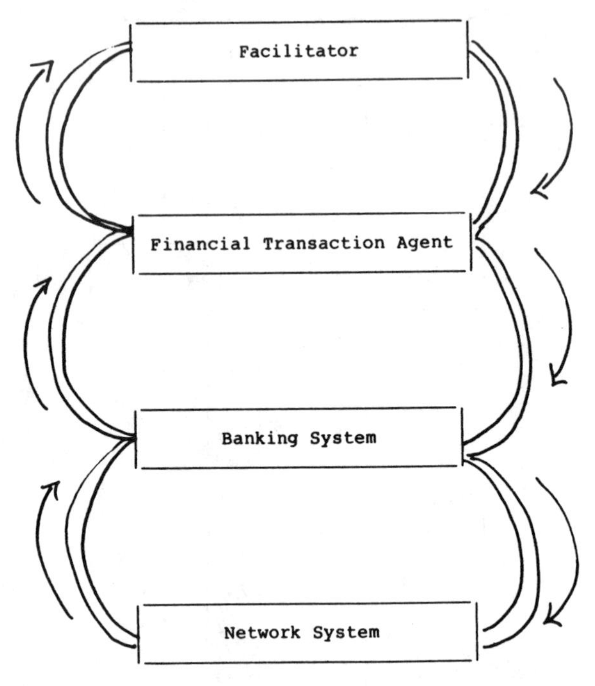

Figure 2-7. Continuous Transaction Paths with Interaction in One Medium

institution. The need for networks to improve the efficiency of financial service, and the trend toward using electronic transfer systems for these networks, combine to create a major influence on the development of the financial transaction path.

Since the economies of scale make the forming of networks a desirable objective, banks try to protect their market position by controlling access to the network system. In some cases, commercial bank networks exclude savings institutions; in other cases, depository financial institutions exclude nonbank financial service providers. A transaction facilitator is not always free to enter the network that would complete an optimal transaction path. Even when an organization qualifies for network participation it may have to decide to install new equipment and modify its choice of transaction medium and configurations in order to participate.

Banks, which were once involved directly in the link between demand and supply (figure 2-8), are now bolstered by networks on both sides. Although this has the advantage of increasing the number of endpoints the bank can serve, it also has the effect of reducing the role of the bank as the transaction agent in the payment process.

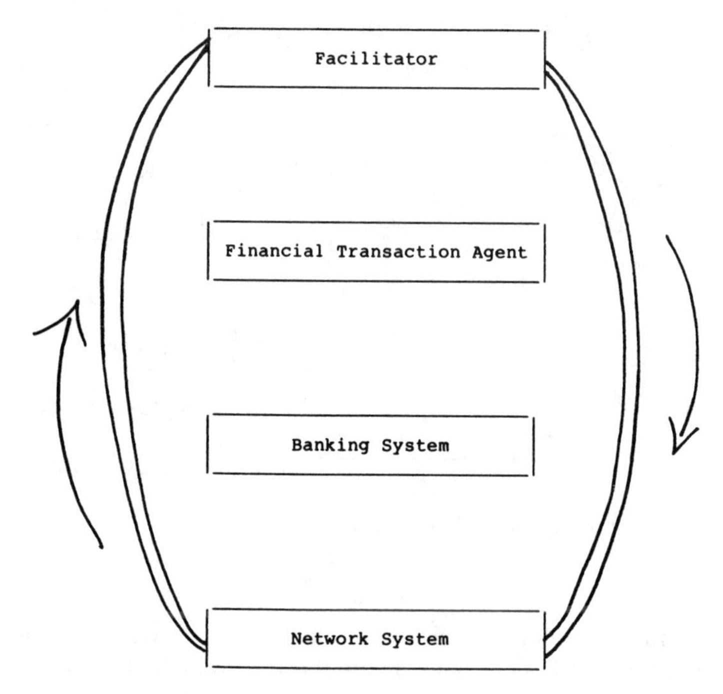

Figure 2-8. Financial Transaction Path with One Medium and One Interaction

It is easy to visualize how bringing the transaction facilitator directly into the network system, with a minimum of intervention from the banking system, simplifies the process of the exchange of value. The role of the bank as an intermediary is reduced. It acts more as a mediator between the financial services consumer and the networks than as the transaction agent. To compensate, banks look for new services and market links to offset their diminished role as transaction agents in the payment process.

The Economic Transaction Chain

Payments and related financial transactions are linked through a chain of needs and actions implicitly or explicitly present in all economic transactions (figure 2-9).

When a transaction occurs between the bank and its customer, the bank is a facilitator meeting financial-service user needs for decision, ownership transfer, and financial management. As they introduce new services, banks seek to increase their role as facilitating agent in meeting other needs in the

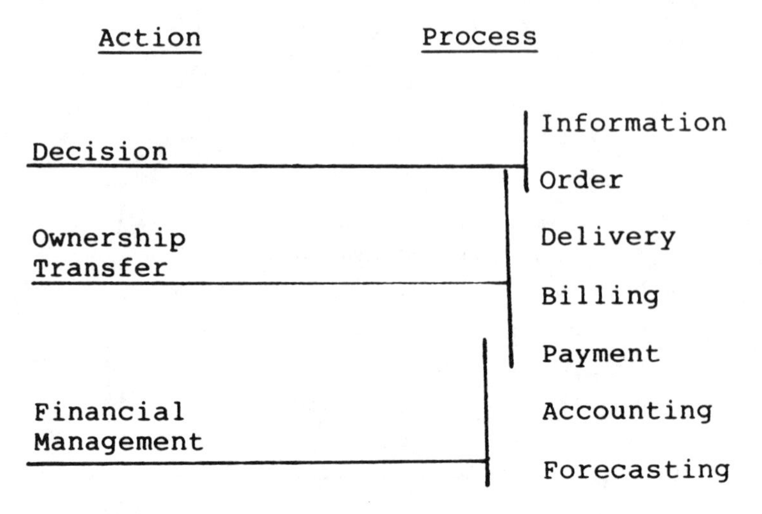

Figure 2-9. Economic Transaction Chain

economic transaction chain. Instead of limiting the provision of information to a statement of a customer's account, for example, banks will offer information on investments—with the objective of capturing the full decision process and receiving the order and its related transactions. In a fully developed chain, banks would be providing financial management services, which would lead to information and new opportunities to capture the decision process. Any provider of financial services that is seeking to maximize market opportunities will try to develop a complete transaction chain.

Before the development of computerized communications and electronic payment methods, each of the steps in the economic transaction chain was discrete, and often laborious and costly to perform. Technology has made it possible to forge an economic transaction chain of electronic links.

Process for Payments and Related Economic Transactions

Depository financial institutions have a key role in the economic transaction chain because of their hold on the payment process. They are also a major user of network services. The banking system is therefore a pivotal player in the development of electronic networks to meet user needs for every link. When they participate in the development of

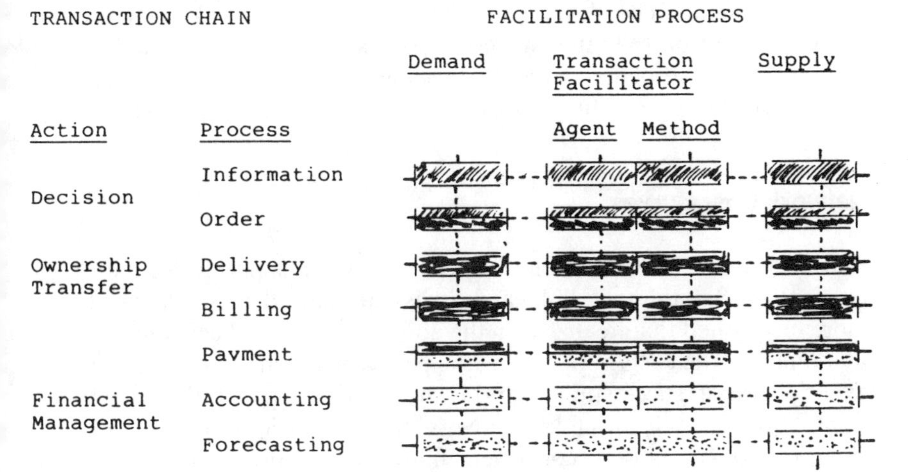

Figure 2-10. Process for Payments and Related Economic Transactions

electronic links for the economic transaction chain, depository financial institutions try to use the electronic transaction paths they have developed for the payment process (figure 2-10).

Transaction facilitators and their agents manage the processes of the transaction chain. Although specialists exist, no single process in the chain is independent of the other processes. Activity among the processes for payments and related economic transactions must be linked by transaction paths. In the belief that optimal economic efficiency is achieved when payments and the related processes are linked electronically for each step in the transaction chain, facilitators are pursuing two paths: vertical integration and horizontal rationalization.

A facilitator who meets one or more needs in the transaction chain and has developed an electronic delivery method to meet the needs of the current market (horizontal links) will seek to expand by meeting additional needs (vertical links) using the same electronic methods. These possibilities are shown in figure 2-10.

At present, electronic transactions which include payment must be cleared through the banking system. Only banks, therefore, can be independent facilitators for every link of a transaction. All other participants who wish to seek the economies of an unbroken transaction process must either include a bank as an agent in the facilitation process, or find a means, such as barter, to exchange value without the participation of the banking system. The development of electronic networks is therefore still dependent on the interest, resources, and capabilities of the banking system. Efforts to benefit from new technology by standardizing the links can be stymied by a refusal of the banks to provide the payment link.

Network Cost Curves

The benefits of integrated electronic networks that permit an unbroken transaction chain among links and across specialized networks are today more envisioned than realized. In the absence of detailed economic studies that quantify the costs of operating the payment system, one can accept the experiences of successful electronic networks as proof that electronic transactions are cheap and effective—or one can look at the problems experienced by poorly conceived networks as proof that electronic transactions are expensive and difficult to manage.

At the beginning of this chapter, the banking system was described as a closed system making economic decisions based on maximizing its own objectives. It was seen that once a bank chose to enter a network it often had to modify its operating decisions to accommodate the requirements for network participation. When a bank seeks to minimize costs through network participation or to maximize its market by adding new services, it increases the number of external variables that can impinge on its economic choices. The public pressure on banks to recognize the social costs and benefits of their operations stems in part from the increase in the diversity of their services and the number of their customers.

Within small, closely controlled networks, an analysis of costs versus benefits leads to an optimal choice of payment media based on operational, not sociopolitical decisions. The customers best served by electronic transactions are those who have quantified the value of the speed with which they can receive information and act upon that information. When the players are known and the transactions are relatively homogeneous, this market can be served efficiently and cost effectively by electronic networks.

As the number of participants increases and the possible combination of transactions multiplies, the costs of providing electronic transaction services increases. Evidence suggests that an increase in costs is exponentially related to an increase in the number of endpoints in a network. Although marginal and hence average costs may approach zero as the number of transactions handled by an individual system increases, it would appear that this does not hold true if the increase in the number of transactions is achieved by increasing the number of endpoints served.

Adding additional participants and additional transaction services increases fixed costs and sets the point at which marginal cost will equal average cost at a higher level of transactions. To get these increased transactions requires either an increasing market of participants who are willing to pay the cost of participation in an electronic network or an artificial pricing policy geared to marginal not average costs. The latter is only viable if this policy successfully increases the number of transactions. The first method, increasing the number of participants willing to pay the actual cost of participation in an electronic network, is complicated by two major environmental factors: users often do not pay the real costs of participation in paper-based networks, and a market of economic participants who have identified the benefits of improved information and transactional efficiency must for the most part be created and educated.

The Payments System as a Public Good

In certain operating environments, electronic technology has been successfully applied to reduce costs and improve efficiency. These situations are characterized by a limited number of participants—demanders, suppliers, and agents—and a common set of information, transaction, and management requirements. When economic players are few and their objectives similar, it is relatively easy to form a network. As the number of network participants increases, the complexity of deciding how to link each step becomes further complicated by the political issues of who will bear the costs of the network services.

As the number of participants in a payment network increases, the system comes closer to being a public good. In today's paper-based networks, the rules for handling cash and checks are rooted in social tradition and defined by law and regulation. The guidelines for participation by government, financial service organizations, businesses, and individuals are established and understood. At present there is a political consensus of sorts regarding the appropriate ways to minimize the costs of a paper-based system while maximizing a set of generally accepted private and public benefits. This consensus does not exist for an electronic-based payment system. The introduction of electronic systems also introduces or reintroduces questions regarding the operation of a payment system as a public good.

One of the characteristics of a public good is that a purely economic pricing system (where goods or services are supplied at a level where the marginal cost equals the market price) is no longer judged sufficient for an equitable allocation of resources. A political system of negotiation supplements or replaces the free-market concept of supplying a good or service at the price that will "clear the market."

The process of establishing the rules for supplying and consuming a public good is essentially a bargaining process. Therefore, it is important that the number of representatives at the bargaining table be a manageable number. Ideally, the goals of each participant will be known by all the players. Since fairness is a major consideration in the provision of a public good, it is important that the representatives be accepted as valid spokesmen and negotiators by the interests they represent. Finally, there has to be in place a mechanism for carrying out decisions; in the case of payment systems, the mechanism requires that the systems be technologically compatible.

The supply of payment services has historically been regulated in those areas where the sociopolitical consensus has deemed that public needs have to be met or protected. The criteria for managing the payment system as a public good have been met for the check-clearing process, which is the base of the present-day payment system. Overlaying the numerous local and specialized check-exchange systems is the check-clearing process of the Federal Reserve System, operated with the participation of the major banks in each Federal Reserve Bank District. These principal players are relatively few and are known to each other. They are therefore able to work together and to communicate effectively when problems occur. They have compatible systems and they are accepted by the other economic players to represent the public interest in managing the existing payment system.

The development of electronic transaction systems requires the participation of new players, who are seeking to establish themselves as valid representatives at the bargaining table. Many of the participants in the economic transaction chain, particularly the depository financial institutions which dominate the payment process, see new technologies as competitive tools. They seek to capture market share through proprietary technology which is better than that offered by their competitors. Consumer preference among competing electronic system alternatives is expected to be established in the marketplace. The winning technology will become the standard for the system.

Contrasting this free market ideal, which is apparently the solution implicitly accepted by current public policy, is the reality of the regulated payment system already in place, which allocates competitive advantages and burdens to different types of players. The players involved in the process for payments and related economic transactions are many more than presently recognized by existing legislation, regulation, and policy.

The alternatives for transactions are numerous; the social and economic viewpoints almost unlimited.

The Future of Electronic Networks

At present, the debates regarding the electronic transaction chain of the future indicate three possible scenarios. These could be described as "fewer networks," "more networks," and "no networks."

Fewer Networks

The solution that the United States banking industry is presenting to the American—and world—economy, is that of a system in which all transaction facilitators and their agents are linked electronically. Payments that occur as part of economic transactions will be captured by the banking industry at the point of initiation and switched through an electronic network. Communication centers will process transaction information and either forward the data immediately to a participating bank or batch transactions for later transmittal. The system is organized around bank account debits and credits.

In this scenario, all the economic activity of the nation will be bundled into transaction packages carried by networks operated by the banking system. The realization of such a network requires that either the number of depository financial institutions in the United States be reduced from 40,000 to 40 or that technology be used to create a massive system of telecommunications links, run by supercomputers, linking the 40,000 institutions to 40 communications centers constructed to handle the nation's electronic payment activity. Evolution to such a system is seen by many as the inevitable result of existing technology, systems applications, management attitudes, and the present structure of the banking system. Debate is centered around who will operate the supernetworks, what the rules of access will be, and how competition can be assured within the banking system.

More Networks

Significantly increasing the number of electronic networks could meet the needs expressed by financial transaction chain participants who operate at one remove or more from the center of banking system power. This group includes community banks as well as the retailers, nonbank financial service suppliers, and other participants in the economic transaction chain concerned about their future in an electronic payment environment.

Existing networks are organized around the criteria most important to the network participants. The criteria for banks focus on account management and fraud prevention. Criteria for other participants in the economic transaction chain may focus on customer needs, inventory control, behavioral research, or interest rate fluctuations, to give just some examples of the nearly infinite possibilities. Nonbank networks that wish to create an unbroken transaction chain must modify their network plans to include the criteria set by the banking system. This increases the cost of operating the network and opens it up to intervention from the banking system, which is often unwanted.

If nonbank networks were permitted to use financial transaction agents that were not depository financial institutions but neutral gateways to the network system, there would be fewer constraints and greater economic incentives for them to create their own electronic networks. Organizing communications centers and switches along product and service lines would open the way to new solutions and applications of technology. These new networks would be developed to meet economic profiles which would include payment criteria determined by the transaction facilitator, not by a depository financial institution. Risks would be assumed by the network operator. However, since each network would be managed by a relatively few number of known players, and participation could be controlled by specific criteria, the costs of security should be easier to identify and control than in a large network with diverse participants. The likelihood that these networks, organized for similar transactions, would also be organized along regional lines would open up new opportunities to local and regional banks to attract accounts.

No Networks

The no-network scenario is theoretically possible if on-line transactions are performed in an off-line mode. One technological solution that could replace telecommunications links is the *smart card* or integrated circuit card. The smart card stores value and information in a computer chip carried on a standard plastic card. The card is used to interact with autonomous terminals located at each transaction point. The card user provides the transaction path by walking from point to point, eliminating the need for electronic links.

In France, where the smart card is being proposed as the electronic money of the future, smart cards will not be used to replace electronic networks. They are expected to reduce demand on existing networks, which will use their freed-up capacity for new applications.

Error Resolution and Fraud

The three network scenarios presented above represent three approaches to reducing payment system error and fraud. The bank-operated networks propose record centralization and interchange in a fully electronic environment as a means of detecting and isolating anomalies. Diversified networks organized along product and service lines would reallocate risk, assigning some of the burden presently assumed by banks to specialists who had evaluated the risks of operating or insuring particular types of networks. The use of the smart card to replace certain types of networks relies on new technology to prevent errors and fraud by giving individual users more control, and possibly more responsibility.

Public Policy Issues

The financial and social costs of human error, systems failure, and fraud are already present in today's paper-based system. The financial cost of fraud and systems failure can be approximated and factored into the costs of operating a payment process. The social costs of systems failures and errors unjustly resolved are the largest unknown costs in the operation of a payment system. The costs and the social questions will be greater in an electronic environment. Rectifying errors is a labor-intensive process which takes away some of the benefit of network efficiency. Furthermore, the increased scope of operations will increase the probability that errors in any one network will be passed on to other networks. The methods for error resolution in such an environment will require sophisticated systems and better-trained customer service representatives.

When networks are small, problems concerning payment errors are resolved at the local level by financial institutions that know their customers. Human judgment is free to operate and to evaluate the factors of each situation. If the trend to fewer networks continues, many financial transaction agents will cease to exist or will relinquish most of their authority in exchange for the right to participate in an electronic network. In a large electronic network, problems are resolved at a service center by employees following system guidelines not equally applicable to each situation. Error resolution can involve many unknown players and requires a specialized labor force that can identify where human intervention and judgment are needed—not always an easy task in systems created to eliminate human intervention. Furthermore, the monolithic nature of these networks makes it theoretically possible to deprive financial service users of access to electronic payment systems at a national and even international level.

At present, electronic networks present the possibility of massive fraud, which frightens the banks and their insurors, and of computer-generated abuse of human rights, which frightens everyone. Judging from the legislation enacted sofar, it seems that the political reaction to regulating electronic systems is to place paper-based constraints on electronic transactions in an attempt to keep the new systems anchored in the familiar paper system with its well-established rules. What is needed are rules that take into account the particular characteristics of electronic transactions. For example, Regulation E—which regulates electronic funds transfer transactions—emphasizes written confirmation of electronic transactions. This increases the cost of providing electronic transactions because of the duplication of information. The systems operators are required to generate costly paper confirmations but they are not required to read them. It is left to the financial services user to detect errors. The consumer is considered to be protected by information about account activity.

Given the speed of electronic transactions and the irrevocable nature of many of them, information that alerts the consumer to an error that has already occurred is slight protection. More emphasis should be put on improving error resolution. Experiences with credit card and electronic funds transfer regulations suggest that it is difficult to legislate human judgment and that systems put in place to ensure strict compliance often eliminate or restrict the application of human judgment in error resolution. When an error is not resolved by strict adherence to credit card or EFT transaction disputes, the only recourse is the courts. Legal provision for binding arbitration by locally elected mediators might be an acceptable solution which could reduce the costs to society of the error resolution process by permitting the timely intervention of an informed, neutral professional.

Regulation E deals almost exclusively with consumer issues. The area of electronic transactions for business, which represents the largest share of the present volume of electronic transactions, is still largely unregulated. The consensus among operators of electronic systems for commercial operations is that the absence of guidelines and clearly defined legal protection has hindered the development of their services.

No comprehensive legislation exists regarding system reliability. In late 1985, a computer failure at a large New York bank threatened the operation of the entire U.S. payment system. The Federal Reserve Bank of New York was able to take actions to prevent the problem, which tied up billions of dollars of electronic transaction, from paralyzing the operations of the other major banks that are part of the same electronic network. Quick action was possible in this situation because the number of players were few and were known to each other.

At present, because of the limited applications of electronic networks, the problem of system failure is manageable by its participants, with or without guidelines. It is not too soon, however, to consider the guidelines needed when the scope of electronic networks has increased to the point where electronic transactions are widely accepted as a means of payment. When a snowstorm shuts down the airport, merchants do not stop accepting checks. When an electronic network is down, direct debit at the point-of-sale is a questionable form of payment. Since an alternative form of payment is cash, network operators should not be permitted to operate both their automated teller machines and their point-of-sale network on the same system. At present such a requirement would be not only meaningless but counter-productive; it is given here as a simple example of the types of legislation that would be useful in an electronic payment environment.

Product guidelines are another form of meaningful consumer protection that have to be developed specifically for electronic transactions. A public agency not unlike the Food and Drug Administration might be an appropriate way to establish rules for the quality of financial transaction services. What is the appropriate waiting time, for example, to gain access to an electronic network for a home banking transaction. In France, consumers often try for 20 minutes or more before successfully connecting with their bank through the national videotex switch. If the system hangs up in the middle of a transaction—*tant pis*.

Electronic network operators serving the general public should be required to file with a government agency and offer proof of their ability to comply with pertinent financial and systems requirements. At present the integrity of electronic transaction networks is assured by the participation of banks that have already met capital requirements and are assumed to have the necessary expertise for operating a network. Because banks control the critical payment link in the transaction chain their presence is artificially required in the development of complete chains. Their presence does not ensure that financial service user needs for security and reliability are met. The fact of being a bank does not make them the best operators of an electronic transaction chain. Since the payment system as a whole is a public good, regulation that meets the needs of all participants is necessary. Payment systems regulation that is rooted in the system requirements of a paper-based system, and therefore recognizes traditional players at the expense of new but potentially better-qualified players, is not meeting the responsibilities of a democratic process for the allocation of a public good.

The resolution of these and many more issues are the major barriers related to the economical operation of an electronic payment system. There appears to be an unwillingness to face the political issues surrounding the use of new technology in the payment process. From a technological point of view, the choices among media are fairly straightforward. But the near total absence of a sociopolitical consensus regarding the appropriate environment for electronic payments artificially loads the costs of existing electronic networks and presents formidable barriers to the introduction of new forms of networks. If public policy is needed to manage the public interest in electronic networks then public policy must recognize that new technology requires new forms of management.

3 TELECOMMUNICATIONS POLICY ISSUES: THE NEW MONEY DELIVERY MODES

Henry Geller

The computer, wedded to new communications delivery systems such as the satellite and the fiber optic, is rapidly leading to a new information order, both domestically and worldwide. The examples are legion and dramatic. When the fire alarm sounds in Malmo, Sweden, the firemen consult a computer base in Amsterdam to find the best route and nearest hydrant. Oil shipments are traced throughout the world by contacting a computer base in Houston. Construction projects in Brazil or Saudi Arabia are managed from computer bases in San Francisco. The computer bases can be used in shifts because of time-zone differences; thus an Ohio computer can be used first in Western Europe, then in the United States, and finally in Japan. The satellite, perched at 22,300 miles in a geosynchronous orbit and distance-insensitive, makes possible this new global information order [1].

This information revolution extends to banking. Thus, there is the SWIFT network—the Society for Worldwide Interbank Financial Telecommunications—used by roughly 700 of the world's major banks to allow their subscribers to transact business virtually instantaneously anywhere on the globe. And individual large banks now have telecommunications networks reaching four or more continents, and allowing the central bank in New York or San Francisco instantaneous access to data in any of its worldwide locations [2].

Domestically, telecommunications links make possible remote banking services (such as home banking or point-of-sale operations); network services to other banking locations (such as for cash reporting, movement, control, and similar management functions); and interbank services, including the ACH (automated clearing houses). It has been estimated that the total network wire transfers in the United States daily come to $500–600 billion, with some banks electronically transferring each day a dollar value that equals two to four times their total deposits [3]. The Fedwire, a system of computers and Telex connections operated by the Federal Reserve Board, is now the principal means by which banks exchange funds in transactions other than those involving checks.

These new developments have raised serious problems for the regulators of the banking system, particularly the Federal Reserve Board. To give but one example, a computer failure at the Bank of New York in November 1985 snarled thousands of government securities transactions and resulted in a brief $32 billion overdraft at the New York Federal Reserve Bank. A concerned Congressional committee was told that on an average day, about $200 billion worth of government securities transactions take place, involving about 27,000 separate transactions. The Federal Reserve Board Chairman told the subcommittee, "Like it or not, computers and their software systems—with the possibility of mechanical or human failure—are an integral part of the payments mechanism. The scale and speed of transactions permit no other approach" [4].

This chapter will discuss the telecommunications policy issues relating to this new electronic banking process. As has been made clear before, banking today encompasses more than the traditional banks, including all the new entrants like investment companies (e.g., Merrill Lynch), American Express, Dun & Bradstreet, Sears, etc. Significantly, these new entrants rely heavily upon telecommunications networks [5].

The discussion will first treat domestic issues, business networks and then residential or home links, and second the international telecommunications policy matters.

Domestic Telecommunications Policy Issues Affecting Electronic Money Transactions—Business to Business

New Technology and the Regulatory Response

The driving force behind the massive changes in this field has not been government policy but rather dynamic technology. Before World War II, the U.S. telephone scene was dominated by one player, American Telephone and Telegraph Co. (AT&T)—a huge *de facto* monopoly providing end-to-end integrated service (along with 1500 smaller telephone companies largely located in small communities). The underlying technology was the paired 4-Khz. copper wire, and that surely militated for one monopoly service. Because it was a monopoly of an essential service, there was close governmental regulation of entry, rates, etc., by the Federal Communications Commission (FCC) and the state commissions to insure that expenditures were legitimate and prudent and that ratepayers received efficient service at reasonable rate.[1] The company, on the other hand, was allowed to recover all such operating expenses together with a fair rate of return on investment.

Because this was a monopoly system, the FCC took several steps to promote universal service at reasonable rates. Thus, it adopted a policy of nationwide pricing uniformity for interstate toll rates (even though the costs are higher over the thin routes). It assigned substantial joint interstate and intrastate expenses (the so-called nontraffic sensitive (NTS) costs of the telephone signaling instrument—the inside wiring, the loop from the subscriber to the central office, and the switch in that office) arbitrarily to the interstate services, to keep local rates low. (For a discussion of this complex subsidy arrangement, see Noam [6].)

Technological advances after World War II drastically changed this cozy monopoly situation. First came the microwave, then coaxial cable, followed by the satellite, and now the fiber optic with its enormous capacity. Switching, so crucial to a common carrier's operation, now became the province of the computer. Packet switching, dependent on the computer, is the ideal transmission mode for the greatly increasing volume of data communications. The trend is clear: from analog, so suited to voice, to digital, able to handle both voice and data. The data processing and telecommunications fields are merging [7].

This can be seen in the equipment field. A Private Branch Exchange (PBX) is now a computer: It can be used one moment for communications (switching) and the next for data processing (inventory), and, of course, should be so used. It can be supplied by an AT&T or an IBM (Rolm), with the latter always totally deregulated. Further, the telephone network itself can perform the same functions as the PBX (e.g., Centrex or enhanced Centrex, which can be programmed by the subscriber). As a further illustration, protocol conversion can be done by equipment (supplied by an IBM); by a data processing/communications service such as GTE's Telenet; or again by the local telephone network, acting as a universal gateway for data just as it does for voice. The computer (integrated circuit) underlies the entire telecommunications information industry [7].

This merging of the computer and the communications industries forced the policy makers to choose between extending regulation to the unregulated (the data processing industry) or deregulating the entire field. Of necessity, the goal must be the latter, for the telecommunications field, like its merging partner, now calls for fast response in the marketplace to changing technological advances. It is no longer suited to a slow administrative minuet where permission from the government must be obtained before introducing some new product or service.

This is not to say that the governmental process toward this goal was sure or carried out with consistency. Thus, the FCC sought to limit competition to the established AT&T monopoly only to the private-line sector (less than 2% of the interstate revenues), and thus hoped to preserve the above-described subsidy scheme. Such market segmentation is inconsistent with the driving technology. Once competition is introduced because of such technology, there is no logical stopping point. Rather, this is the proverbial slippery slope that lawyers talk about. The restrictions erode. (This erosion process is described by Wiley [8].)

Present Telecommunications Policies

As a consequence of that erosion process, the situation today is as follows:

1. The telecommunications equipment field is wide open to competition and completely deregulated (with one exception discussed within). The telephone line is like the power line: Anyone can attach any device so long as it meets certain technical standards insuring compatibility with the network (see Wiley [8], pp. 27–31). So-called "smart buildings," where the landlord installs a large-capacity PBX to handle all the tenants' incoming and outgoing calls, are now a frequent occurrence.

2. The interstate and, increasingly, the entire toll field is open to competition. New competitors like MCI (now combined with IBM's SBS) and GTE Sprint are competing with AT&T with billion-dollar construction programs of microwave, fiber and satellite circuits. Hundreds of resellers have entered—entities that acquire bulk quantities of, say, AT&T's channels and then resell them to the public at discount prices. Many offer value-added services, such as some form of data processing—storage, editing, protocol conversion, etc. (see Wiley [8], pp. 31–37).

3. With the exception of AT&T and its divested operating companies (see below), these competitors are deregulated. There is thus virtually no regulation of the resellers or the new competitors like MCI (called Other Common Carriers or OCCs); they have no market power warranting entry or rate regulation. As for the value-added carriers, the FCC held that

providers of enhanced operations (involving data processing functions like storage or forwarding or protocol conversion) are not rendering common carrier services. Only the basic communications (pipeline) service remains subject to regulation.[2]

4. To prevent AT&T from improperly cross-subsidizing when it entered these new enhanced (and thus deregulated) fields, the FCC required that the company employ fully separated subsidaries (FSS) for these competitive undertakings, so that there would be no common facilities involving the monopoly portion of the enterprise.[3] The Department of Justice, however, believed that much more was needed to insure effective competition in the toll area where new entrants like MCI were coming forward. The Department sought and obtained divestiture—spinning off the local monopolies—which are essential to these new toll competitors, since they have to rely on the local telephone companies to complete the toll call. Divestiture, implemented in 1984, left intact Long Lines, the manufacturing unit (Western Electric), and its R&D support (Bell Labs). In the Department's view, this separated the "workably competitive" (toll and customer-premises equipment—CPE) from the "natural monopoly" (the local exchanges). The latter must afford the OCCs interconnection equal to that given AT&T by September 1986.[4]

Transitional Problems

This is not to say that the United States has now arrived at regulatory nirvana in the telecommunications field. Far from it, we are in the worst of all possible worlds—regulated competition. For there must necessarily be a transition from the monopoly to the fully deregulated market place, and to paraphrase Goethe, "The Devil is in the details of that transition."

First, there is the issue of continuing entry and rate regulation of AT&T. The company argues that it should be deregulated now, since it has divested itself of the essential or "bottleneck facilities" and is subject to growing competition in all its remaining fields. Its competitors strenuously object, pointing to its still large share of the toll market (i.e., 64%, with the divested companies sharing an additional 25% of the market among them). For political reasons, deregulation of AT&T in this decade appears unlikely. But as a practical matter, AT&T does not appear to face serious regulatory obstacles. Many states have deregulated all toll carriers, including AT&T, and the FCC is using a relatively light hand in its processes. Thus AT&T has been permitted to go forward with new private-line services like Megacom and SDN (software defined network) aimed at the large user. Indeed, AT&T seems bent on reconstructing its end-to-end service for these larger users, who represent over 50% of the toll revenues. Further, the FCC is moving to end the considerable inefficiencies and costs involved in the FSS;[5] the large companies now want one-stop shopping tailored to their particular needs. The FCC will rely on accounting to deal with problems of improper cross-subsidization.[6]

Second, there are large problems in moving away from several facets of the entrenched monopoly system. A wide-open competitive environment necessarily drives prices to true marginal costs; artificial pricing and subsidy schemes are inconsistent with the new competitive milieu. It follows that the nationwide average, the pooling arrangements among all exchange carriers, the subsidy scheme referred to above (at 4) should be phased out as quickly as possible. But there is great political resistance to such drastic change in the system.

Take the issue of bypass of the local telephone company's facilities. Such bypass has always been feasible (e.g., private-line facilities). It has become increasingly available, through microwave facilities (of the customer or a carrier, including the local telephone company), cable TV lines, Digital Termination Services (DTS), satellite uplinks, etc. Such facilities can connect the large user directly to the toll carrier of its choice or to its own private network. There is nothing *per se* wrong with bypass; it is simply another name for competition based on the new technologies.

But if the bypass is really aimed at avoiding the present "tax" on the large toll user (resulting from the subsidy scheme to inordinately shift NTS costs to toll), then it represents not a response to new efficiencies but to a false economic signal. Clearly, the subsidy scheme needed to go and as quickly as possible. The FCC therefore moved to shift rapidly the NTS costs to the end user. This, however, would have resulted in considerably higher local rates, and Congress, for short-term political reasons, therefore markedly slowed the FCC process.[7] It remains a festering question to be dealt with in the remaining years of the decade.

A final example of the large regulatory issues still confronting the nation involves the divested Bell operating companies (BOCs). These companies face regulation on three fronts: The FCC, as to their interstate access charges for toll interconnection and the *Computer Inquiry II* requirements; the state commissions, for their intrastate rates; and the Department of Justice and the antitrust District Court, as a result of the conditions set out in the Modified Final Judgment (MFJ). (See note 4.)

Thus, under the MFJ, AT&T is now free to enter any field, with one minor exception (viz., electronic publishing over its lines until 1989). Indeed, this was AT&T's main reason for agreeing to divestiture. AT&T

recognized that it was not just in the telephone business but also in the information business; as the only way to escape a 1956 consent decree greatly hobbling its entry into the information field, AT&T reluctantly agreed to divestiture of the local companies (see Geller [7], p. 33).

However, because of Justice's view of the industry, and specifically, that the BOCs continue to have the essential local monopoly telecommunications pipelines, the BOCs are greatly restricted in what they can undertake. They cannot provide interexchange or information services or manufacture CPE or "any other product or service that is not a natural monopoly service actually regulated by tariff," other than local telecommunications exchange or access services (Geller [7], pp. 33–34).

In my view, these restrictions are poor policy because they are inconsistent with the driving technology. The BOCs—large companies ($16–24 billion) representing over half of the U.S. telecommunications sector—are driven by the technology to seek to provide these information services just as much as AT&T or GTE. Indeed, they may be able to make unique contributions because of possible efficiencies involved in combining data processing with the network. For example, packet network vendors, such as GTE Telenet, provide processing services which allow various terminals to hook up computers on the network, using a standard interface. Essentially, the packet network provides enough "data processing" to translate from a nonstandard terminal to a standard terminal. This processing task is a natural part of any universal service data network. Prohibiting the BOCs from providing this service and similar ones as part of a local data communications network is inefficient (Geller [7], p. 35).

Similarly, the restriction on CPE manufacturing removes the BOCs—half of the U.S. telecommunications industry—from making their contribution to trade and improved productivity. Without manufacturing facilities, the BOCs cannot reasonably be expected to engage substantially in the research and development that is vital to this dynamic sector, where the United States faces increased foreign competition (Geller [7], p. 36).

Because the MFJ restrictions represent market segmentation in conflict with the underlying technological drives, they will eventually erode and finally disappear. The question is when and at what cost to competitive goals during the interim. Neither the antitrust court nor the Department of Justice (and certainly not AT&T) have recognized what I believe will be the largest and most serendipitous benefit from the disruptive divestiture process: that AT&T has been cloned seven times (the seven regional companies owning the BOCs). This introduces much greater pluralism in our telecommunications system; strategic planning is now enormously diversified. The court and the Department of Justice should recognize this great opportunity to promote competition (of course, with safeguards imposed by the FCC and the court), instead of blindly enforcing the decree and, like the Alec Guinness character in the *Bridge Over the River Kwai*, forgetting the real purpose of the endeavor.

Bottom Line for Electronic Banking

While the foregoing transitional problems are important and therefore should be taken into account, the bottom line is the extraordinary contribution that the telecommunications revolution has made and will continue to make to electronic banking. The banking industry is based on transactions—the movement of data—and the development of advanced data communications technologies has consequently greatly spurred electronic banking. As the November 1985 NTIA Report (see note 6) aptly states (at 117):

> Even a cursory look at the electronic banking marketplace produces numbers of staggering proportions. By 1980, approximately $140 trillion was changing hands annually in the U.S. economy, and $6 out of every $7 of this total moved electronically. Taditional paper-based payments methods too have become dependent on modern data processing and communications technologies to cope with the 37 billion checks, 315 billion credit drafts, and the 30 billion shares of securities traded which must be processed in the United States each year.... Nine thousand financial institutions in the United States are members of 175 computerized payments systems.... Of the estimated 45,000 automated teller machines in use in the United States approximately half are linked to one or more of the 200 regional and seven national shared networks. [footnote citations to industry sources omitted]

Because of technological advances and the spur of competition, financial institutions in the future will have even greater opportunities to use or own satellite transponders and earth stations, private microwave or digital terminations systems, fiber optic facilities, cable television instutitional networks, teleports, and sophisticated computerized switches. These communications facilities may be used to link branches within a town or area or to establish national and international packet-switched systems. The clear beneficiaries are the public: Competition among the providers of financial services is spurred, with resulting cost reductions and innovations.

To give but two examples of the enormous coming capacity, twelve entities (including telecommunications firms, railroads, and financial institutions) are planning and constructing long-distance fiber optic networks, five to be national in scope and seven regional. AT&T plans to construct 21,000 miles by 1990, with 4,200 miles in service by 1987. A competitor, United Telecommunications, is investing $2 billion to construct a 23,000-mile network.[8] There are now 27 U.S. domestic satellites with over 400 transponders being operated by ten U.S. companies. By 1990, there are expected to be twice as many companies offering four times this capacity.[9]

Of course these telecommunications opportunities are not without concurrent problems. They contribute significantly to the regulatory disarray now facing the financial service community (an issue not within the scope of this chapter). They raise concerns as to security and personal privacy, and enhance the opportunity for crime and abuse. To some extent, these problems are being dealt with.[10] On the other hand, present federal statutes making it a crime to intercept communications define "intercept" as the "aural acquisition of the contents of any wire or oral communications" and thus do not cover data communications.[11] There is thus a clear need for remedial or at the least clarifying legislation.

Further, banks can face unique problems in entering the telecommunications field. Thus, Citicorp in a 1982 application sought to provide a common carrier Digital Electronic Message Service (DEMS) focused on banking, financial, and economic data in fourteen cities. The FCC, however, rejected the application on the ground that the Bank Holding Company Act did not authorize Citicorp to engage in common carrier communications services without the prior approval of the Federal Reserve Board.[12] It was pointed out that Citicorp was eligible, even without such approval, for private DTS (digital termination services) facilities, which it has since obtained.[13]

Finally, while financial institutions are becoming telecommunications competitors, which includes reselling their excess capacity, communications companies may return the compliment. Thus, AT&T could construct a nationwide system of ATMs (automated teller machines), owned and managed by it but open to financial institutions on a fee basis.

Domestic Telecommunications Policy Issues Involving the Home Residence

One form of electronic banking has existed for some years: telephone bill payment whereby the consumers pay their bills by contacting their financial institution and authorizing it to debit their account and transmit funds to the payee they specify [9]. This is a rather mundane use of electronics and does not bulk large in the average transactional scheme (estimated by

Electronic Banking, Inc., Atlanta, to be 0.04 out of 30.12 average transactions per month per household).

A more sophisticated and truly electronic method would be the use of a home computer or even the touch-tone telephone set, sending data instructions over the telephone line or, less likely, a cable TV line. But here again the use is miniscule. Thus, only about 44,000 people now use their home computers for financial transactions, despite a base of 5 million such computers in 1983, which is estimated to grow to 11 million by 1988 [10], [11]. (Indeed, only 4% of all ATM transactions transfer funds from one account to another; most simply supply cash.[14]) Similarly, the use of point-of-sale terminals for credit and check verification, and eventually direct transfer of funds to the stores is in its infancy [12]. The potential for such use, on the other hand, is enormous: out of an estimated 57 billion transactions involving food and liquor stores, gasoline, retail stores, and miscellaneous outlets, 17 billion are susceptible to point-of-sale handling [13].

Electronic banking could become an important facet of videotext operations—a wedding of computers and their information bases to the home through telephone or cable TV lines [14]. There is no technical obstacle in the transmission line; and that aspect will be still further improved as the local telephone companies increasingly move to digital transmission (including local data transport systems), fiber optics, and even eventually the ISDN system (integrated services digital network). There are some regulatory problems such as the FCC's failure to adopt a single standard that would have provided needed certainty for the market without sacrificing quality.[15] But even had such a standard been adopted, it is most unlikely that videotext would have spurted ahead in the United States. For in the United Kingdom and the Federal Republic of Germany, there is only one system (Prestel and Bildschirmtext, respectively), and neither has prospered.

The main obstacle would appear to be the cost of the service—$600 or more for the terminal and substantial monthly charges. People apparently do not have enough interest in the uses of videotext (e.g., for information, games, electronic mail, and transactions) to pay such costs. Its growth thus appears to be quite slow—perhaps 5% penetration of U.S. households by 1990 [15]. The French government has decided to break this "chicken-and-egg" bind by gradually replacing all printed telephone directory books with an electronic terminal (called Teletel); the terminal would then also be used for financial transactions, airline and restaurant reservations, theater tickets, etc. In short, France is trying to leapfrog into the information society.

The subsidy cost in supplying such terminals is substantial, however, and there is therefore some doubt as to the wisdom and ability of France to implement this ambitious scheme. In the United States there was a proposal to require that all color TV sets have a videotext component, thus gradually putting a terminal into over 95% of the homes (but again at a significant cost—perhaps as much as $50 or more a set in the beginning).[16] This proposal fell on deaf ears, and progress in videotext is likely to continue to be slow. Indeed, it may be that the breakthrough will only come when videotext, including its electronic banking aspect, is an add-on to some other function greatly desired by the public, such as a digital TV set making possible much sharper entertainment pictures. Such a set is quite likely to be in great demand in the next ten years. This kind of breakthrough, combined with a generation trained in schools to use computer keyboards, will then spur rapid development of videotext, with its electronic banking facet.

International Telecommunications Policy Issues

The same technological advances are at work in the field of international communications and have thus contributed vitally to the present global market in finance. These advances will create even greater future opportunities. There are, however, difficult policy issues because of the different nature of international communications, and in particular the differing attitudes of our foreign partners.

There are two main international transmission modes: submarine cables and satellites. The cables are owned collectively by AT&T, the international record carriers (IRCs) like RCA Communications, ITT Worldcom, etc., and their foreign correspondents. The latter usually are government-owned postal, telephone, and telegraph administrations (PTTs) or, as in Japan and Great Britain, privatized entities (e.g., KDD, British Telecom). Several transatlantic cables now terminate in the United States, and one—the 38,000 circuit TAT-8—is a fiber optic cable that will be in service in 1988. The FCC has also authorized two noncarrier transatlantic cables, Tel-Optik and Submarine Lightwave Cable Company (SLC), with enormous projected capacity (60,000 circuits for Tel-Optik and over 200,000 circuits for SLC). The companies would sell space to large users, just as is now done in domestic satellites.

As to satellites, INTELSAT, a 109-nation consortium, owns and manages the global satellite system. There are regional systems like ARABSAT, EUTELSAT, and PALAPA, that have little economic impact on the INTELSAT system. Comsat, the U.S. representative to INTELSAT, owns a 23% share in that organization and provides U.S. international satellite circuits, largely as a "carrier's carrier" (i.e., to AT&T and the IRCs) but the FCC has recently expanded the range of "authorized users" to whom Comsat may render service.[17] The earth stations used in the United States to provide access to the satellites are now collectively owned by Comsat, AT&T, and the IRCs; but again, recent FCC decisions have resulted in shifts in ownership (e.g., to AT&T alone or to new carrier entities).[18] INTELSAT has 15 satellites in operation with 150 transponders, and will add a new satellite system, (generation) VI, in 1986, with a capacity of at least 108,000 circuits [16]. INTELSAT now handles about two-thirds of the world's transoceanic communications and most of the international television transmissions.

In 1983–1985, several U.S. firms (e.g., Orion Satellite Corp., International Satellite, Inc., Cygnus Corp., Pan American Satellite Corp., RCA, Systemics General, Financial Satellite Corp.) filed applications with the FCC to establish systems in addition to that of INTELSAT. The Executive Branch recommended approval of the applications, subject to two main conditions: each system is to be restricted to providing services through sale or long-term lease for communications not interconnected with public switched networks (e.g., specialized private-line services such as data or television); and one or more foreign authorities are to authorize use and to join in the consultation procedures required by the INTELSAT Agreement to insure technical compatibility and to avoid significant economic harm to INTELSAT.[19] Since such private-line services represent only about 15% of INTELSAT's revenues, the Executive Branch paper urged that there will be little adverse impact on INTELSAT. The FCC, on July 25, 1985, did grant the applications, subject to the above noted and several other conditions designed to protect INTELSAT's basic operations. The new entrants are now seeking the necessary foreign partners and, if successful, must then undergo the INTELSAT consultation process.[20]

There are a number of practical caveats to be noted. Thus, the restriction to nonpublic switched services seems to repeat the domestic experience: the conditions did not hold then and would appear likely to erode in the international field over time. There is an even larger caveat: It is highly unlikely that all these new applicants will proceed to build the proposed cable and satellite facilities: the excess over projected needs would be very large.

From the aspect of this article, however, the important point is that financial institutions will surely have available increased telecommunications options. There will be a large-capacity fiber optic cable or cables and in all likelihood the opportunity to acquire or lease facilities on such a cable. There will be new and cheaper satellite facilities available. Thus, INTELSAT is already responding to the new competitive milieu with innovative services such as the International Business Service, which allows large users access to smaller earth stations located close to their business for their data and other communications. New carriers are coming forth to offer such services tailored to individual large users. It is thus clear that the processes at work domestically will not stop at the shore but rather will work their way into the international pattern.

There are difficult legal and practical problems that will have to be resolved before the full benefits of that competitive thrust can be realized. Thus, competition to INTELSAT and Comsat raises serious legal and policy issues in light of the Communications Satellite Act of 1962, the INTELSAT Agreement, and the entrenched positions of these organizations, long established and fostered by the United States. For example, the role of Comsat is subject to considerable strains and doubts in light of the competitive trends. It is the U.S. representative to the critically important INTELSAT Board of Governors; it is supposed to reflect U.S. policies at the Board, but it clearly has a conflict of interest since those policies are now at odds with its own self-interest. Further, its role as the middleman between the users of the space segment and INTELSAT also appears more and more inconsistent with competitive trends. If the rivals of INTELSAT, whether satellite or cable, are offering *direct*, tailored service to the large users, how can INTELSAT compete effectively if it must always go through a middleman (e.g., Comsat)?

There are even larger problems because this is *international* communication and the interests and policies of the foreign partner may be quite different from those of the United States. The following are illustrative.

1. As noted, in most countries, communications services are provided by government-owned or government-controlled monopolies—the PTTs. These entities are thus not interested in promoting competition within their borders; indeed competition would often be inconsistent with subsidy schemes (of local rates or equipment/information industries or the postal service) based on the monopoly telecommunications system. They therefore may well resist the U.S. trend to wide-open competition, including new entrants, resale, deregulation of enhanced services, etc. It is thus by no means certain that the new international satellite entrants will all obtain the necessary foreign partner and even if they do, the conditions could be onerous and disadvantageous to the United States.[21]

2. The PTTs often have close relationships with their national manufacturers of electronic and telecommunications equipment and with

national computer software companies. Because the industrialized countries regard this high-tech area as vital to their future, the PTTs adopt restrictive practices regarding procurement in areas like standards, testing, inspection etc., designed to assure preference of the national product or service. Modest progress has been made to alleviate this situation but much remains to be done.[22]

3. Not only do PTTs disfavor resale and shared use of leased lines, contrary to the U.S. policy, but the very availability of the leased line is in doubt in some countries like Italy and the Federal Republic of Germany. Large users, including the U.S. multinational corporations and financial institutions, find leased lines, rented for a fixed monthly fee, cost efficient and thus most attractive. They accordingly account for much of the growth in communications volume. Since the revenues of the PTTs have not kept pace fully with volume growth because of this factor, some West European nations want to end or limit the use of the leased lines.[23]

4. Governments have also limited or regulated the international flow of information (i.e., the transborder data flow issue). There are certainly legitimate reasons for doing so, such as protection of individual privacy and safeguarding national security. But countries such as Brazil have also acted to protect their own infant data processing industries from more efficient foreign competition. This is protectionism, pure and simple, and can adversely affect the flow of information so necessary to the efficient functioning of the international financial community. In that regard, the Canadian Banking Act of 1980 requires customer data to be stored and processed in Canada, thus forcing U.S. banks to duplicate their record processing in Canada rather than simply rely on existing U.S. facilities.[24]

These illustrative problems are serious and difficult to resolve because they do involve foreign governments and sovereignty and trade considerations. Their resolution over time requires the focused effort of a number of U.S. entities—the Executive Branch, including the U.S. Trade Representative, the FCC, and the Congress. Besides the bilateral efforts, there is a need to use fully such international organizations as the International Telecommunications Union (ITU), the Organization for Economic Cooperation and Development (OECD), and the General Agreement on Tariffs and Trade (GATT), by expanding its common set of rules and procedures for international trade in goods to services.[25]

The problems are thus complex and will only be solved gradually in this international arena. But the bottom line for financial institutions is nevertheless most positive: tremendously enhanced telecommunications opportunities for efficient and innovative services.

Conclusion

Technological advances, leading to competition and related policies favoring fast response to this dynamic technology in the marketplace, have already contributed substantially to improved efficiency and the growth of innovative financial services in this key sector. That contribution will become even larger as the new technologies and their associated competitive regulatory policies come into fuller fruition.

Notes

1. See Title II, Communications Act of 1934, as amended, 47 U.S.C. 201, et seq.

2. See *Second Computer Inquiry*, 77 FCC2d 384 (1980), *recon.* 84 FCC2d 50, *further recon.* 88 FCC2d 512, *aff'd sub nom. Computer and Communications Ass'n* v. *FCC*, 693 F.2d 19 (D.C. Cir. 1982), *cert. denied*, 103 S. Ct. 2109 (1983); *Notice of Proposed Rule Making in Third Computer Inquiry* (Amendment of Sec. 64.702), 50 F.R. 33,581 (August 20, 1985); *Policy and Rules Concerning Rates for Competative Common Carrier Services, Sixth Report and Order*, 57 Rad. Reg. 2d (P&F) 1391 (1985).

3. *Ibid.*

4. See *U.S.* v. *AT&T*, 552 F. Supp. 131 (D.D.C. 1982), *aff'd sub nom. Maryland* v. *U.S.*, 103 S. Ct. 1240 (1983); also Geller [7] and Wiley [8].

5. *U.S.* v. *AT&T*, *supra*, at 7.

6. See *Sixth Report and Order*, *supra* (n. 2); *Notice in Third Computer Inquiry*, *supra* (n. 2); *Furnishing of Customer Premises Equipment and Enhanced Service*, 50 Fed. Reg. 9060, 40379 (1985); Memorandum Opinion and Order, (MEGACOM), FCC 85-584 (Nov. 7, 1985); *Memorandum Opinion and Order (Software Defined Network)*, FCC 85-583 (Nov. 7, 1985); *NTIA Competition Benefits Report*, NTIA Special Publications, 85-17, Nov. 1985 (*NTIA Report*), at 25.

7. See *Memorandum Opinion and Order* in FCC Docket no 78-72, FCC 84-36, released February 15, 1984.

8. See Data Communications, April 1985, at 72–74; *NTIA Report*, *supra* (n. 6), at 55.

9. *NTIA Report*, *supra* (n. 6), at 51.

10. See R. Plesser, Subscriber Privacy, 36 Fed. Comm. L.J. 182 (1984); The Electronics Funds Transfer Act of 1978, 15 U.S.C. sec. 1693; Cable Communications Policy Act of 1984, sec. 551.

11. See Plesser, *supra* (n. 10), at 182–183.

12. *In Re Application of Citicorp. Digital Exchange, Inc.*, FCC File Nos. 10329-CDM-P-82 (Nov. 1, 1984).

13. Id., par. 15.

14. See NTIA Report, *supra* (n. 6), at 117.

15. *NTIA Report*, *supra* (n. 6), at 34.

16. See Petition of H. Geller, D. Lampert, and P. A. Rubin, in FCC BC Docket No. 81-741, filed June 20, 1983.

17. *Authorized User Policy II*, FCC Mimeo 84-633, Dec. 19, 1984.

18. See *Earth Station Ownership*, 90 FCC2d 1958 (1982); *Modification of Earth Station Policies* (CC Docket No. 82-540), FCC Mimeo 84-605 (released Dec. 18, 1984).

19. See *A White Paper on New International Satellite Systems*, Senior Interagency Group on International Communication and Information Policy, at 45–49; Letter of Secretary Schultz and Secretary Balridge of Chairman Fowler, dated November 28, 1985.

20. *In the Matter of Establishment of Satellite Systems Providing International Communications*, FCC 84-1299, at par. 5.

21. See Feketekuty and Arouson [1], pp. 68, 73; Noam [6] pp. 295–301.

22. *Establishment of Satellite Systems*, op. cit. (n. 21), at 69–71.

23. Id., at 72.

24. See Feketekuty and Aronson [1], pp. 76–78.

25. Id. pp. 79–84.

References

1. Feketekuty, G., and J.D. Aronson. *Meeting the Challenges of the World Information Economy*. The World Economy vol. 7, no. 1, March 1984, 63, 67–80.
2. Dizard, W.P. *The Coming Information Age*. Longman, New York (1981), 166.
3. Svigals, J. *Electronic Banking*. Computerworld, Oct. 29, 1984, 1–2.
4. The Washington Post, Dec. 13, 1985, D7–8 ("Computer Snarls New York Bank").
5. Haigh, R.W., G. Gerbner, and R.B. Byrne. *Communications in the Twenty-First Century*. John Wiley & Sons, New York (1981), 141.
6. Noam E. (ed.), *Telecommunications Regulation Today and Tomorrow*. Harcourt Brace Janovich, New York (1983), part 4.
7. Geller, H. *Telecommunications Policy Today: Against Technology*. Issues Magazine, December 1985, 30.
8. Wiley, R.E. The End of Monopoly. In *Disconnecting Bell*. H.M. Shooshan III (ed.), Pergamon Press, New York (1984), chap. 3.
9. Lapis, A.H.,T.R. Marschall, and J.H. Linker. *Electronic Banking*. John Wiley & Sons, New York.
10. *American Banker*. Jan. 28, 1985, 14.
11. *United States Banker*. Feb. 1985. 37.
12. U.S. Congress, Office of Technology Assessment. *Effects of Information Technology on Financial Services Systems*. Sept. 1984, at 19, 124.
13. National Science Foundation. *The Consequences of Electronic Funds Transfer* (1975), at 70.
14. Neustadt, R.M. *The Birth of Electronic Publishing*. Knowledge Industries Publications, White Plains, NY (1982), at 100–02.
15. Bortz, P. Being Realistic About Videotext. In M. Greenberger (ed.), *Electronic Publishing Plus*. Knowledge Industries Publications, White Plains, NY (1985), at 113.
16. Pollack, L., and H. Weiss. *Communications Satellites: Countdown for INTELSAT VI*. Science, February 10, 1984, at 553.

II ELECTRONIC PAYMENTS SYSTEMS LINKS AND RISKS

Most people are familiar with the usual paper payment system arrangements and risks of, say, fraud or nonpayment. The unexpected settlement failure risks arising from electronics we can less easily comprehend. Now "phantom" money can be created and destroyed within the day. This process can be fed by electronic Fedwire or interbank private (CHIPS) wire loans. The former type of loan of reserves is dubbed *daylight credits*, the latter, *daylight overdrafts*. Fedwire provides for guaranteed final payment. Thus the payee (and payee's bank) obtains immediate funds during the day; an accounting transfer of course occurs at that time. However, the payor bank's reserve account is not debited finally until end of day. These Fed's daylight credits of reserves (or new-style electronic float) in theory permit banks to create money during the day through intraday loans. If they hold insufficient reserves at end-of-day settlement time, they can borrow in the Fed funds market to tide them over to the next day.

Meanwhile, on the private CHIPS wire, interbank loans (or debits) are built up prior to end of day "net net" settlement. Low EFT conversion costs and high-speed money transfers can contribute, potentially, to a higher transactions gross, as analyzed by Havrilesky (chapter 7).

A high gross money turnover, or "churning" described by Humphrey, is the flip side of the enhanced money-flow process discussed by Henderson in chapter 1. Stock market speculation and stock price volatility can result (see also Tobin, chapter 6). Another threat is the ultimate new-technology payments disaster, the "unwind" of payments made on large-dollar private wire systems, such as CHIPS. Theoretically, the failure of a bank with many other interbank relationships can impact upon one-third of the CHIPS average daily payments transfers. The fact that an "unwind" has never happened reflects the Fed's rapid use of its traditional lender-of-last-resort function to avert payments crises. Also very important are effective backup safeguards within the regulatory and private payments process.

In chapter 4, Dr. David Humphrey vividly describes these protective payments mechanisms and also risks as they exist today, from his extensive experience within the Federal Reserve System in this area. The author discusses briefly the operational risks, including risk of computer malfunction; he looks at the well-known fraud and credit risks including risk of nonpayment or use by a customer of uncollected balances. All or most of these familiar risks have been internalized, that is, covered by private or public insurance funds. However, unexpected settlement failure on a large-dollar private-wire transfer network creates unknown, potentially much greater, risks to bank stability, payments networks, and financial markets generally. Private transactions costs have not been adjusted, or internalized, to account for this new electronic-generated risk. Because of Fed guarantees of final Fedwire payment a moral hazard or private subsidy problem exists; even transfers on the private CHIPS network are not properly costed because of implied indirect Fed bailout via the discount window, if necessary. Therefore, payments participants do not face the proper economic incentives to internalize settlement risk and reduce it to a socially optimal level.

Humphrey suggests a broad-based private voluntary program to correct this serious deficiency. The Fed through private cooperation can, and has, limited the extent of its own daylight credits and the CHIPS interbank daylight overdrafts which fuel the rising money transactions earlier discussed. Humphrey also believes, as do part I authors, that the Fed system can do more to "cap" the daylight exposure through requiring private voluntary assessment of risk and private payee bank insistence on payor funds guarantees. Greater interstate banking will also reduce the on-other payments transfers, hence reduce system risk and transfer costs. This trend will also heighten financial competition and improve market responses, as discussed in part IV.

Abroad, also, the market response to electronics is an interesting saga, and one of importance to completion of the payments picture. It reads quite differently from the U.S. story just told because of different national institutions and policy emphasis. Dr. Allen Frankel (Chief, International Banking Section, Federal Reserve Board of Governors) and Dr. Jeffrey Marquardt (Bank for International Settlements and Federal Reserve Board) bring to this volume both U.S. and European perspectives and economic and legal expertise. In chapter 5 these authors analyze the changing payments structures abroad and new developments of particular interest. As background they trace the postwar forces at work. Now, they find different choices to be made in an electronic payments environment. To some observers, the U.K. CHAPS (Clearing House Automated Payment Systems) provides a clear prototype design for future national wholesale payments mechanisms. Participants in CHAPS employ standardized SWIFT (Society for Worldwide Interbank Financial Telecommunications) communication of payment messages. Major worldwide "core" banks may also enjoy membership, or access (via correspondents), to the New York-based CHIPS and other international payments links.

The new ten-currency ECU (European Currency Unit) "basket" provides another way to adapt, and is rapidly taking shape on the Continent. The current ECU clearing mechanism is a two-tier arrangement in which nonclearing correspondent banks (the first tier) maintain clearing accounts with one or more of seven core clearing banks (the second tier). The plans now call for the Bank for International Settlements (BIS) to act as the common clearing bank for the monetary-like settlement of ECU operations. SWIFT can then provide the software to feed the interbank clearing lines. There will also be telecommunications links to the large-dollar U.S. payments systems, such as CHIPS, to which some large European banks already belong (see Humphrey in chapter 4). All told, when fully operational, the European ECU can in theory eventually enjoy status as a worldwide settlement unit and reserve currency. Again, dynamic market forces are shaping the evolution of the new systems and their international settlement role. Frankel and Marquardt describe these cost, supply and demand, and behavioral market shifts with realism and skill.

4 PAYMENTS SYSTEM RISK, MARKET FAILURE, AND PUBLIC POLICY

David Burras Humphrey

There are a number of aspects of payments system risk which have recently been the focus of public policy. Everpresent are the operational risks of a computer hardware or software malfunction, such as the one that recently occurred at the Bank of New York and led to a $22.6 billion Discount Window loan, the largest in the history of the Federal Reserve. There are also risks of fraud from bank employees and customers; some of these risks are covered by private insurance. Then there are the standard credit risks banks take on a daily basis when they allow customers to use uncollected or provisionally credited balances prior to settlement. Lastly, there is systemic risk which, at present, is borne by the public. This is the risk that the failure of one payments participant to settle its net position at the end of the day on a provisional funds transfer network will lead to the subsequent failure of other participants in a domino-like fashion.

Except for systemic risk, the cost effects of these risks have been partially or fully internalized by payment participants. The possibility of an unexpected settlement failure on a large-dollar wire transfer network, however, is now recognized to create risks to bank stability, payment

---

The opinions expressed are those of the author alone and do not necessarily reflect those of the Federal Reserve Bank of Richmond or staff of the Federal Reserve System. Comments by Ed Ettin are acknowledged.

networks, and financial markets generally. This situation is one of "market failure," where the transactions fees for flows of large-dollar funds have never been adjusted to reflect this risk and, instead, cover only the operating costs involved in processing the transfer. Consequently, payments participants do not face the proper incentives to internalize this risk—which is now absorbed by the public—and so do not take steps to reduce it to a more socially optimal level. Public policies have recently been devised to make some advances in this direction, however, and further changes are under consideration. This chapter outlines systemic risk, its associated market failure, and the other related public policy issues. The chapter also provides an analysis of the likely impact of current public policies on the institutional structure and operation of financial markets, policies that will likely go a long way to reducing payments risk to a more manageable and acceptable level.

Overview of the U.S. Payments System

The U.S. payments system is made up of the nine types of payments instruments or media shown in table 4-1. In terms of transaction volumes,

Table 4-1. Volume and Value Composition of U.S. Payments–1983

Type of Payment Instrument	*Volume Composition (percent)*	*Value Composition (percent)*	*Average Dollar Value per Transaction*
	(1)	(2)	(3)
Nonelectronic	*99.50%*	*21.50%*	*$247*
Cash	70.41	1.54	25
Checks	25.14	19.80	910
Credit Cards	3.13	0.11	42
Money Orders	0.47	0.03	67
Traveler's Checks	0.50	0.02	35
Electronic	*0.35%*	*78.50%*	*$258,993*
ACH	0.25	0.39	1,800
ATM	0.05	0.00	70
POS	0.01	0.00	30
Wire transfers	0.04	78.11	2,500,000

Source: Computed from Berger and Humphrey, 1986, Table 1-2, p. 18.

nonelectronic payments methods such as cash, checks, credit cards, money orders, and travelers checks are estimated to comprise more than 99% of the payments transactions. Cash transactions alone comprise 70% of all transactions while cash plus check transactions together account for 95% of the total. Electronic payment methods, those using automated clearing houses (ACH), automated teller machines (ATM), point-of-sale (POS) systems, and wire transfers, are estimated to sum to less than 1% of total payment transactions.[1]

A different picture of the U.S. payments system emerges when the total dollar values of payment transactions are examined. While electronic payment methods comprise less than 1% of the number of transactions, they account for 78% of the dollar value. Wire transfer dollar volumes by themselves make up over 99% of the total dollars transferred electronically. Wire transfers plus checks together comprise 98% of all the electronic and nonelectronic dollar values being transferred in the United States.

From a transactions processing standpoint, it is the number of payments made, or transaction volume, that is important. But from an operational, fraud, credit, or systemic risk standpoint (all of which translate into a risk of money losses for payments system participants and the general public), the total dollar flows are what count, along with the average dollar value per transaction. Under both of these criteria, wire transfers become the focus of risk in the payments system since this payments method accounts for 78% of the total dollars transferred.

Types of Payments System Risk

Operational Risks

The recent severe operational problems at Bank of New York illustrate the importance of operational issues in the smooth functioning of the U.S. payments system, in this case the functioning of the market for U.S. government book-entry Treasury securities. In point of fact, operational problems arising from computer hardware, software, or communication lines are a daily occurrence for both funds and security transfer operations. At any time, one or more minor or major payments participants or Federal Reserve Bank processors is likely to encounter an operational problem that affects at least some other payments participant on a large-dollar funds transfer network. Most of these difficulties are handled on a timely basis and the systemic effects of the disruption are minimized. Often payments processors have some sort of disaster plan to cope with possible emergency situations. This typically involves arranging for backup electrical power should a serious electrical outage occur and/or establishing alternative processing sites or procedures for rerouting payments traffic when problems arise. After the Bank of New York experience it is likely that more resources will be directed toward this goal. In addition, Discount Window borrowings for these purposes can in the future contain a special penalty surcharge of two percentage points in order to encourage the development of better backup systems when computer problems arise.[2] Such an extra fee, of course, represents an effort to have private payment participants more completely internalize the perceived externalities associated with operational problems and to induce desired behavioral change that will minimize the probability of the occurrence of these problems in the future.

Fraud Risks

Fraud is another area where payments risk exists. To deal with it, most payments participants perform large dollar funds transfers in areas with limited access and use passwords which are changed daily. When the telephone is used, call-back procedures are followed for assurance that only authorized individuals are initiating the funds transfers requested. In addition, networks utilize reasonably secure "single-use" leased communication lines and rely on authentication and message encryption procedures to obtain the desired level of security. Backing this up are private insurance policies that protect payments participants if certain fraudulent acts accur.

Even with all these controls in place, fraudulent acts costing banks millions of dollars have occurred. The likelihood of fraudulent activities are much greater on what are now small-dollar electronic payment networks, such as the automated clearing house (ACH), than they are for large-dollar wire transfer networks. However, should large-dollar transfers shift from the reasonably secure wire transfer network to the less secure—but also lower transaction cost—ACH network, fraud risks would significantly increase. Consequently, one of the issues involved in controlling systemic risk on wire transfer networks is that incentives to move large-dollar payments off this network and on to the "substitute" ACH network be either eliminated or minimized. In this case, public policies directed at systemic risk can have implications for fraud risk as well.

Credit Risks

When bank customers wire out funds from ledger or uncollected balances, credit risk is created. If covering funds are not received or the balances remain uncollected by the end of the day, then a daylight extension of credit to a customer becomes an overnight loan. Daylight credit extensions should be subject to internal credit judgements by bank loan officers. These judgements in turn should be based on a comprehensive written credit policy adopted by the bank and enforced by a bank's own audit staff. In addition, the credit extension should be coupled with timely monitoring of customer collected and uncollected balance positions across different bank functions and geographic operations (e.g., deposit and loan plus domestic and international activity for the same customer). Today, only a few large banks have this capability, although most are in the process of planning for its implementation in the reasonably near future. Small banks rarely face this difficulty for wire transfers since, given their business mix and orientation, only relatively simple monitoring procedures would be needed for them. Checks, as the E.F. Hutton case has shown, are a different matter; and most banks are aware of the need to improve their customer account monitoring in this area.

While credit risks are the normal business of banking, regulators have sought to limit what they have determined to be excessive risk taking by providing rules and inducements for diversification. Standard portfolio theory, relying on mean returns to different assets and the variance in these returns to determine an efficient set or combination of assets, is not used however. Instead, loan diversification across borrowers is enforced by loan limits to single borrowers, currently limited to around 15% of capital to any single entity. Loan diversification across industry groups is enforced through the examination process, where rough guidelines exist. But these diversification benefits, which reduce the risk of loss from credit risks in general and reduce the risk of failure from any one credit risk in particular, have not been applied to intraday or daylight loans to customers nor to daylight interbank loans.

The connection between daylight customer loans and daylight interbank loans is not one-to-one, so that credit risk from customers need not always result in credit and systemic risk between banks. A bank may incur an interbank daylight overdraft even if all its customers are using only their collected balances for sending funds transfers and vice versa. In general, however, customer and interbank risks are closely interrelated. For example, if bank A never allows a customer to wire out or otherwise use uncollected funds, any interbank daylight net credit extended to other banks (by allowing other banks to send to bank A more than bank A sends to them) could easily be reversed *without systemic effects*. Such a reversal of payment entries may occur if any of the other banks fail to settle their net debit position with bank A on a so-called "provisional" wire transfer network.[3] Similarly, if interbank daylight exposures were not permitted, then problems that could arise when a bank extends daylight credit to its customers—by allowing the customer to use uncollected funds—would be limited to that bank alone and *would not have systemic effects*. Thus a public policy that addresses the interbank systemic effects of a settlement failure should also attempt to deal with the controls and procedures surrounding customer use of uncollected funds (credit risk). This, in fact, is exactly what has occurred.

Systemic Risk

Strictly speaking, any risk can have systemic effects when more than one payments participant is affected. Thus there can be systemic risk associated with operational failures, fraud, and (as just noted) credit risk. However, as used here, systemic risk will always refer to those risks created from a settlement failure, since this is where systemic risk is believed to be greatest. As will be discussed below, the results of a simulation study clearly indicated that the failure of a large or even a small participant on a provisional large-dollar wire transfer network can have important effects on the amount of dollar payments that would be reversed or "unwound" and on the viability of other network participants—even those who did not directly exchange payments with the participant that fails to settle. The risk of settlement failure has the greatest implications for other payments participants and thus has the greatest potential for systemic effects. As a result, settlement failure has been the focus of recent public policy in the payments area.

Domestic v. International Sources of Settlement Risk

For both domestic and international payments, the risk of settlement failure is almost solely a wire transfer issue. This is true for international funds flows because the international use of checks is very small. For domestic funds flows, while check use exceeds the processed volume of wire transfers by a factor of 700, the value of checks cleared between banks is only around 25% of the value of interbank wire transfers (Humphrey 1984, table 4-1). And, in all cases, the legal rights and liabilities regarding check payments are more clearly defined than those for electronic payments, creating less risk to the parties involved than exists for wire transfers, as is discussed next (c.f., Dobbins, *et al.*, 1985).

Large- v. Small-Dollar Payments Networks

There are essentially three classes of payments networks—a small-dollar paper network using checks; a small-dollar electronic payments network using the automated clearing house (ACH), automated teller machine (ATM), cash dispenser, point-of-sale (POS), and credit cards; and finally a large-dollar network using wire transfers.

Check Payments Network

In the check payments network, the average value per transaction is small. It is estimated to be around $900 when both small-dollar consumer and large-dollar corporate checks are included together (see table 4-1). The average value of checks cleared by Federal Reserve Banks, which historically have cleared the smaller dollar value items, is $485 with a median value of only $35 (Federal Reserve Bank of Atlanta 1979, table 10-13). Private check clearing networks typically offer faster funds availability and so have historically cleared the largest value checks, which have on occasion exceeded $100 million per check. In both cases, the frequency distribution of the dollar value of checks is very much skewed to the right toward a very small number of very large dollar value checks.

The average daily total dollar value of checks written in the United States is on the order of $150 billion. This value, while seemingly large, is much less than the $650 billion that is transferred daily on wire transfer networks. In addition, the payment concentration for checks is very diverse. Almost all of the 14,000 banks in the United States pay checks written by their customers while the largest 100 banks in the United States account for over 90% of the dollar value of all wire transfers.[4]

Perhaps more importantly, check payments are provisional payments because of the possibility of returning the check to the original depositor in the event the paying bank fails. Such return items constitute approximately 1% of all checks, although around 85% of all checks returned are returned because the check writer has insufficient funds in the paying bank's account to pay the item.[5] The return item process is clearly delineated in the Uniform Commercial Code (UCC) and has a long history in case law. Consequently, checks are seen to have the best legal framework in place to reduce uncertainty regarding the legal rights and liabilities of the parties in a payment transaction in the event of a settlement failure.

Other Small-Dollar Payments Networks

Substitutes for checks, such as ACH, ATM, POS (debit cards), credit cards, money orders, and traveler's checks are also small-dollar networks. The value processed by these six payments methods totals less than 3% of that for checks, as can be determined from table 4-1. Because few dollars are currently being transferred and because of the small amounts involved per transaction, there is little risk of settlement failure on these networks. And even if there were a settlement failure, the values involved are small enough to not pose a serious systemic problem. The only real area of concern lies with certain large-dollar ACH payments resulting from cash concentration procedures used by corporations. These payments are often over $1 million per transaction and, from a public policy perspective, it would be preferable if these transfers were performed on a wire network where better credit, operational, and fraud controls are in place. However, such a shift to wire transfers is not feasible at this time since no wire transfer network can offer the overnight service that is currently involved in these types of ACH cash concentration payments.

Wire Transfer Networks

The value per transaction on a wire transfer network averages $2.5 million and around $650 billion is transferred on a daily average basis. This dollar volume is divided about equally between the two largest networks which are CHIPS (for Clearing House Interbank Payments System), a private sector network, and Fedwire, a network operated by Federal Reserve Banks. For three reasons—the large values per transaction, the exceptionally large total value being transferred, and the concentration of this dollar volume at large-money center and regional banks—wire transfers create the greatest systemic risk from a settlement failure. Other wire networks currently exist, such as SWIFT and TWX, but because of the specifics of their operation and because of their currently small size they pose less of a problem than CHIPS or Fedwire. In fact, since SWIFT and

TWX are *message transfer* networks which in effect provide instructions to transfer balances between two or more accounts within the same banking organization, these transfers create no credit or systemic risk at all as long as the accounts being debited are prefunded with collected balances and are not run down to negative positions during the day. In contrast, CHIPS and Fedwire are *funds transfer* networks which transfer balances between two or more accounts between different banking organizations. Message transfer networks provide for internal transfers within the same bank while funds transfer networks provide for transfers external to the bank. Both can involve credit risk but the latter is the main source of systemic risk.

On Fedwire, each transaction is also a gross settlement because final funds—here reserve balances—are being transferred between banks for each Fedwire transfer made. On CHIPS, the net of the day's transactions are settled at the end of the day with a net settlement transfer using a special Reserve Bank account to shift reserve balances to make the settlement final.[6] On message transfer networks, settlement occurs when funds are moved between correspondent balances internal to a single bank. In practice, these correspondent balances are funded through Fedwire or CHIPS transfers and may or may not be fully funded with collected funds prior to the movement of funds between accounts within the bank. If large net debits are incurred in the correspondent balances used to settle transfers over message transfer networks, then similar systemic risks exist here as on the funds transfer networks. To date, only anecdotal evidence on unfunded correspondent balances exists although new examination procedures developed by regulatory agencies may clarify the extent that daylight credit and systemic risks are being incurred on message transfer networks.

Growth in Large-Dollar Payments Networks

The simplest way to portray the very rapid growth in large-dollar wire transfers over the last thirty years is as a ratio to nominal GNP. In 1950, the ratio of the dollar value of that entire year's wire transfers to that year's GNP was 1.9. Ten years later, this ratio was 4.8; and by 1970 it was 12.6. There is almost a four-fold increase again by 1980 when it rises to 44.6 and just three years later the ratio was at 61.8. Such an exceptionally rapid rise in the dollar value of wire transfers has been caused by more than the mere processing of payments which are involved in the generation of real goods and services. It involves "churning" which has regularly occurred during the day in financial markets for arbitrage and speculative reasons, where the same financial instrument can turn over many times during a single day rather than being used once for funding or asset portfolio purposes. Such churning has only recently been reduced, as reflected in a decrease in the rate of growth in wire transfer transactions volume following a number of institutional changes in the early 1980s. One such change was the movement from next-day to same-day settlement by CHIPS in 1981.

The ratio of wire transfer dollar volume to GNP is a useful way to illustrate the exceptionally rapid growth in the flow of payments volume to the flow of goods and services production.[7] Another way of illustrating a different aspect of this issue is to compare the growth in wire transfer payments volume to the underlying "money" needed to make the transaction final—reserves held at Reserve Banks. In 1950, the dollar value of wire transfers was only 10% of total reserves, on a daily average basis. In 1960, it was 60% and by 1970 it rose to 200%. Just ten years later, wire transfers were 17 times reserves and three years after that (1983) they were 38 times reserves. Clearly, the dollar volume of wire transfers has far outstripped the underlying "money supply" needed to make these payments, and daylight overdrafts in reserve accounts were the end result.

While both CHIPS and Fedwire growth have been rapid, these networks are quite different in other respects. CHIPS serves 134 U.S. domestic and foreign banks through direct electronic connections while Fedwire serves 7,700 U.S. banks and other U.S. depository institutions through direct computer links, dial-up terminal connections, and telephone. All of the 166,000 daily average Fedwire transactions, accounting for some $366 billion in daily average dollar flows, reflect payments between U.S. depository institutions. In contrast, around 60% of the CHIPS transaction volume of 91,000 a day, accounting for $277 billion in daily average dollar flows, reflects international payments between foreign and domestic banks and between foreign accounts at U.S. banks.

Development of Daylight Overdrafts

In the 1960s Reserve Bank operations were being increasingly automated to handle the rising volume of wire transfers. The extra computer and software costs that would have been necessary to impose real-time monitoring and balance limitations—such as not permitting a reserve account to go into daylight overdraft—were judged at that time to be prohibitive. Prior to this time period, neither daylight nor overnight overdrafts were thought to be a common occurrence and there was little expectation that problems would develop in the future to alter this conclusion. In any case, reserve positions were basically determined at the end of the day by the accounting department so, except for problem banks which were closely monitored on a real-time basis, there was little direct observation of a bank's daylight balance position. The extent of daylight overdrafts on Fedwire was not fully determined until a comprehensive study of their size and incidence was completed in 1979.

Daylight overdrafts on CHIPS, in contrast to Fedwire, were an explicit decision in 1970 when CHIPS began operations. CHIPS participants did not then and do not now transfer good or final funds but rather transfer provisional payments which become final at the end of the day after settlement occurs. In effect, CHIPS participants have always started out the processing day with a zero balance in their "CHIPS account" and settle the net debit/net credit positions incurred over the day at the close of business. Since the CHIPS' account balance starts at zero, just one outgoing funds transfer by its very nature leads to a net debit or daylight overdraft by the sender. CHIPS provisional funds transfers are made final through the movement of reserve account balances at Reserve Banks at the end of the day under a special net settlement agreement.

The use of reserve account balances for two purposes at the same time—an instrument of monetary control and a source of good or final funds for settlement—is economically efficient. But there is another reason for CHIPS' use of reserve balances—rather than specially prefunded interbank correspondent balances—for settlement. This involves the possibility of reduced risk to CHIPS participants in the event of a failure by one of them to settle at the end of the day. It is believed by some banks that the direct involvement of a Reserve Bank in the CHIPS settlement process may confer more timely access to the discount window in the event of settlement failure. The ability of one CHIPS participant to borrow funds from a Reserve Bank if it were otherwise to experience a failure to settle its end-of-day net position confers value to the remaining participants. A discount window loan would also serve to insulate the payments system and financial markets from the effects of a settlement failure. In this instance, systemic risk to the payments system would be absorbed as credit risk by the lending Reserve Bank and, ultimately, the general public.

While interbank credit and systemic risks on wire transfer networks can be eliminated by adding more idle balances to reserve accounts and setting up prefunded accounts on CHIPS so that daylight exposures do not occur, the cost involved, at present exposure levels, would be unacceptable to the banking industry. With each network incurring overdrafts that separately sum to around $90 billion a day (which excludes $47 billion a day in security transfer overdrafts), the yearly cost of borrowing in the overnight Federal funds market to cover this exposure would be $7.2 billion at a funds rate of 8%. Distributing this annual cost among the top 100 banks, which as a group incur around 90% of the total daylight exposure, would mean that the yearly cost would average around $65 million per bank ($65 million = $7.2 billion times 0.90 divided by 100 banks). This cost of eliminating interbank daylight funds transfer exposures with overnight funding would reduce these banks' average 1984 net income of $96 million per bank by two-thirds. While cheaper funding alternatives would likely be found, such as the use of intraday funds at an annual rate of around 100 basis points (which is the typical intraday rate for broker/dealers who borrow a much smaller amount intraday), this alternative will still be costly. Funding the same level of exposure at an intraday rate of 100 basis points, rather than at an overnight rate of 8%, would reduce costs to $8 million per bank and reduce yearly net income by 8%. Even so, the magnitude of these costs are such that it is quite easy to see why the banking industry has to date preferred to deal with the over-draft problem and the risk it creates by procedures that do not rely on funding the exposures incurred.

Simulating the Effects of a Settlement Failure

Possible Responses to a Settlement Failure

Pursuant to the CHIPS rules, the inability of a participant to settle its end-of-day net debit position could result in all its transfers sent and received being backed out of the settlement. In this process, called *unwinding*, a revised settlement position for the remaining participants is then calculated An unwind has never occurred to date and, in the real world, would occur only after an intensive effort to work out a solution that would allow settlement of all activity without unwinding.

Removing the transfers sent and received by a participant would have a different impact on different participants, depending on their net position with the institution that fails to settle. If an institution sent exactly the same aggregate dollar value of transfers to the failed participant as it received from the failed participant, it would have a net position of zero and its net position in the settlement would be unaltered. To the extent that an institution received a larger aggregate dollar value of transfers from the failed participant than it sent to the failed participant, it would have a net credit balance with that institution, and the removal of all transfers between them would reduce the remaining institution's net credit position in the settlement or increase its net debit position. Conversely, failure of an institution with which a bank has a net debit position will reduce the bank's net debit position in the settlement or increase its net credit position.

Because the removal of one institution's payments activity changes the settlement positions of other participants, there is the risk that the failure of one institution can precipitate the failure of others (systemic risk). In contrast, a sender's failure to extinguish its daylight overdraft on Fedwire creates credit risk for a Reserve Bank.[8] Under Regulation J, Reserve Banks provide good and final funds to receivers of Fedwire payments. Thus the failure to "settle" on Fedwire can not impact other bank participants on the network, although the Reserve Bank can suffer a financial loss. As a result, there is no systemic risk on Fedwire although policies have been adopted to limit the risk of loss to Reserve Banks.

A number of factors will affect the degree of systemic risk associated with a settlement failure on a provisional wire transfer network such as CHIPS. First, the more sudden and/or unexpected the shock and resulting default, the less opportunity other participants will have to reduce their daylight exposure to the failed institution. Second, the number of participants affected by a shock (say, a failure to make an expected repayment on a foreign loan), the size of the participant(s) that fail to settle, and the magnitude of the net positions other participants have with the defaulting participant(s) will all shape the outcome.

If a bank is in an expanded net debit position in the revised settlement, it may not be able to recover the additional required funds from customers if the customers have used these funds even though they were provisional. The resulting need for additional funds to satisfy its revised settlement obligation may be met in one of several ways. Up to some point, an institution will be able to handle the revised settlement obligation from its own resources. For institutions with less than $250 million of capital, the "comfort letter" required by CHIPS also obligates the parent to use its resources to meet the obligations of the subsidiary (although an end-of-day failure may preclude any meaningful exercise of this option). Access to the discount window may, for certain institutions, also provide necessary funds as it did for the Bank of New York when it incurred serious operational problems and was unable to settle its U.S. government book-entry securities position. Finally, a settling participant may be willing to settle for one of its associated participants facing a liquidity problem in meeting its revised settlement obligation.

The magnitude of the net position changes that would result from the sudden and unexpected failure of a CHIPS participant can be examined by simulation. This takes the record of transaction activity on CHIPS for a given day and removes all transfers to and from a particular institution and calculates the effect on all other participants. Using such historical data, it is necessary to assume an unexpected failure of a network participant since there is no way to fully simulate other participants perceiving a problem and partially adjusting their exposure. However, this can be at least partly remedied by removing the transactions to and from a participant in a net credit position for the day studied. The failure of a participant in a net credit position means that other participants have extended the failed institution less gross daylight credit than if it were in a large net debit position during the day and, in this sense, is similar to the likely response by network receivers to a questionable participant prior to its relatively unexpected failure to settle.

A Simulation Exercise

Using the actual record of all transactions for a randomly selected business day during January 1983, the settlement position of all institutions before and after the removal of all payments to and from a large settling participant on CHIPS was calculated. It is clearly reasonable to assume that if a participant experienced a position deterioration equal to or greater than its capital and was in a net debit position in the revised settlement, then it too will likely be unable to settle, since if it settled its revised settlement obligation it would in effect fail the bank. This series of iterations—one for each revised settlement—was continued until no participant failed by this definition in an iteration.

The simulations illustrate a dynamic interdependence among participants on a wire transfer network. Overall, there were four simulations, two for the unexpected failure of the same large participant on two different days and two for the unexpected failure of a small participant on two different days. Each simulation had six iterations. All four simulations basically indicated that close to half of the participants and one-third of the total day's payment value could be subject to the CHIPS unwind provisions in the event of an unexpected settlement failure. This demonstrates that systemic risk can be significant, since around one-third of $277 billion in CHIPS payments value could be unexpectedly unwound, or reversed, in a single day. With such a large reversal of payment transactions, the effects on financial markets can be large enough to be a serious problem.[9] Surprisingly, each of the four simulations affected a varying set of participants. This indicates that the participants most affected by a settlement failure can differ as each day's particular pattern of payments changes, making the distributional effects of a settlement failure—but not the total effect—relatively unpredictable.

It should be noted that these simulation results are conservative. This is because the "nonsettlement rule" used was (a) an institution fails to settle when it experiences a reduction in its net credit or an increase in its net debit that exceeds its capital and (b) the institution fails to settle only when it ends up in a net debit position in the revised settlement. Clearly, only (a) may be necessary for nonsettlement. An institution may additionally fail to settle or fail outright if it experiences a reduction in its net credit greater than its capital even if it still has a net credit in the revised settlement. More importantly, an institution may in fact decide not to settle its payment obligations that day if it would incur an apparent loss (at least before court action) of something much less than 100% of its capital. Thus, in these two important respects, the simulation exercise is clearly on the conservative side and, if anything, likely *understates* the impact of a settlement failure on the payments system and financial markets.

Proximate Cause of Daylight Overdrafts

Unfortunately, there is little hard information on the different types of payments and their respective volumes which could be used to help identify those payments that significantly contribute to daylight overdrafts. As well, the information available applies only to Fedwire transactions, not to CHIPS transfers. In what follows, we examine a particular type of payments transaction on Fedwire and show that if it were altered in a reasonably simple (but not costless) way Fedwire funds transfer daylight overdrafts could be significantly reduced or eliminated. Since similar types of payments transactions exist on CHIPS, it is likely that similar adjustments could markedly reduce daylight exposures on this network as well.[10]

Between 1979 and 1981, the dates of two comprehensive surveys of Fedwire payments activity, daylight overdrafts rose by almost 50% at large banks while Fedwire volume rose by less than 45%. Large banks, those with deposits in excess of $1 billion or 2.6% of all institutions using Fedwire, accounted for 91% of the dollar value of all Fedwire daylight overdrafts. Based on Federal Reserve staff analysis, one "cause" of Fedwire daylight overdrafts at large banks appears to be the current institutional arrangements for handling overnight federal funds transactions. Total federal funds transactions are estimated to have accounted for 44% of Fedwire dollar volume in 1981. Daylight overdrafts, in contrast, were around 12% of Fedwire dollar volume during the same period. At that time, many federal funds purchases, although negotiated in the morning, resulted in a gross inflow of funds to the borrowing bank late in the same day. These borrowings were usually repaid (including interest) with a gross funds outflow early in the next business day, less than twenty-four hours after the funds were received. As a result, a large morning outflow of funds occurred from banks relying for funding on overnight liabilities; and a similar reverse flow took place in the afternoon. This cycle has evolved because, in the absence of a policy that forbids or penalizes daylight overdrafts, there is currently little incentive to maintain a positive reserve account balance throughout the business day.

Thus on Fedwire one cause of daylight overdrafts appears to be closely associated with the current institutional arrangements in the overnight federal funds market. On CHIPS, similar types of payments involve overnight Eurodollar borrowings. It is possible to alter the institutional payments structure regarding these types of overnight borrowings and thereby reduce daylight overdrafts. As is discussed in more detail below, daylight exposures can be reduced if:

a. Some portion of overnight funding moves to term or continuing contract funding;[11]
b. Some portion of funding transfers for federal funds, CDs, commercial paper, etc. could be "rolled over" with the same purchaser so that a single and smaller net transfer (which could be zero or just contain the overnight interest) occurs in place of what are now two gross flows; or
c. Payments netting arrangements are developed, backed by new legal agreements, so that one interbank net payment takes the place of many gross payments to satisfy contractual obligations in the forward and spot markets for foreign exchange (to name just one potential application).

These payments system adjustments would all reduce daylight exposures because either the gross payment flows over wire transfer networks would occur infrequently rather than on a daily basis—as in (a)—or because smaller net transfers replace the larger gross flow—as in (b) and (c). The substitution of net for gross flows, however, is only really risk reducing if the underlying legal agreements are altered to reflect a parallel change in payments practices. This basically entails the prior agreement of payment participants to the right of offset, rather than leaving such a determination to a court after one party defaults in its gross payment obligation.

A simple example may be helpful here. Assume that Bank A makes a gross payment of $10 million to Bank B, on the behalf of its customer A1 to customer B2 of Bank B. Later in the day Bank B makes a gross payment of $8 million to Bank A on the behalf of its customer B3 to customer A4 of Bank A. The right of offset implies that when Bank A sends $2 million to Bank B to net settle this series of transactions that Bank A will have debited customer A1's account by $10 million, credited customer A4's account by $8 million, and transferred settlement balances to Bank B of $2 million. Correspondingly, Bank B will have debited customer B3's account by $8 million and transferred this amount plus the $2 million in settlement balance credit to customer B2's account, for a total of $10 million. As seen, customer accounts are credited by using an *internal* transfer of funds between customer accounts within each bank coupled with the *external* movement of funds—the net settlement transfer—between banks. The case today on wire transfer networks is that each transfer between customer accounts is also an external transfer and so increases interbank daylight exposures on a one-for-one basis. If one net transfer is to be substituted for many gross transfers, the legal agreements between banks and between banks and their customers will have to be altered to reflect this. Otherwise, the legal exposure remains the gross exposure rather than the net; and the negative externality—systemic risk—is actually unaffected even though its measured value may be decreased.

In sum, the proximate cause of daylight overdrafts over time, as noted earlier, has been the rapid rise in payments volume (relative to the reserve balances or "money" necessary to fund these payments) and the fact that daylight credit has heretofore been supplied at a zero price. By putting a net debit cap or quota constraint on the value of daylight credit available, current policy will serve to make such credit more costly and lead to changes in payment practices. Pricing of daylight overdrafts would have provided similar incentives. The most likely institutional change will be the use of payments-netting arrangements prior to the value date and rollovers of funding between payments participants so that (smaller) net positions are transferred rather than (larger) gross positions. This development relies on developing a new legal and institutional structure for large-dollar transfers.

Public Policy Issues

The basic public policy issue is the determination of who should bear the risk of loss involved in a settlement failure. Should these costs be borne by society as a whole or should they be somehow passed back to that subset of society made up of wire transfer payments participants? Society could bear the risk of loss involved either directly—without Federal Reserve intervention—or indirectly if the Federal Reserve provided an emergency discount-window loan to an institution so it could make settlement. Currently, society, either directly or indirectly, bears this risk, but the policies being put in place shift some of this risk directly to the payments participants.[12]

Daylight credit provided to the banking system has been free and, as a result, has been overused compared to its true value to the user and the risk to the supplier (and/or society as a whole). Indeed, some banks are able to resell at least part of this free daylight credit to broker/dealers for a fee, typically 100 basis points on an annual basis. The provision of free interbank daylight credit can be considered a case of market failure where the price charged for this credit (zero) does not properly reflect its (risk, value, or real-resource) cost to the primary user. From a public policy standpoint, there are at least three basic ways this type of market failure could be partially or fully addressed (Davis and Kamien 1977). These involve:

1. Regulation: prohibit all daylight overdrafts or regulate the amount that can be incurred.
2. Tax subsidy: provide price incentives to payments participants, such as charging for overdrafts or paying for their reduction.
3. Voluntary action: rely on voluntary efforts by participants, induced by education concerning the risks involved and the use of moral suasion by regulatory agencies.

Current policy relies on voluntary action, implicitly enforced by the perception that if this is not successful then effective regulation is a strong possibility. Flexibility has been retained by the regulatory agencies, since the current approach is considered a first step and future action has yet to be precisely determined.

The current policy, however, involves an aspect of regulation in that private wire transfer networks that net settle using reserve balances at Reserve Banks are required to establish net debit caps for sending participants on their network. This is where a participant is not allowed to create net debits, or daylight exposures, greater than some dollar amount or greater than some percent of their capital position. Thus a net debit cap acts as an interbank daylight loan limit for payments made over a given wire transfer network. The sender net debit cap limits each participant's total daylight exposure. The distribution of this exposure across receiving institutions on the network is governed by the requirement that bilateral net credit limits also be in place. A bilateral net credit limit, in effect, reflects an explicit credit judgement on the part of each receiving institution on how much credit it is willing to extend to each sending institution during the day. Since the sum of bilateral net credit limits across all receivers limits the total net debit a sender can incur, at any point in time either the sender net debit cap *or* the receiver bilateral net credit limits will effectively act as a quota on the amount of daylight exposure that can be incurred on private networks. The voluntary aspect of this part of the current policy is associated with the fact that use of reserve balances for net settlement is not the only way settlement could occur. As noted earlier, correspondent balances can be and still are to some degree used for net settlement, although it is oftentimes argued that this alternative is more operationally complex and expensive (in addition to being more risky to the participants).

A second aspect of current policy involves a voluntary self-assessment by all payments participants using any type of wire transfer network—privately operated or operated by Reserve Banks. The self-assessment involves three criteria related to:

a. Creditworthiness, or the ability to fund unexpectedly large funds outflows or reduced inflows in order to "control" realized interbank daylight exposures;
b. Operational procedures, essentially the ability to monitor and control (if necessary) customer and interbank daylight exposures; and
c. Credit procedures, which relate to specific guidelines for granting customer and interbank daylight credit.

On the basis of these three criteria, a participant chooses a total across-all-networks sender net debit cap which is to be monitored *ex post* by regulatory authorities. The self-assessment results are to be written up, reviewed by a bank's board of directors, and reviewed again by regulatory agency examiners (who, it is noted have *no* enforcement powers). Should an institution choose not to participate in this self-assessment exercise, its Fedwire sender net debit cap would be set to zero. This part of the policy, although voluntary, is thought to provide a strong inducement for participation by banks who now incur daylight overdrafts or who may wish to do so in the future. This, paired with (a) education efforts by the two major banking industry associations—the Association of Reserve City Bankers and the American Bankers Association; and (b) the necessity of board of directors and examiner review; plus (c) the implied threat of future direct regulatory action if voluntary efforts are insufficient, are the inducements built into the current public policy to reduce the systemic risk of a settlement failure.[13]

At the present time, at least three issues are being debated and may in the future be adopted in some form to reduce further systemic risk. The first issue concerns the possibility that the sender net debit caps adopted be reduced over time, directly reducing interbank daylight exposures. A second line of inquiry concerns risk sharing, where the risks involved in a settlement failure be shared more directly by institutions receiving payments. This can be done by having receiving institutions put up the funds needed for settlement in the event of sender failure (as existed on the CashWire network before its demise) but retain recourse to the receiving customer for any losses incurred. This is called *settlement finality*. Or risk sharing can be accomplished by having the receiving bank provide good and final funds to a receiving customer without the right of recourse (as exists on Fedwire); this is termed *receiver finality*. Under either of these alternatives, settlement or receiver finality, the receiving bank can protect itself from losses through the appropriate use of already existing bilateral net credit limits. The third major outstanding issue is the possibility that groups of payments participants or even Reserve Banks may develop and offer a daylight credit facility that makes intraday loans for a fee. This, of course, would be similar to merely pricing daylight credit and letting the market allocate the additional payments transaction costs to end users, which include corporations as well as a bank's own internal funding operations.

How Other U.S. Industries and Other Nations Have Addressed These Issues

Other industries, particularly the U.S. stock and commodities trading industries, do not have a Discount-Window backup for liquidity problems nor do they have federal insurance, like the FDIC, to cover possible insolvency. As a result, these industries have developed their own self-policing policies and have instituted procedures to share the risks of failure, after each participant's security deposit and capital have been used up. The problem of market failure in these industries has been addressed through internalizing the otherwise external costs by passing some of these costs back to each participant as well as having the other participants internalize them in a risk-sharing arrangement. The moral hazard involved in risk sharing is reduced by having the self-policing function follow a set of agreed-upon rules of behavior to minimize these risks.

Certain risk management arrangements are already operational on commodity exchanges. Position limits, collateralization, and indemnification are commonly used by stock and commodity exchange clearinghouses to ensure the integrity and final settlement of transactions. The simplest position limit sets a ceiling on a clearinghouse member's net interest on a contract. A member's net interest on a contract represents the difference between the value of the outstanding contracts in which the member has taken a short position.[14] A member with a net long position incurs losses when the commodity's price declines, while member with a net short position incurs losses when the commodity's price rises. (A member whose net position is neither long nor short does not gain or lose when the commodity's price fluctuates.) Since there are limits on daily price fluctuations, the ceiling set on a member's net interest limits the size of the loss a member can incur (which is also the clearinghouse's potential liability).[15]

Although their collateral requirements vary, every clearinghouse requires each of its members to deposit a specified amount in a special guaranty fund. These guaranty deposits range from as much as $2 million for each member of the Comex Clearing Association having net capital of $20 million or more to as low as $7500 on the New York Cotton Exchange. In addition, all of the clearinghouses have specific procedures to offset the losses of a member defaulting on its obligations. Generally, the defaulting member's obligations are satisfied from three sources of funds: (1) the assets of the defaulting member under the control of the exchange (its open contracts, its margin deposits, its contributions to the exchange's guaranty margin deposits, and its contributions to the exchange's guaranty fund); (2) a reserve representing an allocation of the exchange's net worth; and (3) the guaranty fund deposits of all the surviving members.[16] If these three sources prove insufficient to satisfy the failing member's debts, the remaining obligations are paid off by assessing each surviving member. Each member is assessed either an equal amount or a *pro rata* share based on factors such as its trading volume, open position, financial condition, and the types of contracts it trades. As seen, the risk of settlement failure in other U.S. industries has for the most part been internalized by the individual participant itself or shared with all other network participants. The same approach basically holds for other nations' treatment of banking daylight overdrafts as well.

Other nations do not allow daylight overdrafts to occur or, if they do, require them to be fully collateralized and charge a fee for them. In this manner, the otherwise external costs of a payments system settlement failure are made internal to payment participants and the market-failure issue is eliminated (if the pricing fully reflects the negative externalities). U.S. policy seems also headed in this direction, paralleling risk-control procedures in other U.S. industries where risk of settlement failure exists.

One reason for the different treatment of daylight overdrafts between nations is that the banking system in other countries is much more concentrated than that in the United States. This means that the incidence of daylight overdrafts in other countries would, if they occurred, be much lower merely as a consequence of higher banking concentration since more funds transfers would be internal to a (larger) individual banking organization and less would be functioned over an external, interbank wire transfer network to be measured as a daylight overdraft. This suggests that the increase in U.S. banking concentration which could follow intra- and interstate banking may itself reduce daylight overdrafts, by reducing the need for externally provided wire transfers, and thereby reduce the demand for wire transfer services.

Implications of Current Policy for Financial Markets

Adoption of one or more of the following four settlement risk reduction alternatives—sender net debit caps, receiver-set bilateral net credit limits, settlement or receiver finality, and pricing daylight credit—can significantly affect banks and financial markets in the near future. Such possible effects concern:

1. Changes in the structure and growth of large-dollar wire transfer networks;
2. Shifts in the competitive position among banks, depending on which payments services they specialize in;
3. Improvements in bank monitoring of customer daylight balances and interbank funds transfer positions; and
4. Changes in the institutional structure of financial markets.

Limiting and/or pricing daylight overdrafts can have the effect of reducing the rapid annual volume growth experienced by wire transfer networks and may reduce incentives for new suppliers to enter this market compared to a situation where daylight credit is free and few limitations exist.

Pricing and quantitative limitations can also affect the competitive positions of banks that have been frequent users of daylight credit. Because of the proposed different treatment of funds transfer daylight overdrafts and U.S. government book-entry securities, related daylight overdrafts—which are to be collateralized because of the importance of this market for monetary control—banks that have specialized in securities transactions may be affected less than others. Banks that have chosen to specialize in third-party funds transfers, and/or interbank trading in overnight funds in excess of their need for these funds for their own internal use in asset funding, will likely be affected the most. And, of these banks, those in unit banking states have suggested that they would be more significantly constrained than banks in branching states (Chicago Clearing House Association 1984). Unit banks typically rely more heavily on overnight funds than do branching banks, which use core deposits developed internally within their branching network and often incur lower net positions in overnight purchased funds.

These different impacts by type of payments specialization, by involvement in intraday trading for only trading (not funding) purposes, and by unit or branch organizational structure, will all lead to different costs being experienced and therefore affect the competitive structure between banks. The costs associated with risk reduction, of course, will over time be directly passed on to the various internal bank profit centers affected and, subsequently, to banking customers. This shifting process is made easier if a price for daylight overdrafts develops than if only quantitative limitations are adopted. Pricing, which may result in any case, would lead correspondent banks to reexamine and reprice most or all of their payment services, at times changing their price by more than that attributable to the cost involved in order to practice Ramsey pricing.

Risk reduction will likely lead to important institutional changes in financial markets. These changes concern the development of new procedures and increased reliance on existing methods which reduce the impact of overnight funding on the measurement of daylight overdrafts. Banks that typically purchase overnight funds from the same respondent institutions can attempt to bring these funds "in house" using book-entry procedures or a continuing contract. Alternatively, borrowers could return the *net* value of borrowed overnight funds rather than sending a morning return for the gross amount borrowed the previous day with a receipt in the afternoon of the gross amount reborrowed if the funding is rolled over with the same lender. Still other changes may involve a shift from overnight funding to term funds. Depending on the yield curve (which can change slgnificantly due to changes in interest rate expectations) the extra costs involved with term funds could be positive or negative, but typically below 50 basis points when they are positive. This could lengthen bank liability structures and decrease the usefulness of liability management as a tool for flexible response to unexpected deposit flows and loan takedowns. A related development would be the payment of basis points by borrowers to induce lenders to send borrowed funds earlier than now typically occurs (say one hour after the amount and rate for that day have been negotiated by phone). Alternatively, borrowers could compensate lenders for delayed return of funds borrowed the previous day. This would provide for a closer matching in time for gross sends and receives and reduce the duration of daylight overdrafts (and in some cases their amount as well).

The basic result here is to encourage a better match between a bank's book position regarding funds purchased and sold with the actual operational position regarding funds received and sent. This will be facilitated if reasonable standards are adhered to regarding the time lag between when a trader makes a commitment to sell funds in the federal funds market or buys a financial instrument (such as a CD, a banker's acceptance, or commercial paper) and when the funds are finally wired to the receiving customer. Without such a standard, a "delayed send" problem can easily develop. The problem is that if more than just a few payments participants delay the sending of funds, then the tactic of shifting one bank's daylight overdraft problem to someone else by delaying funds sent will succeed only in creating a problem for all participants and no one participant may gain.

Outlook for the Future

In the near future, *ex post* monitoring procedures will be used to obtain more information on daylight overdraft growth and thus to determine the effects and effectiveness of the current voluntary risk reduction measures. Following an assessment of these effects, sender net debit caps may be reduced in the future, as long as such a reduction would not be unduly disruptive to the payments system.

During this period of time regulatory agency and banking industry representatives will address pending issues, such as the adoption of payments finality on all private wire networks and the provision of "overline credit" at a fee to cover the daylight overdrafts that occur. Most importantly, payments netting arrangements are now being pursued and specific legal contracts are being developed to reduce both measured daylight exposures and actual risk, as discussed above.

Over the next decade, two future developments—payment of interest on demand balances and/or widespread interstate banking—can on their own reduce the problem of systemic risk in the payments system. If interest were to be paid on demand deposits under the existing structure of banking firms, there would be much less incentive on the part of bank customers to consolidate their idle balances from many different banks in different geographical regions and then invest these funds overnight in short-term liquid assets. This may reduce some third-party transfers and thereby decrease customer and interbank daylight overdrafts. And if the structure of banking firms becomes significantly more concentrated in the future, say through regional or national interstate banking, then third-party payments that now go between different banks would more likely go between different accounts at the same bank, further reducing interbank daylight exposures. In addition, the need for interbank funds transfers—for overnight funding, for securities transfers, or for foreign exchange contracts—would be much reduced. These types of transfers are currently processed externally using wire transfers and would shift to internally processed transfers within one (larger) banking firm. Interstate banking, in sum, could greatly reduce or eliminate systemic risk, although credit risk from the now internalized transfers would remain.

Notes

1. The ATM transaction volume used here relates to bill payments, which are only 1 to 2 percent of all ATM "transactions." Most ATM transactions involve cash withdrawals and so facilitate the use of cash in the final payment transaction when the payment media is exchanged for a good or service purchased.

2. Such a suggestion was contained in a statement to Congress regarding the exceptionally large Bank of New York Discount Window loan (Volcker 1985) and recently became policy.

3. Today, there are essentially only two wire transfer networks in the United States. One provides final funds to receivers of payments and is operated by Federal Reserve Banks. The other is owned and operated by a relatively small number of large commercial banks in New York City and provides for provisional funds transfers during the day with finality occurring through net settlement using reserve accounts at the end of the day.

4. The top 100 banks all have over $2 billion in deposits and account for upwards of 90% of the interbank daylight credit exposures on wire transfer networks.

5. This, of course, holds for consumer accounts. Corporate checking accounts typically have bank approved arrangements whereby checks are paid out of uncollected funds or through specific overdraft arrangements.

6. Strictly speaking, on CHIPS only the settling participants settle all the day's transactions between each other and for their respondents at the end of the day. This is called *net net* settlement, since the netting process is done twice prior to settlement.

7. This measure, of course, is quite different than the more typical money/GNP ratio used in economic analysis. In the money/GNP ratio, money is measured as a stock at the end of the day while GNP (and wire transfer dollar volume) is a flow during the day.

8. The CashWire network, before it closed down, contained a special legal agreement whereby a receiving bank would cover any net credit extended to a failed sending bank. In terms of systemic risk, CashWire was thus between CHIPS and Fedwire. CashWire was characterized as having settlement finality where the end of day settlement is assured but the receiving bank or the receiving customer or both share in the losses which result from a participant's failure to settle. Systemic risk existed on CashWire to the extent that either the legal agreement was not honored or, if honored, the resulting loss was so large as to lead to the failure of the receiving bank. The latter event was unlikely since the risk of loss from a

settlement failure would have been internalized to CashWire participants and appropriate risk limiting controls put in place (e.g., bilateral net credit limits).

9. Tables showing the detailed results of these simulations can be found in Humphrey (1986).

10. Note that it is impossible to eliminate daylight overdrafts on CHIPS. This is because, due to the way CHIPS was initially set up with zero balance accounts, there is no "money" with which to cover any net debits that are incurred. On Fedwire, in contrast, reserves are positive and offer the opportunity to cover payment net debits if these net debits can be reduced to the point where the level of reserves is adequate to cover them.

11. When last measured, some 25% of the federal funds market was estimated to be term or continuing contract. Analyses have indicated that if an additional 15 percentage points of the total market moved in this direction, then *on average*, Fedwire funds transfer daylight overdrafts would be eliminated (c.f., Humphrey 1984, pp. 86–89). While this figure is manageable for the average bank, it implies that for some institutions *all* of their overnight federal funds would have to be put into term or continuing contracts, which would complicate liability management.

12. A related problem concerns competition from private networks and nonbank access to the payments system along with support at the Discount Window or by the deposit insurance funds. Some have contended that large-dollar payments are just too important to continue to allow private-sector providers to compete since these suppliers have little incentive to recognize the external costs of a payments system failure in attempting to minimize their internal costs. This is another aspect of the market failure situation noted above. Current policy, however, has rejected this reasoning by establishing methods by which systemic risk can be addressed across all types of wire transfer networks—private or Reserve Bank operated—and for all types of depository institutions.

13. Other policy responses were considered, but rejected. For a review of these alternatives, see Humphrey (1984) pp. 99–102.

14. Net interest on a commodity futures contract is analogous to a commercial bank's net position in a foreign currency.

15. Within the net settlement context, the payments network is analogous to the clearinghouse, and position limits would represent ceilings on a network user's net credit and debit positions.

16. Within the wire transfer context, the margin deposit is somewhat analogous to a correspondent balance or a balance maintained at a Reserve Bank. The difference is that unlike the balances required by correspondents and the Federal Reserve, the required margin deposit fluctuates on a daily basis in response to changes in the risk exposure of a commodity clearinghouse member.

References

Berger, Allen N., and David B. Humphrey. 1986. The role of interstate banking in the diffusion of electronic payments technology. In *Technological Innovation, Regulation, and the Monetary Economy*. Colin Lawrence and Robert Shay (eds.), Ballinger, Cambridge, MA.

Chicago Clearing House Association. 1984. *Daylight Overdrafts*. Chicago, ILL.

Davis, Otto A., and Morton I. Kaimen. 1977. Externalities, information and alternative collective action. In *Public Expenditure and Policy Analysis*. Robert Haveman and Julius Margolis (eds.), 2nd ed., Rand McNally, Chicago, ILL.

Dobbins, Edward F., Richard M. Gottlieb, and Eugene P. Grace. 1985. *Wire Transfer Customer Agreements*. Bank Administration Institute, Rolling Meadows, Illinois.

Federal Reserve Bank of Atlanta. 1979. *A Quantitative Description of the Check Collection System*. Vol. II, Atlanta, GA.

Humphrey, David B. 1984. *The U.S. Payments System: Costs, Pricing, Competition and Risk*. Monograph Series in Finance and Economics, New York Univesity, NY, nos. 1 & 2.

Humphrey, David B. 1986. Payments finality and risk of settlement failure. In Anthony Saunders and Lawrence White (eds.), *Technology and the Regulation of Financial Markets*. Lexington Books/Salomon Brothers Center Series on Financial Institutions and Markets, Lexington, MA.

Volcker, Paul A. 1985. Testimony. Before the Subcommittee on Domestic Monetary Policy of the Committee on Banking, Finance and Urban Affairs, House of Representatives, U.S. Congress (December 12).

5 INTERNATIONAL PAYMENTS AND EFT LINKS

Allen B. Frankel and Jeffrey C. Marquardt

This chapter takes a broad look at changing international banking arrangements, or structure, for making international payments in the postwar era. We would not dispute that the concept of an international payment has become increasingly ambiguous in the emerging environment of electronically linked global markets for trade and finance. Nevertheless, prototypal structures for international payments may be usefully identified and analyzed, particularly, with respect to arrangements for U.S. dollar-based activities. The dollar structure has undergone, and is undergoing, changes with respect to clearing and settlement. Furthermore, it is being adapted for transactions in other major currencies and the European Currency Unit (ECU).

The focus is on the international structure for making what are often called "*large-value*" payments: large-scale daily money (including foreign exchange) market and capital-market transactions almost always depend on the large-value payment systems, which are the centers of clearing and settlement in their respective currencies. They are critical because the normal operation of a sophisticated monetary mechanism is conditioned on

---

This paper represents the views of the authors and should not be interpreted as reflecting the views of the Board of Governors of the Federal Reserve System or members of its staff.

the realization of anticipations about the levels of payments volume, cut-off times by which monetary transfers can be made for a given value date, and the solvency of participants in the system.

The emphasis is not on comparing and contrasting the major national payment systems.[1] We are fully aware that historical events, as well as differences in political and economic views, undoubtedly create the bases for differences among national monetary mechanisms. Nevertheless, important common economic forces are now affecting their development. Again, these forces can be usefully described by reference to a global structure that is subject to change from common forces affecting the demand for and supply of large-value payment services. In turn, we would argue that such a recognition leads to important implications for the operation and supervision of national and international payment mechanisms.

Classic Postwar Structure

Taking the industrial countries as a group, the classic structure for making large-value private payments had at least four notable characteristics (see figure 5-1). First, a small number of core banks have been the main

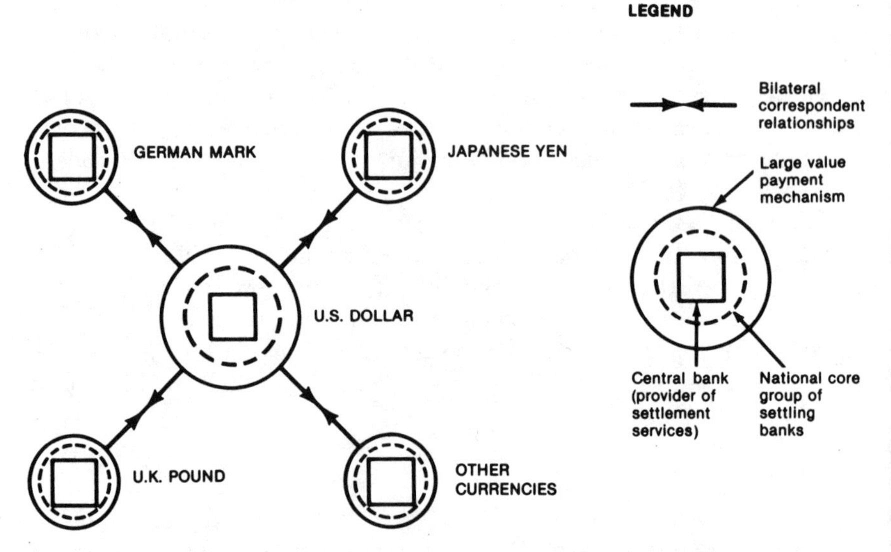

Figure 5-1. Classic Postwar Structure of the International Payment Mechanism

providers of large-value payment services, particularly those involving monetary transfers between countries. Second, banks have specialized in providing transfer, clearing, and settlement services in their home-country currencies. Third, central banks are involved to some degree in the clearing and/or settlement of transactions in the currency of their country. The degree of involvement, along with policies regarding short-term credit extensions, heavily influences the functions taken on by the core group, and even its composition. Finally, the time-honored correspondent banking device of establishing a clearing account for another banking institution has been the principal means by which members of each currency's core group have provided payments services to other banks. Often these accounts were and are established on the basis of reciprocity. The arrangements between members of different core groups, together with the core groups and settlement arrangements, formed the structure for making, clearing and settling monetary transfers in convertible currencies.

Institutional Links

There are a number of forms in which an international payment can be made. They range from paper draft to wire transfer. Depending on currency, even a wire transfer may involve ultimate settlement through a check clearing system. To provide context, it is useful to mention briefly some of the current systems for making large-value interbank payments, transactions which core groups routinely process.

The Clearing House Interbank Payments System (CHIPS), an electronic fund transfer (EFT) system operated by the New York Clearing House, is the core system for making large-value international dollar payments. Such activity can also take place over the Federal Reserve's Fedwire system, although a number of factors have limited its use for these purposes in the past. The Clearing House Automated Payments System (CHAPS), an EFT system, together with the paper-based London Town Clearing, form the key sterling payment mechanism. The Bundesbank's telex-based giro system for interbank payments is the main German mark-based system. Clearing house arrangements for paper drafts, and arrangements for delivering and settling Bank of Japan checks form the core of the Japanese yen-based system. Both the Bundesbank and the Bank of Japan are engaged in efforts to create sophisticated EFT systems, as are several other central banks, such as the Netherlands Bank and the Swiss National Bank.

If two banks or banking offices both participate in one of these systems, they can send payments directly to each other using the electronic or paper media of the particular system. If not, they typically employ one or more correspondent banks. Payments can be made by simple deposit-account debits or credits if two banks have the same correspondent. Frequently banks employ different correspondents and in this case payments are completed by transfers between the correspondents through a core system.

At present, there are two main types of payments communications systems that link banks in one country with their correspondents or other banks in different countries. The Society for Worldwide Interbank Telecommunications (SWIFT) provides the premier form of electronic payment communication, involving sophisticated network architecture, highly formatted messages, and wide international participation. An advantage of using the SWIFT system is that messages can be sent between two or more banks, reformatted electronically, and sent through an EFT system such as CHIPS without intervention, thereby reducing errors and delays. The use of traditional telex systems provides the second main type of international communication. A third means of communication is through proprietary networks maintained by large commercial banks.

Reasons for the Classic Structure

To understand the forces that are changing the international payments structure, it is necessary to appreciate the forces that shaped it during the postwar era. These forces can be classified as those that affect the demand to make payments, and those that affect the costs of offering payment services and hence the supply of payment services. A third category comprised of official policies relating to payments, short-term credit extensions, and international banking can also be separately identified.

The point of view taken here is that "payments" and "payment services" each have a dual nature. A *payment* is a discrete message—in electronic or possibly paper form—containing two types of information. Identifying information indicates accounts to be debited and credited. Monetary information regarding currency, payment amount, and a value date is also contained in a payment message. *Payment services* also have two other aspects. One is financial: the provision of short-term credit to bridge gaps between the initiation and receipt of a transaction is an important example. The other does not appear to be financial. The time required for full execution and variability in this length of time are examples. This dichotomy, however, can be deceiving, since nonfinancial timing considerations can have important effects on the portfolios of account holders and actors in an economy more generally.

Core Groups

The core groups in each currency have typically been composed of relatively few banks chartered by the country associated with the currency cleared and settled through the core group. Not all core groups perform the same functions. Central bank policies, for example, have had important effects on organization.

Although the functions performed by various national core groups differ considerably, two main types of organization may be usefully set out. There are clearing house type arrangements in which banks participate in a cooperative arrangement for exchanging payment messages and effecting settlements for the net value of payments exchanged. Settlements are completed by transfers between reserve or clearing accounts at central banks. There are also central bank operated systems, in which payment messages are exchanged through a communications or clearing facility run by a central bank. Again, settlements are effected by additions to or subtractions from reserve accounts, made by the central bank as it processes individual messages or batches of messages.

These two types of systems are not as different as first appears. Central banks can be viewed as entities that manage private cooperative arrangements among banks under their jurisdiction. Moreover, central bank operated systems can be viewed as an institutional embodiment of cooperative arrangements, possibly influenced by public policy concerns. Hence it is not unreasonable to treat bank participants in both types of system as members of core groups. The functions performed by a particular core group, of course, depend on the role assigned to the central bank.

Demand for Home-Currency Payments

Differences in the distribution of the demand to make payments across banks are important determinants of core group structure. For historical banking reasons, home-currency payments have tended to be concentrated on banks chartered by the home country. The inability of foreign banks to participate effectively in home-country banking markets has been one factor. The reasons range from the official maintenance of banking cartels to the practical difficulties outsiders have in penetrating banking markets dominated by traditional alliances. The close linkage that has existed in the past between the provision of payments and other banking services reinforced the concentration of home-country currency payments on home-country banks. A related factor is that the lack of explicit pricing for payments services in the era prior to deregulation tended to discourage challenges on the basis of price competition to the provision of payments services by home-country banks.

Cost

There are at least three general types of costs associated with various clearing and settlement techniques. First, there are real costs of equipment, systems development, and on-going operations. In a centralized clearing-house-type arrangement, these costs include shares in fixed investments in clearing house computers and switching equipment or less advanced accounting and data processing devices. There are also quasi-fixed costs associated with communications with a central clearing house. These costs may arise from investments in check-sorting equipment and transportation arrangements for paper-based systems. Investments in electronic terminals for communication with a central computer, interface devices to link various electronic message transfer systems, and software development to meet clearing problems as they are encountered are required in centralized electronic systems. In both cases, accounting systems and security arrangements are needed to monitor and confirm settlement obligations in order to meet agreed deadlines.

There are important bargaining elements in the creation of cooperative agreements covering the technical and financial aspects of a clearing system's operation, such as the specifics of settlement deadlines. For example, the choice of a stringent settlement deadline provides only a limited time interval between the clearing and settlement of a business day's payments. Consequently, it should be favored by those system participants with existing excess capacities to provide for real-time monitoring (and control) of their own, and customers', transactions cleared through the system.

The second general type of costs are the financial costs of meeting settlement obligations established in cooperative agreements, or adopted as rules for central bank run systems. It is the relative magnitudes of these financing costs that affect the structure of core payment groups by giving financial cost advantages to a few large banks. In economies with developed money markets, these are the banks that because of balance-sheet size, trading volume, creditworthiness, access to central bank finance, and other factors, form the core of the interbank money market associated with a particular payment system. In economies that do not rely on market adjustment of clearing imbalances, the terms of, and access to, central bank adjustment credit are the dominant factors.

Third, there are also what may be called regulatory costs that affect the composition of core groups. Central bank short-term credit policies that favor particular banks have already been mentioned. There can also be outright prohibitions by governments on entry into core clearing systems. Such prohibitions have typically been rationalized through expressions of concern about the undermining of the effectiveness of a central bank's day-to-day money market operations.

Central banks that directly operate payment systems, such as the Federal Reserve and Bundesbank, have adopted policies of nonrestrictive access to their systems. These policies can significantly reduce the costs of a shared system to low volume users, particularly when development costs are partly underwritten by central banks and payment charges are directly related to the average per message cost of operating the system. These policies operate to enlarge core payment groups. Nevertheless, the marginal costs of payment equipment and systems internal to banking organizations, demand, and other factors appear to have had an important limiting effect on core group size even in countries such as Germany and the United States. In the United States, for example, small banks have been participants in the Federal Reserve's Fedwire system, but have not been significant processors of large-value payments, either domestically or internationally.

Correspondent Clearing Accounts for Foreign Currency Payments

Cost Advantages of the Correspondent Method

The volumes of cross-border payments denominated in U.S. dollars were relatively low until the 1970s; those denominated in other major currencies were low until the 1980s. Therefore, the correspondent banking method appears to have been the low-cost method of clearing and settlement. Correspondent methods of clearing and settlement do not impose fixed costs from joining clearing house or other cooperative arrangements, nor are there the organizational and development costs of setting up local clearing arrangements. There are costs from setting up a bilateral correspondent relationship. However, these appear to be minimal and may be spread over a number of banking functions, allowing the payments function to benefit from economies of scope. Similarly, the fixed costs of communicating with a correspondent appear either to be minimal or to be subject to important economies of scale. If messages are sent and received using paper-based technologies, the costs of communication are essentially per-item mail charges. If electronic interbank communications systems such as SWIFT are employed, then fixed costs are subject to economies of scale.[2] These systems allow communication of messages in virtually any currency, hence marginal communications costs depend—in addition to explicit per-message charges—on the total volume of foreign currency payments, not the number of payments in a particular currency. These economies can be important since core clearing and settlement arrangements in a particular currency typically call for investments in special equipment for communicating with participants in that system.

Formal clearing and settlement arrangements all involve deadlines for communicating individual messages, in the case of electronic systems, or batches of messages, in the case of paper-based systems. There are also deadlines for accomplishing net settlements in systems using this principle, or deadlines for required adjustments to reserve accounts in central bank run systems using the reserve-account transfer method for making individual payments. The ability of banks to meet these deadlines depends on the speed at which accounting functions can be performed as well as the volume of payment messages to be processed. Foreign banks with lower payment volumes in a currency other than their own would, in the past, have faced higher marginal costs of processing payments than home-country banks, even if *communicating* with other banks were costless. This is because fixed costs of internal computing and handling equipment as well as the need for control systems probably created economies of scale in processing at lower payment volumes.

The formation of localized clearing and settlement groups for foreign currency payments is subject to the same technical and cost problems as direct foreign bank participation in core clearing groups. Participation in these systems involves the "local" offices of banks agreeing to net payments among themselves and settle net differences at the end of a clearing period.[3] Except for volume levels and possibly the formality of arrangements, these local systems are similar to core clearing systems. It is not surprising that local clearing arrangements involving netting groups had not been seriously considered until recently when changes in technology and international banking may be reversing traditional cost calculation outcomes.

Finance Costs

Costs of finance may also be lower to banks using correspondent clearing and settlement techniques. The compensation for providing correspondent services has, in the past, been largely in the form of interest earned on compensating balances. Moreover, balance levels have been calculated on a time-averaged basis—for example, average balance over thirty days. Such arrangements have several effects. First, they allow a time interval for a bank purchasing this service to meet the average balance requirement, time which can be very important if a bank and its correspondent are operating in time zones whose business days do not overlap or only partially overlap. Second, because the purchasing bank is allowed to offset above-average balances against below-average balances, it is being permitted to borrow from, and lend against, future clearing balances. This opportunity serves to reduce the costs of finance relative to those charges that would have been incurred if the bank itself engaged in limited amounts of its own, day-to-day, money market transactions.

Finally, when the interbank market in a particular currency is not well developed, bilateral averaging can be viewed as an implicit interbank borrowing and lending arrangement.[4] Adverse clearings leading to below-average balances can be viewed as triggering an automatic loan to the correspondent's foreign bank customer. Favorable clearings leading to above-average balances can be viewed as triggering an automatic loan from the customer to the correspondent. Only net deficiencies over a longer time interval need to be explicitly financed.

Correspondent balance and credit arrangements may also be viewed as a substitute for real investments in monitoring and control equipment as well as expenditures on labor that are necessary to meet deadlines. A bank purchasing correspondent clearing, settlement, and credit services essentially contracts to have another bank monitor and control balances in that account within established guidelines in order to avoid investments to meet its obligations. Purchasing a credit facility from the *same* correspondent eliminates the need to request, verify, and coordinate transfers of funds from other lenders, which require investments in monitoring and control systems.

An implication of this reasoning is that if a bank has invested in account monitoring and control equipment, then its rationale for preferring to purchase a credit commitment from its correspondent clearing bank would be undercut. Indeed there has been considerable pressure on international correspondent banks to unbundle the package of traditional services.[5]

Official Policy

Official policy also imposes costs or outright restrictions on the choice of clearing and settlement techniques for different currencies. Outright prohibitions on foreign bank entry into a country's banking system or its core payment system are obvious examples. In this case, use of correspondent banking relationships for clearing and settlement have been the only practical alternative, since offshore localized clearing and settlement systems have not until recently become economically viable. Cartelized banking systems with restrictions on entry, including entry by foreign banks, have at times also been able to limit the ability of foreign banks to participate directly in core clearing and settlement systems. When cartels have at times been overtly or tacitly sanctioned by authorities as part of a much broader strategy for monetary or credit control, the restrictive effects on payment system organization have in a sense been incidental to more fundamental policies.

A more subtle form of official policy that affects clearing and settlement arrangements is the policy toward official extensions of credit. In the United States, for example, the Federal Reserve under its new "daylight over-draft" policy distinguishes between domestically chartered and foreign depository institutions with respect to the amount of uncollateralized credit it will provide during the day. (See Federal Reserve Board 1985, pp. 22–28.)

In other cases, restrictions on access to official overnight credit, in particular, may affect the willingness of other banks to agree to participate with a foreign bank in a core clearing system that involves net end-of-day settlements. A central bank's policy of refusing to lend increases the probability that disagreements and gamesmanship on the part of other system participants regarding the resolution of a financial problem could disrupt the ongoing operation of the system. In fact, it is possible that such considerations might precipitate outright refusals to cooperate with foreign banks in core payment arrangements.

Demand Characteristics

Opportunity costs are generated by different clearing and settlement techniques that affect the demand for payment services and consequently the exploitation possible of scale economies. These opportunity costs arise from both the average length of time and variation in the length of time it takes to make payments using different techniques. Clearing and settlement techniques relying on correspondents have tended to increase the average length of time to complete payment transactions because they involved more processing steps.

These timing considerations can create float costs, particularly for nonbanks who have to deliver good funds to their banks at the initiation of a payment rather than on its value date. Risk-averse payers have additional float costs because they initiate payments even earlier than others, in order to guard against failure to have payments reliably delivered on value dates. Even risk-neutral payers often must pay *net* interest costs associated with failure to deliver payments on time, a problem for both banks and nonbanks. Moreover, banks can suffer reputational costs from consistently failing to deliver payments on value dates.

The experience of the postwar era until the early 1970s included low interest rates, stable exchange rates, and lower volumes of foreign currency payments. In this environment, opportunity costs apparently were insufficient to generate the demand for faster and more reliable international payment service that would have justified direct participation by foreign banks in non-home-currency clearing and settlement systems.

A further question, however, is why residents in a particular country would use banks chartered in that country to make foreign currency payments rather than branches or subsidiaries of banks from the core clearing group in that currency. One might expect internal bank funds transfer systems to be faster, less variable, and possibly to have lower marginal costs than systems involving correspondents. Several factors, however, inhibit the use of these branches or subsidiaries of core clearing banks.

Availability and cost probably played some role. Overseas banking networks of banks from major countries grew rapidly in the 1970s as international banking expanded. Before that time, limited numbers of foreign offices of banks from core clearing groups may have made widespread use of those offices to make foreign currency payments unattractive. Moreover, these offices did not necessarily have the equipment and procedures in place to efficiently process significant amounts of customer payments. Investments in such equipment would have required large and risky investments by foreign banking organizations. This could have given locally chartered banks with the appropriate equipment lower marginal costs and faster processing times for third-party payments, even though a correspondent bank connection was used for clearing and settlement.

Demand characteristics were probably also important, however, and these continue to inhibit foreign branches and subsidiaries from making the investments to become competitive with local banks in foreign currency payment processing. First, if the bulk of a commercial firm's payments were in the home currency, then a bank chartered in the home country would likely have been chosen for clearing and settling the home-currency payments. These banks would have been members of core clearing groups, or other local arrangements, leading to the fastest and lowest marginal cost processing of home-currency payments by virtue of high payment volumes that predated foreign bank offices in particular countries. Having chosen such banks to process home-currency payments, a firm would have established an account relationship with that bank for managing its cash position. The costs of establishing additional accounts at branches or subsidiaries of foreign banks and the costs of making and coordinating transfers between accounts at different institutions would have provided incentives for nonbanks to forego the use of foreign banks to make foreign currency transfers. In addition, firms have normally received higher quality or priority service from banks at which they concentrate banking functions. If so, they would have had incentives to purchase packages from domestic banks combining foreign currency with home-currency payment services and short-dated deposit and credit facilities.

Changes Affecting the Postwar Structure for Making Payments

In addition to new technology, important changes exogenous to the global payment structure yet affecting its characteristics have occurred during the 1970s and early 1980s. Foreign currency trading developed rapidly after major currencies were allowed to float; international capital and money markets developed rapidly during the 1970s for a variety of regulatory and financial reasons; and major financial firms from a number of countries increased their scale of banking activities in each other's countries. These changes are reflected in heightened scale and more diverse currency distribution of the large-value payment services.

Developments in Dollar Arrangements

Significant changes occurred first with respect to U.S. dollar payments. Non-U.S. chartered banks participated increasingly in dollar-based money markets and foreign exchange trading, and as a result, generated increasing volumes of dollar payments. In addition, increased international trade and financial activity by customers increased the demand to make third-party dollar payments. As a result of higher potential payment volumes, foreign bank participation in core U.S. clearing and settlement systems no longer carried as great a cost disadvantage as previously.

At the same time, higher levels of dollar interest rates raised the opportunity costs of long and variable payment completion times. Banks and firms became willing to pay more for the faster and more certain execution of payments made possible by direct participation in core dollar clearing and settlement systems. Real costs of direct participation also fell as small computers became less expensive and computer software became more flexible. Finally, as a consequence of these factors, and perhaps for reasons associated with marketing and advertising, the participation by non-U.S. chartered banks in CHIPS expanded dramatically.[6] And as a result, this EFT network became the preeminent dollar-based clearing and settlement mechanism for international payments.

In the 1980s the development of local (outside the United States) electronic clearing and settlement systems among non-U.S. chartered banks also appears to be gaining interest. Again, payment volumes between local groups of banks have risen, with general increases in foreign exchange and other financial market dealings employing the dollar. Investments in treasury management equipment and systems were made in the late 1970s to control foreign currency funding activities of many of these banks. Important investments were also made in electronic payment handling and accounting equipment to control the rising volume of foreign currency payments during this period, and these investments are continuing. Given these existing investments, the only additional investments required to create a local payment netting system are in interbank communications lines, interbank payment accounting systems, and software. Such components are available to groups of banks outside the United States from organizations such as SWIFT, other organizations with experience in providing international financial communications, and banks that have developed proprietary communications and cash management services.

Other developments

Two other recent developments also point out how a changing economic environment is altering traditional payment system structures, one involving payments in sterling and the other in European Currency Units (ECUs).

Sterling Payments. In December 1984, the ten member banks of the Bankers Clearing House of London published a report recommending an organizational restructuring of a number of sterling clearing and settlement arrangements. One of the significant recommendations is to allow at least one non-U.K. chartered bank (Citibank) to participate directly in the core clearing systems—the paper-based Town Clearing and the EFT-based

CHAPS system. The logic of the recommendation suggests that membership in the core sterling mechanisms should be generally open to all qualifying banks, that is, banks with established presence in sterling-based markets. (See Banking Information Service 1984.)

To some observers, CHAPS provides a clear prototype for the design of future national large-value payment mechanisms—see figure 5-2. Participants in CHAPS payments are able to employ standardized SWIFT techniques for funds transfer, that is, CHAPS highlights the considerable flexibility that SWIFT has introduced into payment arrangements. CHAPS demonstrates that links among potential participants in a net settlement network can now be readily established. Furthermore, links between bank participants and specialized facilities, such as automated ledgers to monitor the total network credit of individual participants, require only adaptations of standard software. The design of the CHAPS mechanism thus appears to embody a relatively low-cost solution to the problem of establishing national EFT mechanisms that can be readily embedded in the established dollar-oriented international payment mechanisms.

The CHAPS mechanism involves the assignment of risk-management

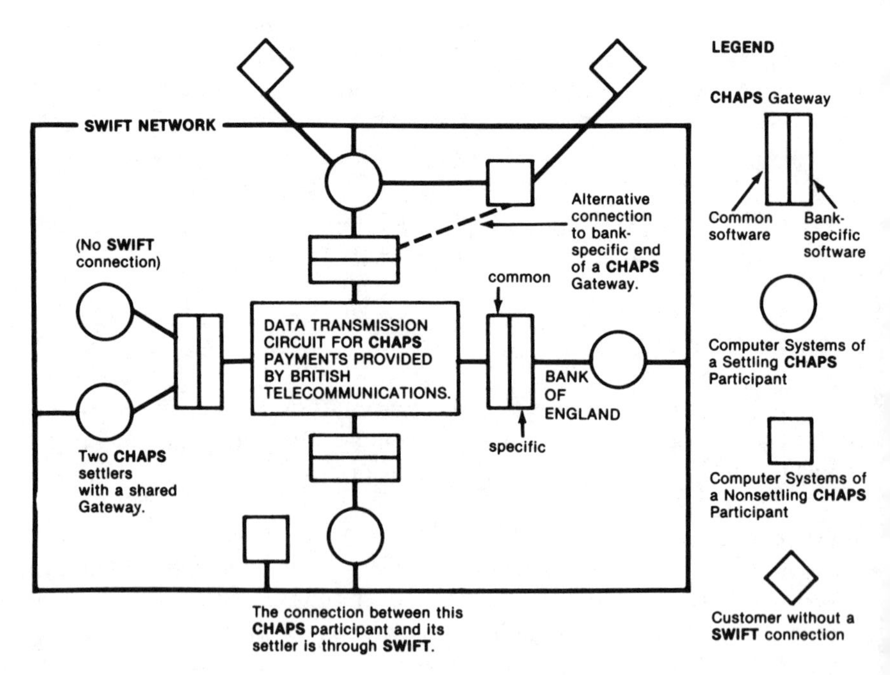

Figure 5-2. CHAPS

responsibilities for sterling payments arrangements to the U.K. clearers as a group and individually. U.K. authorities have not indicated any interest in explicitly supervising the terms on which the U.K. clearers will admit other participants to the CHAPS network, a policy based on the view that CHAPS network relationships ought to be described and maintained by the banks "responsible" for the day-to-day operation of U.K. payment arrangements. Notwithstanding such assertions, it is clear that the Bank of England's responsibilities as the central bank for sterling and as the settling agent for CHAPS do not permit a totally hands-off policy. Moreover, the criteria for obtaining a settlement membership on the Town Clearing and CHAPS include an "ability to establish settlement account facilities at the Bank of England". (See Banking Information Service 1984, p. 10.)

ECU Payments. Perceptions of greater exchange rate risk have led economic actors to seek various means of cover through various financing arrangements. Currency composites like the European Currency Unit (ECU) provide an alternative to more sophisticated (and more costly) hedging techniques such as trading in foreign currency options. Overall, the ECU's considerable popularity must be attributed primarily to the success of efforts of the European Monetary System (EMS) in establishing credibility as to the maintenance of reasonable stability of the ECU in terms of its ten component currencies.[7] By inference, this argument would also explain the lack of interest in other currency baskets, such as the International Monetary Fund's SDR that includes the U.S. dollar and the Japanese yen.

The use of the ECU for denominating financial obligations created a demand for a complementary infrastructure which now has been established. The availability of such an infrastructure has operated to reduce the need to resort to the process of unbundling (in terms of ten currencies of the ECU valuation basket) to complete a single ECU transaction. For example, a bank covering a newly created ECU-denominated deposit need not make offsetting purchases of forward, or spot, foreign exchange contracts in the component currencies.

The deepening of ECU-related financial capabilities has produced a softening of the ECU's basket nature. The ECU market is producing new instruments, with characteristics that are no longer the simple weighted average of existing instruments in the component currencies. The widening range of similarly denominated financial instruments has tended to lower the cost of their use, partially reflecting the economies introduced for ECU-denominated payments by the interbank clearing mechanism that has been established.

The current ECU clearing mechanism is a two-tiered arrangement in which nonclearing correspondent banks (the first tier) maintain clearing accounts with one or more of seven core clearing banks (the second tier). Payments in ECUs between banks whose accounts are with different core clearing banks are made by entries to Mutual ECU Settlement Accounts (MESA) maintained by each of the seven clearing banks. Net balances or overdrafts between the seven clearing banks are settled by paying out component currencies when amounts exceed agreed credit limits.

To broaden the effective coverage of ECU clearing arrangements, a multinational association of commercial banks has been formed. The association has developed and agreed upon a plan to create a multilateral ECU clearing mechanism in association with the Bank for International Settlements (BIS) (see figure 5-3). These plans call for the BIS to act as the common clearing bank for the monetary-like settlement of ECU operations, and for the SWIFT organization to provide the software to run the communications links, and accounting function, for the interbank clearing system. This architecture demonstrates again how easy it has become to create the essentials of a payment system based on slightly modified versions of existing communication software. Furthermore, it may be anticipated that the number of clearing banks will be increased once the system has passed through a probationary period. It is not, however, clear that the European authorities will be willing to accommodate a fuller monetary status of ECU-based exchanges between central banks and commercial banks using the BIS as an intermediary.[8]

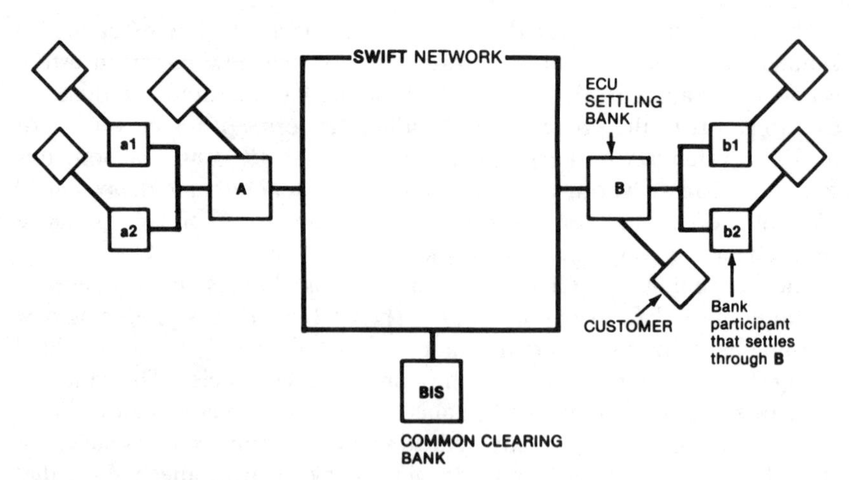

Figure 5-3. ECU-Based Payment Mechanism

A Newly Emerging Structure and Its Implications

At the heart of the postwar structure for making large-value payments were core groups of large domestically chartered banks in the major currencies. Banks in one group cleared and settled payments in the currency of another group via a system of correspondent accounts. Changes in the level of financial, and possibly real, activity have dramatically increased the number of payments in dollars and in other currencies. Banks also expanded the scale of activities in each other's countries. At the same time, investments in automated communications, accounting, and control systems increased as the fixed costs of these investments fell with technological advances and declines in computer prices. Moreover, the opportunity costs of long and variable payment execution times have increased as interest rates have risen and, along with exchange rates, have become more volatile.

These factors have made it economical for non-U.S. chartered banks to become participants in the core U.S.-dollar clearing and settlement system. Similar factors also created pressure to open the core sterling interbank payment systems to non-U.K. chartered banks. Other countries have experienced or may yet experience pressures for foreign bank participation in core systems. Japan, for example, has four foreign participants in the Tokyo Clearing House arrangements for large-value draft and check clearing. These pressures will probably increase as new electronic interbank payment systems now being developed in a number of countries become operational. Hence the trend—mirroring the trend in international banking generally—is toward multinational participation in core clearing and settlement systems for the currencies of major countries.

The logical extension of current trends suggests that the authorities may find themselves—without design—facing a new structure for the international payment system (see figure 5-4). Old core groupings of banks in each major currency, chartered by the authorities in the country associated with each currency, may no longer form the basis of interbank payment systems. These groups would be replaced by a single transnational group composed of the major multinational banks, which are chartered by various countries. In the extreme case, this single group would form the interbank system for clearing and settling payments in a number of currencies through local offices in the major countries.

In a sense, of course, the participation arrangements for the new ECU clearing system foreshadow the development of a single transnational clearing group. A system that contemplates participation by banks from most or all countries in the European Community is, by construction,

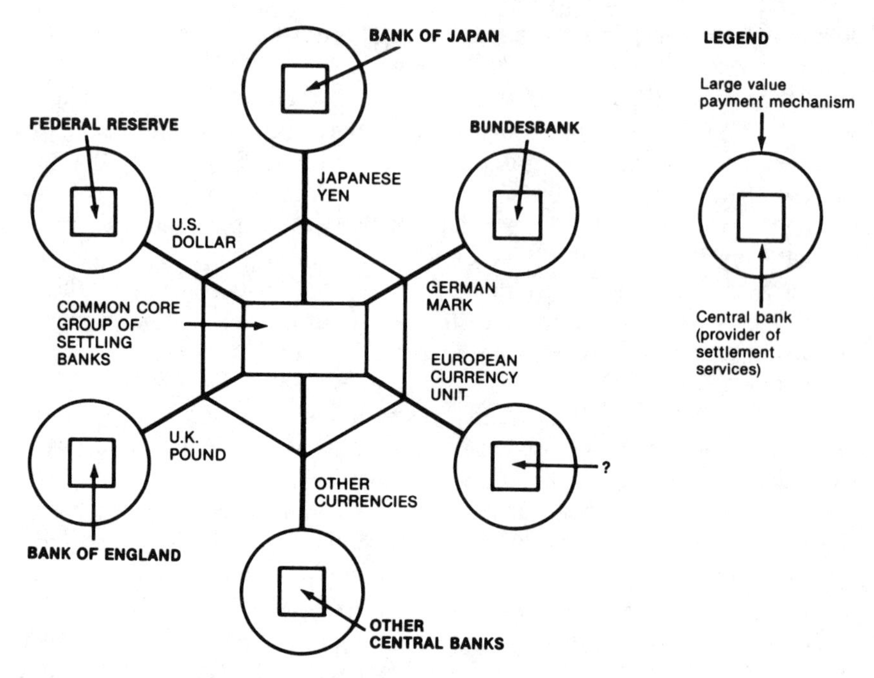

Figure 5-4. New Structure of the International Payment Mechanism

transnational. The implications of the development of a single group, however, transcend the questions raised by the development of the new ECU arrangements. In particular, the emergence of a multinational core clearing group offering international payment services in several currencies may weaken the bargaining positions of individual central banks in negotiations with commercial bank participants in their home money market.

A second issue is broadly supervisory.[9] Most central banks recognize a duty to supervise the monetary mechanism with which their country is associated. The provision of official emergency credit presents a related difficulty. As the general allocation of supervisory responsibility for core banks becomes more diffuse, traditional assumptions about credit extensions between central banks and particular commercial banks may also break down.

Another issue, which is likely to become topical in the near future, is both supervisory and monetary in nature. It is possible under the newly emerging international payment structure to have clearing and settlement arrangements for more than one currency within particular financial centers such as London, New York, and Tokyo. The issue is now most pressing for dollar-clearing arrangements in Tokyo. However, in a world of competing international currencies, other possibilities exist.

The issue is which central bank is responsible for ensuring settlements in "foreign" currencies made by banking offices located in the traditional territorial jurisdiction of another central bank such as the Bank of England or Bank of Japan. The answer to this question is unclear. In the past, such settlements have not typically been highly organized or taken place on a large scale. If scale and organization increase, and they are increasing, then orderly settlements in financial centers outside the traditional home country of a currency may become important to international financial stability, and call for more than reliance on the traditional home-country central bank.

Finally, questions of policy become even more complicated if one considers extending the group of possible participants in core clearing systems to include nonbanks. Marginal costs of participation have presumably fallen for large nonbank companies as well as for banking organizations. Moreover, these companies are becoming more and more sophisticated in their intraday cash control strategies and in their level of direct financial market participation. If the thrust of official policies is to require such entities to make payments through banking organizations, it is important to understand the reasons for this restraint on arrangements that would likely increase the speed and lower the costs of making payments. Increasing the stability of payment arrangements by insulating them (partially) from risks originating in nonbank sectors might be an important part of the answer.

Notes

1. For this type of review, see Bank for International Settlements (1985b).
2. SWIFT is a cooperative company created under Belgian Law. It is wholly owned by member banks. SWIFT provides an international transaction processing network to which only banks (or bank-owned organizations) may connect.
3. These groups might settle through payments on the books of correspondents through the adjustment of reciprocal balances, or perhaps through payments over a core system. Current dollar clearing arrangements among banks operating in Tokyo appear to be one example. Proposals for Scandinavian dollar-clearing arrangements as well as enhanced London dollar clearing are other possibilities.
4. An interbank market is assumed to encompass both the borrowing of funds with payments in that currency and foreign exchange trading.
5. In-depth coverage of this topic may be found in various issues of the *International Correspondent Banker*, a monthly trade journal published in the United Kingdom.

6. CHIPS, with more than 120 (mostly non-U.S. chartered) bank participants is operated by the twelve-member New York Clearing House Association. About twenty CHIPS participants settle for themselves, with half of these settling for one, or more, of the other CHIPS participants.

7. The ten component currencies of the ECU basket are: The pound sterling (United Kingdom), the German mark (West Germany), the franc (Belgium, France and Luxembourg), the lira (Italy), the guilder (Netherlands), the krone (Denmark), the pound (Ireland), and the drachma (Greece). The United Kingdom and Greece, however, do not now participate in the exchange rate mechanism of the EMS. See the discussion in Bank for International Settlements (1985a). For a discussion of how the ECU clearing system will work see Bank for International Settlements (1986), pp. 172–173.

8. For a thoughtful discussion of future developments within the European Monetary System relating to the ECU, see Padoa-Schioppa (1986). For an exploration of the question "Does the ECU need a lender of last resort?" see Allen (1986), pp. 44–48.

9. The problem of allocation of general supervisory responsibility is not new and has been partly addressed for banking groups by the Basle Concordat (see Committee on Banking Regulations and Supervisory Practices 1983).

References

Allen, Polly Reynolds. 1986. *The ECU: Birth of a New Currency*. Group of Thirty Occasional Papers 20.

Bank for International Settlements. 1985a. *Fifty-fifth Annual Report*. Basle.

Bank for International Settlement. 1986. *Fifty-sixth Annual Report*. Basle.

Bank for International Settlements. 1985b. *Payment Systems in Eleven Developed Countries*. Revised edition, Basle.

Bank Information Service, 1984. *Payment Clearing System Review of Organization Membership and Control*.

Committee on Banking Regulations and Supervisory Practices of the Bank for International Settlements. 1983. *Principles for the Supervision of Banks' Foreign Establishments*. Revised, Basle.

Federal Reserve Board. 1985. *Reducing Risks on Large-dollar Electronic Funds Transfer System*.

Frankel, Allen B., and Jeffrey C. Marquardt. 1985. Payments Systems: Theory and Policy (processed).

Padoa-Schioppa, Tommaso. 1986. *Lecture before the European University Institute on 2/20/85*. Revised and released by the Bank of Italy on 2/17/86.

III MACROECONOMIC POLICY UPDATED

Will EFT and redesigned network architecture, discussed earlier, reduce the central bank's future effectiveness? That issue is central to part III of this volume. Practically all the elements involved in Fed/money-supply links seem certain to change in a rising EFT payments mode. In the years 1985–2000, the Fed's leverage over money creation may be reduced either because (1) it is not clear what money is in the world of exotic new technologies; (2) the money multiplier shifts unpredictably; (3) money is not subject to reserve requirements and therefore not directly under the Fed's control; or (4) network architecture is such that EFT systems can clear funds in large part outside the Fed funds system.

Another set of linkages important to the effectiveness of monetary policy switches the focus from money supply to money demand and the macroeconomic variables: real growth, employment, prices. Hence, more questions follow. In an EFT-dominated world, what will happen to the secondary linkages between money aggregates, interest rates, and real-sector variables: prices, income, and employment? Part III seeks to answer these questions, in two different theoretical models.

By way of background, table III-1 shows the tools of Fed policy (I) and the secondary links (II). With quantitative and qualitative

Table III-1. Monetary Policy/Macroeconomic Links

I. *Fed Policy Tools*

- Quantitative
  - OM operations, Discounts — affect reserves
  - Reserve requirements — affect money multiplier*
- Qualitative
  - Moral suasion
  - Other selective credit controls

↓

II. *Operating Targets*

Bank reserves (money base)
Monetary aggregates (M_1, M_2, M_3)
Fed funds rate
Bank credit, domestic nonfinancial debt

↓

III. *Ultimate Policy Targets*

GNP, Real output growth
High employment (or reduced unemployment)
vs.
Price stability (or acceptably low level of price rise)
Exchange rate stability
Balance of payments equilibrium

* $M_1 = mR$, where M_1 = money supply; m = money multiplier; R = reserve base.

instruments (I), the Fed hopes to achieve the ultimate policy goals (III) of price and dollar stability and economic growth. Given practical realities, the Fed first aims at money, interest rates, or some nonmonetary intermediate "operating" goals.[1] For example, the Fed hopes to achieve price stability through stable money growth, which in turn affects spending behavior of the public. In the process of controlling money here or the dollar's value abroad, however, the manager of the Federal Open Market Committee (FOMC) may not permit interest rates to rise above some unacceptable upper limit known as the "fed funds constraint."

Monetary theory is the key to understanding these links. Theory analyzes the relationships between money growth (once one succeeds in controlling it) and the positive elements identified in the economy: stable prices, real growth, balance of payments equilibrium.

The "new classic" and monetarist models, developed here by

Professor Havrilesky (chapter 7), emphasize the links between money, permanent income, and prices with interest rates of minor importance. Money change is then the major determinant of short-run changes in nominal and real income, and policy makers must focus on controlling growth of the monetary base. The Tobin portfolio model (chapter 6) stresses the importance, however, of interest rates as well as gross national product and employment. Because interest rate expectations change frequently, this second interpretation suggests an uncertain relationship between money and prices or income. Hence, policy makers must choose at their own discretion from among a variety of monetary and nonmonetary targets, including interest rates and credit extension as well as final output.

Crucial to the macroeconomic linkages, under whatever theory one happens to believe, is the stability of money velocity or its reciprocal, money demand. That is, will the public's desire to hold money be subject to short-run unpredictability until technological change settles down in the next ten or fifteen years? Havrilesky and Tobin both address this central issue too.

One critical question is whether money demand shifts, recently inspired by user experimentation in the new technology, are likely to be permanent and predictable, leaving intact the Fed's ability to move from money to prices and income in the manner of the classic monetarist story. Or do long-run unstable money demand relationships suggest, rather, the better central banking use of both monetary base and nonmonetary targets? From about the time of the 1951 Fed-Treasury "accord" until the new monetary targets emphasis in 1979, Fed policy was largely of a discretionary nature among a shifting blend of intermediate targets (II) shown in table III-1. Between 1979 and late 1982 money supply was, at least on paper, the central bank's major policy target. Now, with the post-1982 money revolution, theoreticians and policy makers both have become more uncertain about the proper path to follow. The role of narrow (M1) money has been downgraded by policy makers since fall of 1982, and the macro theories presented here suggest still further future policy shifts in emphasis to money base (Havrilesky) or real-sector variables such as GNP (Tobin).

Some developments can already be assessed. Credit cards have reduced the public's cash-holding habits, while ATMs permit cheaper and faster access from money to interest-earning accounts, or lower "conversion costs." The payment of market rates of interest may cause future economizing in narrow transactions money (M1) holdings. At the same time, an underground economy interested in moonlighting and/or tax evasion has increased currency demand and the implicit desire to escape the computer's scrutiny and trail.

The year 2000 will likely see further sweeping changes in demand for money to hold. Through improved quality of service, private suppliers may succeed in persuading users to alter check-payment patterns. Payors may send greater proportions of money payments electronically via private-bank wire systems, as shown by Henderson and Moore (chapters 1 and 2). People may initiate money transfers on-line from videotex home computers or smart-card terminals via satellite in Geller's scenario (chapter 3). The rate of use of the public's dwindling transactions money balances, or velocity, will likely rise as users economize further on zero or low-yield transactions money balances and take advantage of cheaper, faster, more efficient payments opportunities. Professor Havrilesky's innovative macro model develops the possible outcome and policy implications. Havrilesky also synthesizes his original work with earlier theories, and develops a strong program for effective monetary reform including a stable policy environment.

Professor Tobin, too, examines money- and real-market equilibrium in the new technology era, and analyzes step-by-step its impact. The likely future behavior of market participants including banks and their customers, given market-determined rates on transactions money as well as money substitutes, is explicitly set forth. Tobin's lucid analysis indicates, as does Havrilesky's, the need for some monetary reforms and revision of theoretical concepts. In particular, for reserve requirement purposes Tobin's model downgrades bank deposit liabilities in favor of all the bank assets that banks can buy with the electronic short-lived loans.

Both authors stress the need to examine all the transactions the new money can fuel. Their models mesh with the earlier work in this volume, which suggest that the elusive and often ghostly nature of short-term money creation and destruction these days demands some rethinking of the policy targets, concepts, and rules. Tobin and Havrilesky both focus upon the widest variable in a reserve or money demand equation, transactions and all the assets financial institutions can buy with the new money flows.

However, Havrilesky recommends the targeting of the reserve rather than money base; he notes that there is greater stability in base velocity than in money velocity, hence its greater reliability as a target for open-market policy. Havrilesky also urges the establishment of a more predictable and open monetary regime, free of money policy surprises, in which raw data promptly are made available to market participants.

Tobin suggests the reapplication of reserve requirements to depository institution assets (less capital). The things the new money can buy for banks will in that manner be more completely reservable, and subject to the influence of Fed policy. The Fed umbrella will cover money created by the new nondepository short-term liabilities as well as transactions deposits money creation.

Deregulation, according to Tobin, is also making the new money demand more interest-inelastic. It is fulfilling the monetarists' dream of an interest-inelastic money market equilibrium, or *LM* curve. The policy solution is not to be found, however, in the development of a "supermonetarist" policy which offsets any financial shocks at the expense of sharply higher interest rates. Rather, the authorities may better pursue a discretionary monetary policy that seeks to attain optimal levels of gross national product. They may therefore more successfully avert the unfortunate kinds of delayed reactions suffered to monetarist policies of the 1979–1980 period during the recession aftermath. Both Havrilesky and Tobin believe that, given policy shifts of emphasis, monetary policy and open market operations can operate well in the brave new world.

Note

1. See Henry C. Wallich, "Recent Techniques of Monetary Policy," *Economic Review*, Federal Reserve Bank of Kansas City, May 1984, 21–30.

6 MONETARY RULES AND CONTROL IN BRAVE NEW WORLD

James Tobin

The regulatory, institutional, and technical environment of banks and competing financial enterprises has changed rapidly in recent years. More changes are on the way. Most analysts focus attention on the microeconomic consequences, how the changes affect the various types of financial institutions and their customers, both depositors and borrowers. This chapter concerns the macroeconomic effects, how the monetary system is altered and how the central bank, the Federal Reserve System in the United States, can and should operate in the new environment. Monetary policy is the government's principal instrument for controlling the overall course of the economy. Consequently, in this industry much more than in others, these macroeconomic effects are of the greatest importance.

The chapter examines the implications for central bank monetary policy of two significant developments, the deregulation of interest payments on deposits (part I) and the coming of automated payments (part II).

Part I adapted with permission from Tobin, J. *Financial Structure and Monetary Rules. Kredit und Kapital* 2: 155–171, 1983.

Part II reprinted with permission from Lawrence and Shay's *Technological Innovation, Regulation, and the Monetary Economy*. Copyright 1986 by Ballinger Publishing Company.

I. Deregulation of Interest on Deposits

Legal ceilings on deposit interest rates are disappearing, even on checking accounts. Related proposals would pay interest on bank reserves at a rate indexed to the central bank discount rate, and would in turn index the discount rate to market rates. These changes alter the properties of the monetary system, in response both to central bank operations and to nonpolicy shocks. A short-hand summary is that they make the Hicksian *LM* curve very steep. Different monetary rules distribute differently, among interest rates, output, and prices, the effects of various kinds of shocks. These distributions are significantly altered when the financial structure changes. Both the desirability of structural reforms and, if they are adopted, the suitability of particular rules of monetary policy depend on these alterations in the properties of the system.

Monetary Policy and the Conversion of Shocks into Macroeconomic Outcomes

Rules governing the monetary policies of central banks determine the response of the economy to various macroeconomic shocks. The shocks are of several kinds. Three of the most important are the following: Real demand shocks affect the aggregate demand for goods and services. They may arise from the spending behavior of consumers, from business investment, from exports, and from government fiscal operations. Financial shocks affect the demand for monetary assets relative to their close portfolio substitutes, whether by banks or by other private agents. Price shocks affect current and expected prices of goods and services; they may arise in world commodity markets, in exchange rates, or in domestic wage and price settings by trade unions and businesses. Monetary policies may be invariant to these shocks, at least for a time, because they cannot be discerned or anticipated or because on principle the authorities choose to ignore them. In any case the monetary rule distributes the shocks among several macroeconomic variables, of which the most important are real aggregate output, real interest rates, and prices. Different monetary rules distribute the various shocks differently. One important consideration, in choosing among competing rules, is evaluation of their conversions of shocks into the macroeconomic variables of social concern.

This mode of analysis has been well known at least since *William Poole's* celebrated article in 1970. *Poole*, using the standard *IS-LM* framework, compared a monetary policy fixing the interest rate (both real and nominal, as he abstracted from price and inflation effects) with one fixing the quantity of money. He assumed that the central bank could, if desired, respond quickly to observed interest rates but that output was not observed soon enough to be included in a monetary rule. He showed that pegging the interest rate protected the economy from output variation due to purely financial shocks but transmitted real demand shocks into output fluctuations. A monetarist rule, on the other hand, would convert both types of shocks partly into output changes and partly into interest rate changes. Output would be less vulnerable to real demand shocks and more vulnerable to financial shocks than under the interest rate rule.

These conclusions were based on the standard assumption that the *Hicks*ian *LM* curve, taking account of the monetary rule, would be horizontal in conventional output/interest rate space under the interest-pegging policy and upward sloping under the monetarist rule. A vertical *LM* "curve" would protect the economy completely from output fluctuation due to demand shocks, converting them entirely into interest rate volatility, while rendering output highly vulnerable to financial shocks. But a fixed-M policy would not insure a vertical *LM* curve unless the demand for that M were wholly interest-inelastic. Otherwise, to achieve a vertical *LM* curve and the shock distribution it would imply, would require a supermonetarist policy, namely one that changed the quantity of money systematically in the opposite direction from observed interest rates.

Figures 6-1a, 6-1b, and 6-1c picture graphically the three situations: pegged interest rate and horizontal *LM* curve; monetarist rule with upward sloping *LM* curve due to response of velocity or central bank or both to interest rates; vertical *LM* curve due either to inelasticity of velocity or to supermonetarist policy. In each case the expected outcome is point *E* and the shaded zones encompass outcomes with some $x\%$ probability given the joint distribution of real demand shocks displacing *IS* and financial shocks displacing *LM*, assumed uncorrelated in the illustration. The shapes of the zones, differing from diagram to diagram, show how the different *LM* shapes distribute the shocks differently as between output and interest rate deviations from *E*. In the extreme case of zero real demand shocks, outcomes are always on the central *IS* curve, solid in the diagrams; in the other extreme case, zero financial shocks, outcomes are always on the solid *LM* curve.

If a classical situation, with supply-determined output and flexible prices, is assumed instead of the *Keynes*ian situation of the *Poole* article and of figure 6-1, the *Poole* analysis is still applicable. Just reinterpret the horizontal axis in the *IS-LM* diagram to refer to price level rather than to

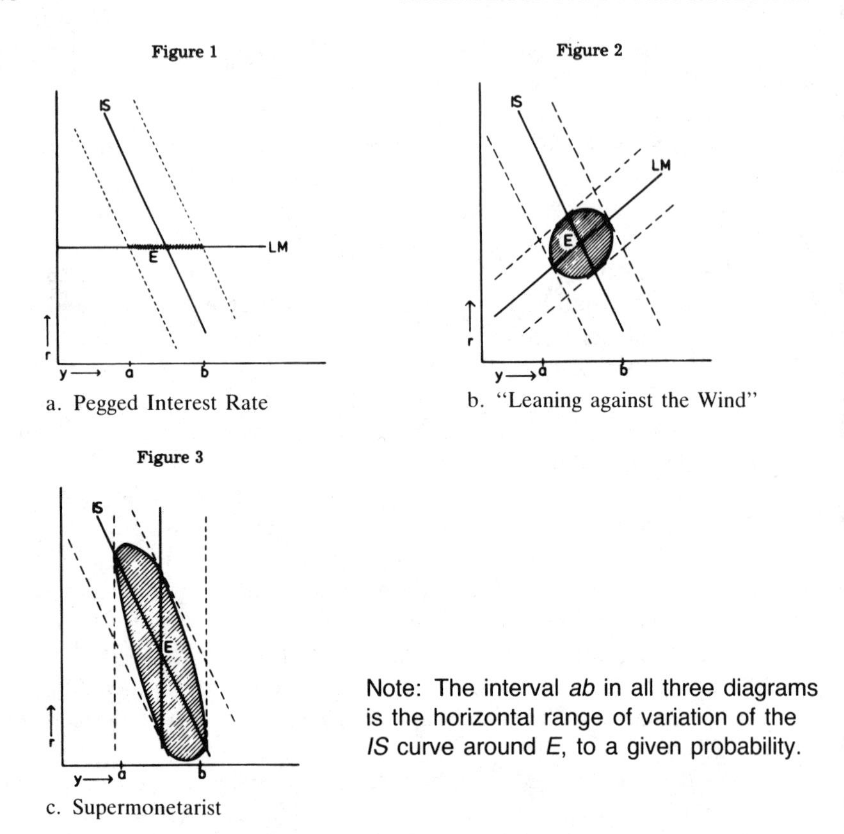

Figure 6-1. Output and Interest Variability under Demand and Financial Shocks: Three Cases

real output. Because of the *Pigou-Patinkin* real balance effect, the *IS* curve will still be downward sloping.

One monetarist proposition asserts the stability of money demand, the unimportance of financial shocks relative to real demand shocks. This argues for a monetarist policy rule, as against a pegged interest rate, in the pursuit of output stability—and of price stability insofar as variations of real demand are absorbed in prices rather than quantities. But the logic of this monetarist argument would seem to call for a vertical *LM* curve, as in figure 6-1c. If nature does not provide one, then a super-monetarist policy would be in order. Nature would provide one according to the old-fashioned quantity theory of money, which denied or ignored the interest-elasticity of money demand. I have the impression that this view has been abandoned under the weight of theoretical logic and empirical findings.

In general, the optimal shape of the *LM* curve depends on the joint distribution of *LM* and *IS* shocks (e.g., on their variances and covariance). This is true even if the objective is simply to minimize the variance of output (or price or some combination of the two) regardless of the variance of interest rates. There is no justification at all for assuming that the optimal *LM* shape is the one that corresponds to a fixed money supply. The optimal money supply rule could be either less accommodative than that, supermonetarist, or more accommodative; by "accommodative" I mean in this context positively responsive to interest rates.

How the LM *Curve Distributes Demand, Financial, and Price Shocks*

The *Poole* analysis can be extended to take explicit account of supply price shocks along with the other two types. Here is a simple short-run model, from which may be derived the effects of each of the three kinds of shocks and the way in which these effects are altered by changing the slope of the *LM* curve.

(1)	$Y - E(y,r,p) - u_1 = 0$	Goods and services (*IS*)
(2)	$r - lY + (l/k)(m - u_2)/P = 0$	Money (*LM*)
(3)	$p - S(Y) - u_3 = 0$	Price level

The symbols are the following: Y real output; r real interest rate; p price level; u_1 real demand shock; u_2 shock to excess demand for nominal money; u_3 shock to supply price of output; l slope of *LM* curve, account taken of both private agent money demand response to interest rate and of the central bank's supply response; k income effect on money demand; m constant in money supply function.

The following are standard assumptions regarding:

the derivatives of the aggregate demand function E with respect to its arguments: $0 < E_y < 1$; $E_r < 0$; $E_p \leq 0$ (the *Pigou-Patinkin* real balance effect);

the derivative of the aggregate supply function S: $S_y > 0$;

the parameters of the *LM* relation: $l > 0$; $k > 0$; $m > 0$.

This is a *Keynes*ian model, as equation (3) indicates. It is not possible to discuss nominal supply price shocks in a classical model where price is completely flexible and wholly endogenous. I spare you the standard comparative statistics calculations which support the qualitative results summarized in tables 6-1 and 6-2.[1] These confirm those of the *Poole* analysis already discussed for the first two kinds of shocks. As one would intuitively expect, a positive price shock lowers real output and raises the price level. Steepening *LM* accentuates the output effect and mitigates the price effect. For those who are concerned more for price stability than output stability, this is a reason for preferring a more monetarist structure.

An external price shock, dramatically typified by the two OPEC crises of the 1970s, combines a positive supply price shock and a negative real demand shock. If the *LM* curve is close to vertical, there will be a much larger output loss but less of a general price increase than if monetary policy is more accommodative.

The price shock in the preceding analysis is an increase in price level, present and future, leaving expected inflation unchanged. An increase in the expected inflation rate is a shock of a different kind. It is indeed equivalent to a reduction in demand for money at a given real interest rate. The nominal interest rate rises relative to the real rate. But the result is that the real rate falls, as table 6-1 says. The analysis indicates that inflationary expectations are expansionary. If this seems strange in these times, it is because the analysis assumes a fixed monetary rule while

Table 6-1. Effects of Shocks on Macroeconomic Outcomes

	Variable		
Shock	*Real Output*	*Real Interest Rate*	*Price Level*
Excess real demand	+	+	+
Excess money demand	−	+	−
Increase in supply price	−	−	+

Table 6-2. Effects of Steepening *LM* Curve on Strength of Shock Effects

	Variable		
Shock	*Real Output*	*Real Interest Rate*	*Price Level*
Excess real demand	−	+	−
Excess money demand	+	+	+
Increase in supply price	+	+	−

+ means absolute size of effect is increased.

experience has led people to expect that monetary policy itself will become more restrictive on news of higher inflation. In the model, a positive expected inflation shock would be correlated with a positive shock to excess money demand, delivered by the central bank.

Reforms of Financial Structure and Their Macroeconomic Implications

The above review was intended to prepare the ground for the main point of the chapter. Once policy is defined by a rule, it essentially modifies the structure of the system. Policy and structure become inextricably combined. Their joint product is what matters, as illustrated by the shape of the *LM* curve in the example above. One way to alter the operating properties of the system, specifically the way shocks are distributed among various outcomes, is to change the policy rule. Another way is to change the structure. Moreover, if structural reform occurs, whether for reasons connected with macroeconomic policy and performance or not, then most likely the policy rule should be changed too. That is, the rule that was optimal given the old structure will generally be no longer optimal under the new. For example, suppose that changes in financial technology, institutions, and regulations twist the *LM* curve of figure 6-1b toward the vertical one of figure 6-1c. Then if a monetarist rule was previously optimal, a more accommodative rule would now be optimal, with policy offsetting the nonaccommodative consequences of those structural changes.

The example is, it happens, realistic. Structural changes of the kind described are now occurring rapidly in the United States. Financial deregulation is making the *LM* curve vertical. Quantity theorists were wrong in the past in arguing as if it already was, as if money demand were interest-inelastic. But now monetarists are in the front line of advocates of reforms of financial structure that will make the world over to their design. Let me explain in some detail.

The most important reform is that legal ceilings on interest rates on bank deposits are being removed. Even demand deposits will bear market-determined rates. Deregulation conforms to the spirit of the times. Economists instinctively support free price competition among banks as among airlines or trucks or dairy farmers. Monetarists are especially strong in free market instincts, but they have macroeconomic objectives as well. They wish to tighten the central bank's control of money supply, and to hold GNP more tightly to the money supply in the face of shocks to aggregate demand.

For these reasons, their agenda for "reform" include the introduction of flexibility in other interest rates too. They would have the Federal Reserve pay interest on banks' reserve balances, presumably at a rate indexed to market rates. They would index the Federal Reserve discount rate, making it equal a market rate plus a constant penalty. Along with contemporaneous reserve accounting, these reforms are designed to tighten the relation between the supply of unborrowed reserves and the deposit component of M1. In this monetarist vision, there will also be uniform reserve requirements on M1 deposits, which are transactions media, and none on other liabilities, which are not.

The pace of deregulation has accelerated. Banks and other depository institutions were, beginning in December 1982, allowed to offer deposits payable on demand, with interest rates uncontrolled. Since the number of withdrawals by check were limited to three per month, these deposits are not quite transactions media on the Fed's current M1 criterion, "checkable." Congress in 1982 rushed through legislation authorizing these new deposits in order to enable banks and other regulated depository institutions to compete with money market mutual funds. The new deposits are free of reserve requirements and are insured by the federal government, an advantage over the funds.

The following year an even more decisive step was taken on the road to deregulation of deposit interest rates. Beginning in January 1983, banks and other depository institutions were authorized to offer insured demand deposits with unlimited checking and prearranged transfer privileges. The only legal restrictions were a minimum balance requirement (then $2500) and the ineligibility of businesses to hold accounts of this type. These deposits are called "super-NOW" accounts. Regular NOW accounts have been available nationwide for nonbusiness depositors since January 1, 1981. They originated as interest-bearing savings deposits on which checks could be written provided they were called by another name, "Notices of Withdrawal." Like regular NOW accounts, super-NOW deposits are subject to reserve requirements and are counted in M1.

As deposits come to bear competitive interest rates, monetary theory—models of money supply and demand and of the transmission of control measures and shocks through financial markets to the real economy—will have to be rewritten. Standard theory assumes that "money," whatever its other characteristics, bears an exogenously fixed nominal interest rate, set by law, regulation, or institutional convention. It may be zero, as it is on currency and has been on reserve balances and conventional demand deposits. It may be an effective ceiling above zero, as formerly on passbook savings, and on most time deposits. Demand for monetary assets of these kinds is specified in our models to depend on the endogenous market-determined interest rates on substitute nonmoney assets and on other variables. The differential between those uncontrolled interest rates and the fixed nominal rates on monetary assets is compensated by the nonpecuniary services of money, which are thought to be inversely related to the real quantity held.

Consider how this traditional property differentiates "money" from assets with uncontrolled endogenous interest rates. When, for example, the supply of treasury bills is increased, one adjustment that can induce people to buy and hold the new supply is the fall in the price of bills, the increase in their interest yield. This is not the only adjustment, but it is the obvious first-order vehicle of equilibration. For fixed-interest money, however, this first-order effect does not occur. If the supply of money is increased, the public has to be persuaded to hold it by changes other than in its own interest rate—notably other interest rates, transactions volumes, prices. Indeed in standard theory this is precisely the reason why monetary control powerfully affects nonfinancial variables. When market rates are paid on money too, the transmission mechanism is significantly altered.

Currency, it is true, will continue to bear zero nominal interest, but the currency exception is probably not very important. Currency demand does not appear to be sensitive to interest rates when they are already very high. Moreover, interest-induced substitutions for or against currency are likely to be almost wholly with transactions deposits. Consequently, when deposits bear market-determined rates, it will not be a bad approximation in modeling money demand decisions to regard those rates as applying to the whole transactions money supply. Likewise when and if interest comes to be paid on reserve balances at the Federal Reserve, it will not be inaccurate to model bank demands for reserves inclusive of their currency holdings as dependent on that interest rate. In both cases, marginal adjustments will be made in interest-bearing form.

In the old regime, and in the standard model, the "market" for fixed-interest deposits is in disequilibrium. Depositors' demand is smaller than the amounts banks, individually and in aggregate, would like to supply at the controlled rates. Banks will gladly accept, on prevailing terms, any new funds the public would like to deposit; no one will be turned away. When rates are uncontrolled and competitively determined they will clear the market. Banks will be supplying all the deposits they wish to offer. They will accept deposits to the point where their marginal cost, including interest, equals the marginal revenue expected from lending or investing the funds. Of course deposit interest rates will be, like loan rates now, administered prices. But, also like loan rates now and uncontrolled rates on certificates of deposit as well, they and the other terms of deposit agreements will be readily changed under competition. The United States system of banks and other financial institutions is, unlike the system in most other countries, decentralized and competitive, though monopolistically competitive.

In the new regime, the interest differential between bank assets and deposit liabilities would meet the costs of intermediation. These costs include the risk that deposit withdrawals and the accompanying reserve losses would impose extra costs, borrowing at a premium in the market or at the Federal Reserve discount window. A bank's choice of asset composition, as between illiquid loans and variable-price securities on the one hand, and excess reserves or other liquid assets on the other, would reflect that same risk.

The marginal costs of intermediation are probably fairly constant over normal ranges of variation in the volume of bank deposits and assets. Thus the competitive deposit rate will be below the rates on bank loans and other assets by a fairly constant differential. The public's demand for deposits, on the other hand, depends principally on the interest differential and on transactions volume. If the differential becomes a constant, the demand for deposits will be independent of the level of interest rates. A rise in market interest rates will not reduce the demand for deposits as it does in the old regime and in the standard model, because the rate paid on deposits will rise too. The old monetarist assumption of interest-inelastic money demand will apply, though for a reason quite different from its original motivation.

Figure 6-2 pictures the new regime. It shows a family of deposit demand curves, for various transactions volumes proxied by money income Y_p. The higher curves correspond to higher income levels. As indicated, deposit demand depends inversely on the interest differential. But given constant costs of intermediation, the bank's supply of deposits is perfectly elastic at the interest differential that meets those costs. Thus equilibrium volume of deposits depends solely on the income level.

Equilibrium also requires demand = supply balance in reserves, shown in the bottom panel of figure 6-2. The supply of unborrowed reserves is determined by the central bank by its open market operations. (Actually these operations affect directly the unborrowed monetary base, only part of which takes the form of reserves. The remainder is currency outside banks. The Federal Reserve has to estimate, with some error, the public demand for currency.) The demand for unborrowed reserves has two components. Required reserves, as indicated in the diagram, are approximately proportional to deposits. From this demand must be subtracted net

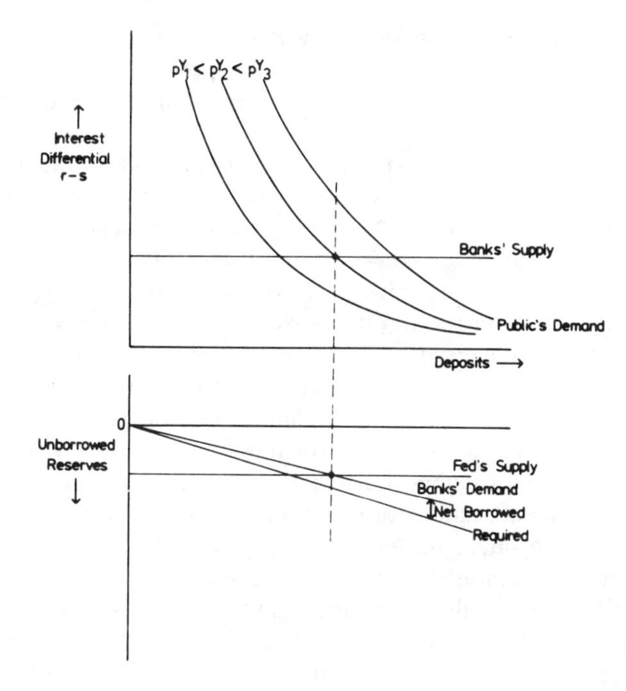

Figure 6-2. Financial Structure and Monetary Rules

borrowed reserves, borrowings from the Federal Reserve less reserves held in excess of requirements. At present net borrowed reserves vary directly, in the short run at least, with market interest rates. The discount rate charged by the Federal Reserve is constant, so that an increase in the market rates that can be earned on bank assets is an incentive to borrow and to economize holdings of excess reserves. Once interest geared to market rates is paid on reserves and interest charged on borrowing from the central bank is similarly indexed, this relationship will be nullified. Banks' net borrowed reserves will be essentially a constant fraction of deposits and required reserves, as pictured in figure 6-2.

As a result, the central bank will control pretty tightly the volume of deposits by fixing the supply of unborrowed reserves. And thus the central bank will also determine quite closely the level of money income (pY_2 in the upper panel). These linkages will, moreover, not be loosened by variation of interest rate levels, as they are today. An interesting sidelight, pointed out by *Hadjimichalikakis* (1982), is that innovations in financial technology which either raise transactions requirements for holding money or reduce costs of intermediation will reduce money income unless the central bank responds by increasing the supply of reserves.

The main outcome, as foreshadowed in my first section, is to fulfill the monetarist dream of a vertical *LM* curve.

Of course in the very short run the control of deposits and money supply via fixing unborrowed reserves will not be as tight as figure 6-2 and accompanying text depict. As now, it will take action by the Federal Reserve, adjustment of reserve supply targets, to correct observed deviations from the desired track of monetary aggregates. But the corrections will be faster and the deviations smaller, because some of the adjustments that now require central bank action will occur automatically.

To appreciate the change, it is necessary to understand how the Federal Reserve operates in the present regime. The basic targets are, or at least were until late 1982, announced growth tracks of monetary aggregates, M1 in particular. Primary importance has been attached to meeting numerical targets announced in advance for money growth from the final quarter of one year to the final quarter of the next year. Interim targets for each quarter are also announced in the course of a year. These long- and short-range M-targets should be distinguished from the one-month operating instructions to the New York Federal Reserve Bank regarding open market operations. Since the celebrated announcement of October 1979, these instructions have been designed to obtain a supply of unborrowed reserves consistent with the short-run M targets. Suppose however that bank loans and deposits, and thus required reserves, rise beyond expectation. Money market interest rates will rise as banks scramble to meet their reserve tests. Banks will borrow more from their Federal Reserve Banks at the fixed discount rate and cut down their holdings of interest-free excess reserves. Monetary aggregates will rise above their desired tracks. Correction will come later, by downward adjustment of next month's reserve supply and possibly by upward adjustment of the discount rate.

In the new regime, if and when it is fully established in future, the adjustment will occur sooner by automatic increase in the discount rate. The same assumed shock will raise interest rates more and money supplies less than in the old regime.

This is one buffer or safety valve that the proposed structural reforms remove. The other one, more consequential in the longer run, is the increase in monetary velocity now induced by the rise in interest rates. This will be nullified as the rise in rates extends to money itself. There is no doubt some elasticity in the transactions velocity of money even at constant interest differentials. That is, households and businesses can find ways of handling increased economic activity with the same cash holdings, at least in the short run. As *Akerlof* and *Milbourne* (1979) have shown, depositors who follow an *S-s* strategy for their inventories of cash will handle larger transactions volumes with the same average cash holdings as long as they keep those *S-s* thresholds unchanged. They may change the thresholds when and only when they regard a new volume of transactions as permanent.

In the end the removal of these buffers will make the *LM* curve more nearly vertical in the short run and the longer run, given the same operating and targeting procedures by the central bank.

Dangers of Combining Monetarist Structure and Monetarist Policy

Monetarism has already steepened the *LM* curve considerably. Intermediate-run targets for monetary aggregates made money supply less responsive to demand than pegged interest rates in the forties or the "bill rate only" policies of the early 1960s or the "leaning against the wind" approach of other postwar years. The October 1979 change in operating procedures further removed the short-run accommodative buffers implicit in the previous practice of instructing the open market desk to hold the market interest on overnight interbank loans of reserves, "federal funds," within a narrow range decided monthly by Federal Reserve authorities. The 1979 procedures substituted unborrowed reserve supplies for interest rates in these instructions. M1 targeting makes *LM* steeper than targeting on unborrowed reserves over a longer period, because it commits the Fed to reverse any lasting changes in the relation of required reserves to unborrowed reserves. The indexing of interest rates on reserves and discounts would automatize and accelerate such reversals. As we would have expected from figure 6-1 and have already observed, monetarist targets and operating procedures have made interest rates much more volatile, and the fulfillment of the monetarist vision will make them more volatile still.

For several reasons, we could expect the location of the *LM* curve to be even more stochastic in the full monetarist regime than it is now. Once M1 deposits bear competitive market rates, depositors will have much less reason than now to "fine-tune" their allocation of funds between M1 deposits and other assets, including noncheckable deposits in banks and the new "money market" deposits with restricted checking and transfer privileges. Moreover, the transactions for which M1 balances are held are by no means solely GNP transactions. Indeed most debits to checking accounts are for other transactions, largely financial, and the two types are by no means perfectly correlated. The turnover of checking accounts for financial transactions is extremely high (more than four times a day, judging from New York "debits"). In the new regime, moreover, M1 holdings for financial transactions would be much larger, and GNP-velocity would be more seriously distorted by variability of finance-related holdings.

Another source of *LM* volatility is connected with intermediation and disintermediation, as these are influenced by borrowers' and lenders' perceptions of the relative risks of short and long commitments. As experience since 1979 suggests, increased uncertainties about future interest rates lead borrowers and lenders to shift from long markets, where banks and other suppliers of checking accounts are not active on the demand side, to short markets, where they are active on both sides. The shift increases the size of monetary aggregates that include the short liabilities of those intermediaries. Those bulges are not connected with positive *IS* shifts, but indeed possibly with the reverse. Ross Starr has documented this effect for M2. In the new regime, the effect could spill into M1.

When banks expand loans to their customers, they must somehow induce the public to hold more of their liabilities simultaneously. As borrowers expend the balances credited to their checking accounts, the direct and indirect recipients have larger balances. At least during the time it takes them to adjust, an M1 bulge accompanies an expansion of lending. When the loans are financing real investments, both are indicative of an *IS* shift which it is the purpose of M1 target policy to oppose. Sometimes, however, as observed in recent recessions, the loan demand reflects distress borrowing, designed to protect or rebuild liquidity for the borrower and his suppliers. It is a byproduct of a negative *IS* shift damaging to cash flow, rather than a positive one. In this case a constant M1 rule aggravates an undesired decline in income. This instability would be magnified in the new regime.

I have argued that in the new regime *LM* would be very steep even in the very short run. In my view *IS* is already very steep in the short run. That is, saving and investment decisions are interest-sensitive only with a lag. In a month or a quarter, expenditures on goods and services, investment and consumption both, are largely the execution of previous decisions, constrained only by current liquidity. Over a longer period, the decisions are reconsidered and remade, interest rates matter a great deal, and the *IS* curve is more gently sloped.

On the other hand, the *LM* locus has been significantly steeper in the longer run than in the short run. That is, the accommodative buffers previously discussed were allowed to operate for a while, but the central bank until recently opposed with increasing strength lasting deviations from its targets for the economy or for the aggregates. The move to tighter targets, enforced more promptly, was motivated by the belief that cumulative inflationary movements in the economy got out of hand before the Fed could or would arrest them. But, as I think we have also seen, there is danger in moving too far in this direction. A restrictive nonaccommodative policy, a steep *LM* curve, makes interest rates shoot up while having little immediate effect on GNP, as one would expect if *IS* is also steep in the short run. But the big rise of interest rates sows the seeds of subsequent collapse, as the high rates take their eventual toll.

During recession, moreover, the distress borrowing and liquidity syndromes previously described postpone the remedial decline in interest rates that should be the other side of the monetarist coin. As the 1981–1982 case illustrates, the collapse may be so great, the relief may be postponed so long, the real determinants of investment may become so unfavorable, that interest-sensitive expenditures are difficult to revive.

It is hard for me to believe that the Federal Reserve intended or anticipated that its M1 targets and operating procedures for 1981–1982 would produce the dismal GNP history actually experienced. One reason they did, according to the Fed itself, was a positive financial shock, increasing the demand for M1. Of course, it is for reasons of this kind that I favor gearing year-to-year Fed policy to more consequential economic variables like GNP, unemployment, and inflation rather than to any intermediate aggregate.

Whatever the Fed's targets, however, I advise caution in moving further toward a monetarist structure of the system. The buffers we have had, even those we still have, serve useful purposes. We can, it is true, have too many buffers and too much accommodation. Since demand (*IS*) shocks, financial (*LM*) shocks, and price shocks, are all likely, the optimal *LM* curve will be upward sloping, neither vertical nor horizontal, neither completely unaccommodating nor wholly accommodating. I suspect we have already made the *LM* curve steeper than optimal. We should not make it vertical. This means that if the structural changes I have described are adopted for microeconomic reasons—and I am by no means convinced they should be—then the central bank should offset their macroeconomic effects by adopting more accommodative operating procedures and targets.

II. Automated Payments

Will effective monetary control of the economy still be feasible in the brave new world of structural change and automated payments? Yes, I think, via a transmission process not much different from the present one. Some adaptations will be needed, both in the laws and regulations applying to banks and other financial intermediaries and in the operating procedures of the central bank. But these seem to me to bring no insuperable difficulties. They continue a process of adaptation that has gone along pretty successfully for a long time.

After all, Congress and the Fed have adapted to other striking technological, institutional, and regulatory changes, confounding many predictions that these innovations would render monetary control ineffectual. Think back to the development of the Federal Funds and Eurodollar markets, the facilitation of transfers between deposits subject to reserve test and other bank liabilities, the erosion of Regulation Q, the inauguration and spread of NOW accounts, the generalization of checkable deposits to intermediaries other than commercial banks, and now the payment of uncontrolled interest rates on transactions accounts.

The Reserve Test

In the United States the fulcrum of monetary control is the reserve test. To judge the future of monetary control in a system of automated payments, we must ask whether and how a reserve test will work in that system. I begin by reminding you how it works now.

Designated "depository institutions"—I shall call them all *banks* for short—must pass a reserve test periodically. Large banks, which account for the bulk of deposits, must do so every two weeks; some others have to pass it only quarterly. The pecuniary sanction against failing does not seem formidable; an interest rate two points above the Fed discount rate is charged on the reserve deficiency, and this penalty is mitigated by allowance for some carry-forward of deficiencies to subsequent test periods. The more important sanction *de facto* is presumably the bank's fear that failures will impair access to Federal Reserve credit in the future.

To pass one of its periodic tests, a bank must hold *eligible reserve assets* during its *reserve-maintenance period* in daily amounts averaging no less than its *requirement* for the test. There are two eligible reserve assets, currency and deposits at Federal Reserve Banks. (They differ in reserve-maintenance period. I am going to gloss over this and similarly inessential technicalities.) The requirement depends, now almost proportionally, on the amounts of certain types of liabilities to nonbanks. Liabilities subject to reserve requirements are now mostly confined to transactions accounts, that is, accounts payable on demand and on order by check or wire to third parties. The *requirement-computation period* leads the maintenance period for reserve balances in Federal Reserve Banks by two business days; thus, since February 1984, reserve accounting is essentially simultaneous.

An essential requisite of monetary control via reserve tests is that the government, via the central bank, monopolizes and controls the aggregate supply of the eligible reserve assets, the monetary base. This the Federal Reserve does by open market operations and by setting the rates and other terms on which it will lend reserves to the banks. Another requisite, also met in the United States, is that the banks subject to reserve tests are in aggregate weighty enough participants in financial and capital markets so that central bank operations affect importantly the quantities, prices, and interest rates determined in those markets.

The question is whether the mechanism just described will apply in a new payments system, and how it will need to be amended. To consider that question, I need first to describe a new payments system as I imagine it.

An Automated Payments System

Here is my vision of the brave new world.

1. Payments will be made at time of purchase or settlement on the initiative of the payor. They will be made from computer stations connected to banks and Federal Reserve Banks, located at banks themselves but also in stores, offices, and homes. I suppose this network will somehow use the telephone system. Plastic cards will be used, as at interactive automatic teller stations today. The payor will enter or confirm information about the transaction by keyboard or telephone dial.

2. Four things will happen when the transaction is executed, either at once or at a future time designated by the payor: (a) The payment will be debited to the payor's account. (b) Simultaneously it will be debited to the payor's bank's account at the Fed, and (c) credited to the payee's bank's account at the Fed, and (d) credited to the payee's account. There will be no float, either for depositors or for banks. Note by the way that this is a greatly accelerated version of the European giro system, which always seemed to me a more efficient flow of information than our check system: from payor to payor's bank to payee's bank to payee rather than from payor to payee to payee's bank to payor's bank.

3. Banks will allow *overdrafts* up to previously established credit lines like those now defined by bank credit cards. Indeed extensive use of overdrafts, long common abroad, is the principal innovative byproduct of the new system for the United States. A transaction will be completed

if and only if it would not result in an overdrawn balance exceeding the prearranged limit.

4. Interest will be credited to positive balances and charged to overdrafts, both of course automatically. I assume that interest rates will be uncontrolled by law or regulation, as the trend of legislation in the United States already suggests; but this is not essential or germane to our present topic. Almost surely the rate for overdrafts will exceed the rate on positive balances.

5. Automatic transfers via the same machinery will be possible to and from nonmonetary accounts at banks and other financial institutions. Nonmonetary accounts would be those not payable or transferable on demand, or those redeemable on demand but variable in value (like shares in variable-price mutual funds). The network could not be used to transfer the ownership of a nonmonetary asset to a third party, but only to buy such an asset by transfer from a monetary account or to order the sale or redemption of such an asset and deposit of the proceeds in a monetary account. Any financial intermediary institution which would wish to use the network for transfer of ownership of its liabilities or shares would have to become a "bank" subject to reserve tests and associated regulations.

Reserve Tests and Monetary Control in the Automated System

The likely extensive use of overdrafts would make it necessary to revise the present base for calculation of bank reserve requirements. If reserves were required, as at present, only against positive liabilities of transactions balances, use of the overdraft facility could make them very small or even zero for many banks. This would be even more likely if overdrafts were netted out. These schemes would, moreover, give banks incentive to offer generous credit lines in order to minimize costly required reserves. Evidently it will not be practical to stick solely to reserve requirements against liabilities. Milton Friedman taught that only the liability side of bank balance sheets should concern us and the central bank. That proposition can be rescued from absurdity only if unused overdraft credit lines are counted as a liability, perhaps a "reserve" charged against the capital account.

The most natural revision might be to set reserve requirements as a function of the bank's net transactions account balances plus aggregate credit lines. This corresponds to a rationale often given for basing reserve requirements on transactions deposits today, that they represent balances immediately available for making payments. A related rationale is that the demand for such balances, of which M1 is meant to be the contemporary aggregate, is a stable and predictable function of nominal income, prices, and interest rates. To be enforceable, this revision would require that the overdraft limit to a depositor be precisely defined and that, as described in the previous section, the automated payment be blocked if it would transgress the limit. It would also require that the bank report, in connection with each reserve test, the total of its credit lines to depositors.

While this revision would be feasible, so far as I can see, I do not think it is the best way to proceed. I have never found the above rationales for reserve requirements on immediately transferable deposits very convincing. It becomes less so when interest on deposits deters their use in payments to acquire other assets, and *a fortiori* when high interest charges on overdrafts would deter use of credit lines. There is precious little econometric evidence for the stability of demand for money in this sense, and I suspect there will be even less in a regime of automated payments.

Effectiveness of the reserve test mechanism does not depend on scaling reserve requirements to deposit liabilities, actual or potential. The mechanism will work however the requirement is computed, so long as the Federal Reserve controls the medium of interbank clearing. A bank loses reserves when it comes up short in check clearings; the same will be true when it is short in automatic transfer clearings. To avoid the fate of running out of liquid federal funds with which to meet deposit losses and negative clearing balances, a bank may hold excess reserves; and if these are depleted, the bank will sell securities, curtail lending, bid for deposits of all kinds, borrow from other banks or from the Fed. All these responses to actual and potential reserve scarcities restrict bank credit and raise interest rates. Any reserve test system that evokes these responses will work; it does not have to require reserves against transactions balances, even though it is mainly through shifts of transactions balances that reserves are moved from bank to bank.

In principle the system will work even with *zero* reserve requirements, with the same penalties against overdrafts at the Fed in excess of vault cash holdings that now apply to reserve deficiencies. That is not a good practical idea, for two reasons. One is that banks' total demand for reserves would be at least as volatile and unpredictable as net free reserves or excess reserves are today. The other concerns equity between banks and other taxpayers; required reserve ratios have already been greatly diminished.

I propose gearing the reserve requirement to bank assets minus capital liabilities. Assets include overdraft advances to depositors. Assets covered by capital liabilities would be free of reserves. It seems to be desirable also to exempt assets covered by subordinated debt, i.e. liabilities on which there is explicit understanding that they are not insured either *de jure* or *de facto*.

My proposal in effect extends reserve requirements to "nontransactions accounts," time deposits and CDs. In the new system banks will be using these funds to advance overdraft credit to holders of transactions accounts. And these "near-moneys" will be even more easily transferable on maturity or sale into transactions accounts than they are now. It seems to me more appropriate to "tax" overdrafts in use than unused credit lines.

In an automated system of the type imagined, M1 will not be a very interesting statistic, for much the same reasons that render deposits unsuitable as the base for reserve requirements. However the monetarist savants decide to redefine M1, its velocity will probably be even more volatile than it is now. But monetary policy will be no less effective. Variation of the Fed's instruments, open market operations and discount rates, will still affect the monetary base and will be transmitted to macroeconomic variables that really matter. Mechanical monetarism, targeting of monetary aggregates, will be dead, but monetary theory will be very much alive. The payments system will be more efficient and convenient.

Note

1. A further assumption, beyond the standard restrictions listed in the text, is required for the entries for Y and p in the third row of table 6-2. It is that the *Pigou-Patinkin* effect E_p is relatively weak. To understand it, imagine the (1) and (2) are solved to eliminate r and to derive an aggregate demand relation of p to Y, which will be negatively sloped. This, together with equation (3), the positively sloped aggregate supply relation of p to Y, determines p and Y. As in ordinary demand/supply analysis, an upward shift of the supply curve will lower Y and raise p. It will lower Y more and raise p less the gentler the slope of the demand curve. The question in table 6-2 is how steepening LM alters the slope of the aggregate demand relation of p to Y. Two price effects on aggregate demand are present in the model. One is the *Pigou-Patinkin* effect: a price increase lowers real financial wealth and increases saving. This effect is smaller when LM is steeper, because it is offset to a greater degree by a decline in the interest rate. The other is the indirect monetary effect: a price increase lowers the real money supply and raises interest rates. Making LM steeper accentuates this effect. The first effect tends to make aggregate demand less sensitive to the price level, the second effect to make it more sensitive. The assumption of table 6-2 is that the monetary effect dominates, so that the aggregate demand relation of p to Y becomes flatter. Technically, it is that $(m - u_2)/p$, the absolute value of the real money supply change due to a price movement, exceeds $-E_p/(1 - E_y)$, the "multiplied" *Pigou-Patinkin* effect.

References

Akerlof, G., and Milbourne, R. 1979. Irving Fisher on His Head: Part I. *Quartery Journal of Economics*. 93(2):169–187.

Hadjimichalikakis, M. 1982. *Monetary Policy and Modern Money Markets*. Lexington, MA: Lexington Books.

Poole, W. 1970. Optimal Choice of Monetary Policy Instruments in a Simple Stochastic Macro Model. *Quarterly Journal of Economics*. 84(May):197–216.

Starr, R. 1982. Variation in the Maturity Structure of Debt and Behavior of the Monetary Aggregates: The Maturity Shift Hypothesis. San Diego Discussion Paper #82–9. University of California, March.

7 MONETARY MODELING IN A WORLD OF FINANCIAL INNOVATION

Thomas Havrilesky

Sufficient information has been amassed regarding Electronic Funds Transfer Systems (EFTS) to allow intelligent guessing about the outlines of the financial system that will emerge. This chapter begins by sketching some key elements of the type of macroeconomic model that would be consistent with that system. It then presents an intuitive model of the interface between regulatory and market forces which motivate financial innovation. Having considered the macrotheoretic end point and the forces propelling us toward that point, the chapter then examines ongoing changes in monetary and nonmonetary behavioral relations and how they are likely to affect monetary policy.

The specific types of technological innovations that are labeled Electronic Funds Transfer Systems (EFTS) are discussed in detail elsewhere in this volume and need not be reviewed here. For larger business firms and financially sophisticated households the primary monetary impacts have been a closer synchronization of payments and receipts, a reduction of collection times and a related sweeping of transactions balances (M1) into "investment" accounts (non-M1) on a frequent basis. As unit costs

---

This chapter has benefited from discussions with Fred Furlong, Jurg Niehans, Mike Rose, Bharat Trehan, Ross Taylor, Paul O'Brien, Robert Schweitzer and William Yohe. Responsibility for error is this author's.

decline new techniques will eventually enable medium-sized firms and less-sophisticated households to adopt new microprograms for the timing of receipts and disbursements, such as direct computer links to financial services firms. On an industrywide level, these impacts have already permitted the development of firm-to-firm payments systems for large businesses. Except for the automated clearing house network, systemswide applications within the financial services industry have been rather slow in emerging. However, dramatic changes are expected. Ultimately these developments will increase the speed at which funds and information are transferred from account to account, will reduce day-ending transactions deposits to near zero, and will shrink to a minimum the risky carrying of currency.

While these *ultimate* impacts have been discussed in a number of compendia, there remain strong disagreements regarding their implications for *current* money demand behavior and *current* monetary policy. In addition, there is little discussion in the literature of the ultimate *non*monetary macroeconomic impacts of EFTS (on expenditures and production relations). This paper will consider the implications of EFTS for *both* monetary and nonmonetary macroeconomic behavioral relations. It will attempt to resolve some of the disagreements regarding current behavior and current policy by appealing to the ultimate macroeconomic model toward which the financial system is evolving as well as to an understanding of the interaction among financial innovation, financial regulation, and monetary policy.

Some of my fellow economists may consider ventures of this sort to be excessively speculative. I shall attempt to demonstrate that further work on theories of financial innovation, financial regulation, and monetary regimes and their incorporation into empirical money demand research and monetary policy recommendations are absolutely essential.

I. The Macroeconomic Model with Zero *Nonbank* Transactions Balances

The seminal models of the demand for transactions balances of Baumol, Tobin (1956), and Miller and Orr predict that as the explicit fees and time costs of converting from nonmoney assets into transactions balances fall, as collection uncertainty is reduced, and as payments and receipts are better synchronized, the demand for a stock of transactions balances will shrink. Since the literature on EFTS indicates that unit asset conversion costs will approach zero, the demand for a stock of transactions balances can be expected to become very small.[1] Assuming that the nonbank demand for a stock of transaction balances is zero, the conventional transactions balances multiplier and transactions balances velocity are no longer meaningful.

What will be the role of money and the properties of the macroeconomic structure in a world of zero conversion costs and no legal intermediation restrictions? Such a world has been called "nonmonetary" by Fama and McCallum; associated with unlimited price level increases by Gurley and Shaw; linked to an indeterminate price level by Patinkin and Pesek and Saving; and labeled as invalidating the quantity theory of money by Black. I believe that these descriptions are in error. They arise from a failure to specify realistically the role of banks as asset-transformers with strong ties to clearinghouses in an unregulated system. In what follows, it will be shown that this view of the banking system preserves all of the traditional properties of monetary economies.

The Bank Demand for Reserves

Let us assume that banks have zero legal reserve requirements. (An alternative assumption that has a similar effect is that they receive interest payments on their reserve balances that are tied to the interest rate on short-term marketable securities. For brevity's sake we ignore that alternative.) This assumption does away with the "tax" on bank revenues from funds garnered from checking account customers and eliminates this particular incentive for banks to hold reserves and to induce customers to switch between reservable and nonreservable accounts.

Banks are viewed as asset transformers who sell divisibility services to borrowers and liquidity services to depositors. Maturity risk arising from the bank's balance-sheet mismatch and the stochastic deposit flows of individual customers is dissipated but not eliminated by the consolidation of these flows within the bank. Credit (default) risk is also dissipated but not eliminated by portfolio diversification. Banks have an incentive to absorb the residual interest rate risk which cannot be completely diversified away or completely shifted away through hedging. This profit incentive is the liquidity premium that is normally embedded in the term structure of interest rates.

Niehans has invoked a perfect markets (zero asset conversion costs) model to contend that if banks could invest unexpected surplus reserves at the same market-clearing rate at which they could borrow, there would be no reason to hold reserves. I believe, however, that even with zero legal reserve requirements and zero nonbank transactions balances, there would still likely be a demand for a stock of risk-free liquid assets (reserves). These assets would probably be the medium in which interbank clearings are settled.

The ability of those depositary institutions that are at the vortex of the clearing-settlements mechanism to act as standby sources of liquidity in times of stress is central to the stability of financial markets. Stress arises when there are sizable deposit shifts from certain troubled banks which must be recycled back to these banks at a crisis-propelled, high interbank interest rate. Stress is exacerbated by currency withdrawals, which absorb reserves that could have been recycled. Specialized depositary institutions (bankers' banks) with inventories of reserves could profit continuously from taking orders to sell these reserves at favorable rates whenever the overnight interbank rate rose beyond certain thresholds. Timberlake shows that in the nineteenth-century these specialized institutions were the locus of the interbank clearing network.[2]

To settle accounts, clearinghouses must be able to transfer an asset accepted as a final means of payment. Historically that asset has always come from outside the banking system. Thus, as pointed out by O'Driscoll, the existence of a stock of reserves is essential to the concept of a competitive, asset-transforming (banking) industry.

The aggregate demand for reserves would vary inversely with the interbank rate and directly with the liquidity premium, a scalar (scale of operations) variable, and the overall perception of interest rate risk. The elasticities of this relation would obviously be sensitive to the pricing efficiency of the services of a governmental lender of last resort and deposit insurer.

If a residual nonbank demand for currency remained (while transactions deposits were zero), that is, if the services of currency and the services of an EFTS system were imperfect substitutes, the monetary base demand function would still have the aforementioned properties. It is unrealistic to believe that currency is an endangered species. Osborne indicates that with all the innovation that has taken place in the past 100 years, the demand for currency as a percentage of GNP has declined only about one-third. However, the traditional properties of monetary economies, such as price determinacy and the quantity theory of money, do not hinge, as both McCallum and Fama seem to contend, on the thin reed of the existence of a nonbank demand for currency. They rest instead on a more substantive foundation, the bank demand for perfectly liquid reserves.

If such a demand relation exists in an economy with a zero stock of nonbank transactions deposits, the monetary base remains a viable policy instrument. Open-market operations would work pretty much as they do today.

The Properties of the Model

In the discussion that follows it is assumed that the economy is closed and that government debt claims are not part of aggregate private wealth such that monetary policy is neutral. Debt claims are not part of aggregate wealth if the present value of future tax liabilities for interest payments and principal repayments on these claims equals the present value of their interest income. Anticipated open-market purchases in which the Treasury or, if one is established, the central bank swaps claims against itself for less liquid, public or private, nonmonetary claims, could impart to the financial system undesired real liquidity that would be immediately swept into other nontransactions accounts and then eroded by swift increases in the nominal prices of assets, goods, and productive factors, with no effects on aggregate real income or ex ante real interest rates.[3] There is a unique price level that clears the markets. If there is a bank demand for the real monetary base (as posited above) it would be unaffected in the new equilibrium. Thus, in a zero stock of nonbank transactions balances (EFTS accounting system of exchange) world, the quantity theory of (base) money is perfectly valid.

Open-market purchases that are not anticipated by market participants would generate unanticipated increases in nominal prices and thereby provoke short-run increases in productive effort which temporarily boost aggregate real income. Temporarily higher real disposable income and associated more optimistic attitudes toward risk would result in an increase in the supply of real funds (net of the real deficit-financing credit demands of government) in credit markets and lower ex ante real interest rates during the cyclical boom. However, inflationary expectations would increase the level of nominal interest rates and make steeper the yield curve. Thus, there would be a cyclical decrease in the (bank) demand for a stock of real reserve balances. Assuming a unitary income elasticity of the demand for reserves, base velocity would rise.

A regime of persistent monetary surprises would increase interest rate risk and boost the liquidity premium that is embedded in the term structure. This would permanently increase the bank demand for real reserves and would serve to reduce base velocity. Thus, in a world of zero nonbank transactions deposits, the stability and predictability of the bank demand for a stock of real reserve balances would hinge on the stability of the monetary policy environment.

Allowing a positive demand for noninterest-bearing currency-in-circulation would yield a small multiplier and a large velocity of nonbank transactions balances. The nonbank demand for a stock of real transactions balances would respond strongly to the level of nominal interest rates and less than proportionately to the level of real income. The nonbank demand for real transactions balances would not be affected by anticipated open-market purchases. An unanticipated open-market purchase would lower real and nominal interest rates and raise real income and, therefore, increase the nonbank demand for real transactions balances. However, if open-market purchases embarked on a higher growth path over time, thereby increasing nominal interest rates, the demand for real transactions balances would fall. The multiplier would reflect the confluence of the aforementioned responses in the demand for the base and the nonbank demand for transactions balances to various types of open-market postures by the monetary authority.

Thus, at the conceptual end of the road of financial innovation the monetary macroeconomy will not differ substantially from today's environment. In a world of zero nonbank transactions balances, the demand for the real base and its velocity should be quite predictable. If there were a positive nonbank demand for currency, its velocity and the multiplier should be similarly predictable.

A twist is imparted to the preceding analysis if the interest-bearing debt of government is as liquid as its noninterest-bearing counterpart (while retaining the assumption that neither are part of aggregate net private wealth). The analysis of Sargent and Wallace indicates that with no binding legal restrictions on intermediation, in a zero conversion costs-zero nonbank transactions balances ambiance, the banking system would hold a desired proportion of government debt as reserves. The balance of the government debt would be retained as nonmonetary assets in private portfolios.

It seems to me that the main claim to fame of this model is the neat property that if the interest rate exceeds the growth rate of income, growth in the debt-to-income ratio would directly fuel increases in the price level, because interest-bearing government debt becomes superfluous. Anticipated open-market purchases that attempt to swap liquid claims against the central bank for equally liquid government debt would be pointless since private market participants could convert back at zero cost with the real liquidity of portfolios unaffected. It is, however, incorrect to infer, as does Kareken, that in a Sargent-Wallace world of no legal restrictions on intermediation, other types of open-market operations are ineffective. As mentioned at the outset, interest rate risk is imbedded in the yield curve and creates a demand for the liquidity services of certain (short-term) assets. (To put it in Sargent-Wallace's and Kareken's terms, "intermediation costs" vary directly with term-to-maturity). Whatever asset is inventoried for its unique liquidity services by the specialized clearing-house banks, described earlier, could be labeled (a use of) the monetary base. Openmarket operations that swap these claims for less liquid claims would have all the conventional properties described in modern macroeconomic theory, such as neutrality.[4] In an environment of no legal reserve requirements, no legal intermediation restrictions, and zero asset conversion costs, there would still be a demand for the monetary base.

III. Theories of Financial Innovation and Financial Regulation

The Theory of Financial Innovation

Much of the macro finance literature views innovation as the attempt to make less binding the physical and political constraints on wealth-seeking activity. Economists do not generally model innovation as an endogenous process. Yet in many cases failure to incorporate policy-induced innovation will produce misleading empirical results and short-sighted policy recommendations. Later, I will contend that it is precisely this type of failure that plagues recent empirical money demand research and confounds recommendations for monetary policy.

Historically, the focus of human inventiveness is not a random walk; rather it is directed by wealth-seeking activities. In the mercantile societies of the fifteenth through early eighteenth centuries man's inventiveness was first concentrated upon improving navigation. Then it naturally evolved to focusing on the perfection of sailing vessels. In the manufacturing societies of the late eighteenth and early nineteenth centuries an enormous amount of innovation centered around the application of combustion engines to industrial activity. As industrial and corresponding political empires grew geographically in the late nineteenth and twentieth centuries, man's inventiveness shifted to improving his ability to communicate across vast distances.

Recent financial innovations are obviously an offshoot of the latter process. Modern theories of financial innovation properly examine private market attempts to harness new telecommunications technologies. Greenbaum and Haywood show that in a world of fixed-unit portfolio costs secular increases in nonhuman wealth generate a growing *demand* for a wider diversification of (new types of) financial claims. Regulatory constraints and monetary policy surprises increase costs, change relative prices faced by financial services firms, and spur their efforts to *supply* new types of financial claims. Technological innovations which reduce asset conversion costs increase the supply of claims at all prices. Despite the questionable status of conventional patent protection, innovating financial services firms enjoy sufficient reputational market power to appropriate the returns from innovation. Their efforts reduce the costs imposed by regulatory constraints on wealth-maximizing activity in financial markets.

Given the preceding supply and demand paradigm, the basic theoretical problem is to predict *when* innovations will occur. In the sparse literature on the subject emphasis has been on innovation to circumvent regulatory constraints rather than on innovation in direct response to changes in consumer preferences or production methods that give rise to a gap in the menu of available financial claims. An example of a broader view that incorporates both types of innovation is provided by Silber.

Private market participants historically seem to be able to circumvent constraints more quickly than regulators and politicians erect new ones. One reason for this seems to be that information processing and feedback mechanisms in the private market work with easily understood and assimilated market signals (prices). In contrast, the informational mechanisms of government regulators must process and respond to complex nonmarket signals such as executive, legislative, and judicial inquiries; new laws; and expected voting outcomes. In addition, the economic theory of bureaucracy imputes objectives to regulators; and the redistributive theory of financial regulation imputes objectives to politicians that impede efficient regulation. For these reasons, private market participants seem to stay steps ahead of regulators in the (regulatory dialectic) struggle envisioned by Kane.

Since the supply of new types of financial claims depends on the circumvention of regulatory constraints, useful theories of financial innovation as well as Kane's regulatory dialectic should be premised on a theory of financial regulation. Historically, political control of financial activity often seems to have been predicated on the desire of politicians to dispense privileges (redistribute income) in order to enhance electoral outcomes.[5] Valuable insights may be gained by viewing modern monetary policy and financial regulation from this perspective. Some of these are discussed below. However, the dominant rationale for and theory of regulation of financial markets in recent times has been based on the concept of market failure.

The Market Failure Theory of Financial Regulation

According to this theory, the primary objective of government is to reduce a classic "externality," the risk of breakdown of the nation's payments system. In an environment of high maturity risk (associated with stochastic deposit flows and the liquidity premium embedded in the term structure of interest rates) and low barriers to entry, the cyclical implosion of deposits (historically associated with a massive flight to currency such as occurred during the classical financial panics of 1873, 1878, 1893, 1908, and 1932) leads to the exit of firms.[6] The resulting threat of breach of deposit contracts is seen as having the potential to cripple the nation's payments mechanism and, thereby, to inhibit trade.

The government provides two types of guarantees to the nation's payments mechanism: it acts as a lender of last resort (via the Federal Reserve Act of 1913) and as a deposit insurer (via the Glass Stegall Act of 1933). Both types of guarantees produce moral hazard, because both encourage banks to be less liquid, to acquire riskier assets, and to sustain thinner net worth positions.

Government's apparent reaction to this particular moral hazard problem has been to erect even more regulatory barriers: pricing restrictions (ceilings on deposit rates of interest), geographic and product line restrictions (branching and bank holding company laws), entry restrictions (branching, bank holding company, and chartering statutes), and balance sheet restrictions (legal reserve requirements, asset proscriptions, and capital requirements). Seen within the context of the regulatory dialectic, the direction taken by financial innovation simply reflects the (moral hazard) incentive provided by deposit insurance and lender-of-last-resort guarantees to private market participants to circumvent this particular web of ancillary regulations. Government presents regulated firms with glowing incentives to take inordinate risk and then imposes barriers to risk-taking that these firms can evade faster than new ones are built.

In addition to the incentives provided by government, competition from unregulated firms, such as money market mutual funds, has forced regulated depositary institutions to substitute away from regulated areas by changing their production methods, product lines, and organizational forms.[7] As pointed out earlier, this process exploits the advances in communication technology that reduce the marginal cost of handling customer transactions in deposit and nondeposit claims, in loans, and especially in complementary services. Thus, management of depositary institutions innovates by offering unregulated and less regulated products within growing, geographically expanding, and diversifying organizations. Depositary institutions are expanding their electronic linkages with their customers and sharing both the linkages and the customers with less-regulated financial services firms. A wide variety of financial claims and services are becoming available in nationwide delivery systems.

The Response of Bureaucratic Regulators

With the circumvention of regulation, it has become apparent that the financial services industry is overspecialized and underconcentrated. The new environment has contributed to the technical failure of large numbers of depositary institutions. The reaction of regulators to this shakeout has recently assumed disastrous proportions. By permitting thousands of *de facto* insolvent depositary institutions to continue to operate, regulators have tacitly extended federal guarantees to a wide assortment of formally uninsured financial claims offered by firms that now compete in far riskier markets than in past decades. Thus, the cost of taxpayers' covering the dollar liabilities of technically failed institutions in excess of the true market value of their assets could easily rise to hundreds of billions of dollars.[8] Kane (1985) argues that *de facto* insolvency is disguised by forced mergers, subsidized takeovers, and regulator operation of failed institutions. To this list should be added the FSLIC consignment program, the issuance of "income capital certificates" to insolvent thrift institutions in exchange for FSLIC notes which they speciously count as capital. By continuing to cover up such insolvency, regulators hasten the day when a large portion of the nation's financial services industry will be nationalized as the only way to pay its debt to the taxpayers.

Repeated academic demands for a more efficient pricing of lender-of-last-resort and deposit insurance guarantees, reforms that would help to prevent insolvencies and forestall government takeover, are rarely endorsed by regulators. Academic economists have long argued that moral hazard leading to inordinate risk taking by depositary institutions could be reduced by calibrating deposit insurance premiums and coverages to reflect a depositary institution's balance sheet risk and by systematically assessing the creditors and stockholders of failed institutions. Consistent with the economic theory of bureaucracy, cost-minimizing FDIC officials, with few exceptions, have balked at the responsibility of systematically penalizing managers, uninsured depositors, and stockholders, and of closing failed institutions.

For decades academic economists have also contended that moral hazard could be reduced by pegging the discount rate near the short-term market interest rate, thereby automatically rationing credit only to the most distressed firms. Consistent with the economic theory of bureaucracy, perogative-maximizing Federal Reserve officials have insisted on nonprice rationing of loans at a discount rate often fixed well below the market rate. In fact, since 1984 the Fed's extended credit program has increased its lending commitments to depositary institutions that are in long-term straits. Moreover the same Federal Reserve officials who resist reforms of the discount mechanism, which would help to reduce financial crises, unabashedly promote themselves as "crisis managers." Indeed, since 1981 every recent alleged financial crisis seems to have been used to justify further extension of Federal Reserve authority.[9]

A Redistributive Theory of Financial Regulation

The preceding discussion suggests that the market failure theory of financial regulation cannot explain today's insolvency problems without invoking the bureaucracy theory of regulator behavior and/or the assumption of government myopia. The insolvency problem would not exist without regulatory barriers to entry and these are not explained by the market failure theory.

A superior theory should explain why barriers to entry persist. The redistributive theory of regulation purports to do this. The essential development of this general theory of regulation was done by Stigler; it was refined by Peltzman and expressed as a cross-subsidization theory by Posner. The latter was tested in financial services markets by Tucillo.

In applying the redistributive theory to financial markets we can only conjecture about fruitful directions. One possible course would be to model each political party as promising, over a relatively long planning horizon, a regulatory policy platform. Each platform would establish a set of regulations, such as taxes or entry barriers, which would implicitly be understood to redistribute income to the party's supportive constituency of protected firms and their customers. In this way the regulatory policy platform would yield the optimal (expected-vote and campaign-contribution maximizing) number, size, and degree of specialization of financial services firms. Regulatory policy platforms would be modified as new firms appeared or as new distributions of earned income and voting rights altered each party's supportive constituency. Because income redistributions are not possible without explicit or implicit taxes, regulatory policies that are electorally optimal would be viewed as economically wasteful, for example, they would result in overspecialization.

Obvious manifestations of economic waste, such as massive insolvency problems, may, after a time, have adverse electoral consequences. These problems can often be covered up with monetary surprises that are directed at lowering real interest rates or keeping them from rising. Thus, according to this model there would be a link between the regulatory redistributive regime and monetary policy. In form, it would not be unlike the connection between the fiscal redistributive regime and monetary policy modeled by Havrilesky (1987) but operating over a longer planning horizon. My conjecture is that the greater the economic losses generated by regulatory policy, the greater the subsequent potential for attempts at monetary surprise.

Earlier in this section it was suggested that the financial system is evolving toward consolidation. It was indicated that this process is clouded by a recurring threat of insolvency and periodic monetary policy surprises to ease that threat, such as the ones that occurred during the LDC debt crisis in 1982 and the Continental-Illinois crisis in 1984. The preceding discussion suggests that a major roadblock to consolidation is the risk that a financial regulatory reform package will follow in the wake of the failure and effective nationalization of a large number of the nation's depositary institutions. Regulatory bureaucrats can be expected to use this opportunity to extend their domain (see note 9).

III. Macroeconomic Behavior in a World of Ongoing Financial Innovation and Interaction Between Regulatory and Monetary Policy

As the financial system evolves toward a world of a zero stock of nonbank transactions balances, a number of questions arise concerning changes in the demand for transactions balances and other behavioral relations. Knowledge of the forces that are propelling us toward a zero nonbank balance endpoint may provide hypothetical answers to these questions.

Predictability of Changes in Transactions Demand

There has been considerable dissatisfaction with the empirical estimation of the demand for transactions balances. Discord has risen to such heights that investigators such as Rose now question whether the construction of simultaneous and static money demand equations is theoretically possible. Other analysts, such as Judd and Scadding, Hamburger, Tatom, and Hafer and Hein, do not go quite so far. They contend that changes in transactions demand would not be unpredictable if the proper explanatory variables were to be included and appropriately specified.

The question of appropriate specification of the transactions demand for money raises a number of difficult questions. To begin with, there are very loose links between theoretical advances, such as models incorporating cash-in-advance constraints, and empirical work. Even more importantly, while practically all researchers agree that "unstable" monetary policy and regulatory environments impede the search for stable adjustment patterns in the demand for transactions balances, there is insufficient research being done to explain how and why these environments change, or to deal with these changes in empirical work. For example, it is widely recognized that the parameters and lags in the macroeconomic structure are sensitive to the policy regime. However, empirical money demand studies merely tend to collapse that sensitivity into estimates of the coefficient on the lagged dependent variable. As another example, Havrilesky (1985) shows that the interest elasticity of the demand for money may be sensitive to the policy regime, as measured by the variance of nominal income. Nevertheless, at this writing, only the empirical money demand models of Carr and Darby, Coats, and Hetzel have been developed to account for switches in monetary regimes.

While the absence of quantum leaps in financial reregulation or a financial reform panic, discussed above, would improve matters, it seems unlikely that regulatory policy will remain frozen and monetary policy will ever assume a "stable" trajectory. Policy changes are not a random walk. There are systematic linkages between monetary regimes and changes in regulatory policy. For example, the (commercial loan theory of banking) monetary regime that is implicit in the Federal Reserve Act of 1913 begat the changes in the regulatory environment in the Glass Steagall Act of 1933. As another example, the activist monetary policy regime that was established by the Accord of 1951 led to the regulatory upheavals of the Depositary Institutions Deregulation Act of 1980.

Furthermore, as discussed in the previous section, there appears to be a link between the regulatory regime and attempts at monetary surprise. The Federal Reserve is impelled to ease the pressure on insolvent and near-insolvent depositary institutions. Surprises often coincide with financial crises during which the Federal Reserve portrays itself as "crisis manager" (see n. 9). As insolvencies mount, attempts at monetary surprise are bound to increase.[10]

Despite this track record, theories of financial innovation (e.g., Greenbaum and Haywood or Silber), theories of financial regulation (e.g., extensions of Stigler or Peltzman), and theories of monetary/fiscal regimes (e.g., Havrilesky 1987, or Frey and Schneider) have not been explicitly built into empirical money demand work. The predictability of changes in transactions demand as we evolve toward a world of zero balances will continue to be problematical as long as the determinants of monetary and regulatory policy and their interrelationship are neither modeled nor incorporated into empirical research.

Conversion Costs

It is now recognized that empirical money demand relations need to employ better explicit measures of asset conversion costs, including brokerage and time opportunity costs. Lieberman showed that the failure to account for these costs will lead to spurious estimates of the demand for money. Important dynamics are omitted and inconsistent estimates are introduced by the exclusion of this contemporaneous but temporally dependent variable. To the extent that the adoption of EFTS is related to the rise in interest rates and conversion costs are related to the true interest opportunity costs, discussed below, the omission of conversion costs will raise the estimated elasticity of transactions balances with respect to the market rate of interest. To the extent that the adoption of EFTS is correlated with the secular rise in income, the omission of such measures will lower the estimated income elasticity of transactions balances. Finally, because the average level of transactions balances is trending downward, the omission of conversion costs will lower the estimated intercept of the transactions balances demand relation. All of these problems will yield systematic forecast errors. Thus, the steady-state estimates that are implicit in existing empirical work are of almost no value. The development of reasonable measures of conversion costs is a fruitful area for further research.

Interest Opportunity Costs

A consensus has emerged that the appropriate opportunity cost in the demand for transactions balances is the difference between the after-tax short-term rate on market instruments and the after-tax own rate on transactions balances. The implicit return reflected in this measure can change over time. As conversion costs fall, if deposit insurance coverage is reduced, and if interest is paid on reserve balances or legal reserve requirements are reduced, the differential will narrow. Nevertheless, because there is (residual) risk associated with asset transformation by depositary firms, the differential will not disappear. Simpson (1984) argues persuasively that it will vary less in terms of basis points than the market interest rate, although perhaps in the same proportion. In the long run this characteristic will greatly lower the interest elasticity of the demand for transactions balances and reduce its cyclical volatility.

However, in the near term, the interest sensitivity of transactions balances will be difficult to tie down as it depends on the adjustment of own rate-setting bahavior by depositary institutions. For example, if conversion costs fall and own rates do not quickly adjust then the interest elasticity of transactions balances will temporarily rise. Substitution among different assets will cause the relative growth rates of M1, M2, M3, etc., to vary in the short run.

Scale Variables

As the impact of interest opportunity cost on transactions balances falls, the ratio of these balances to scale variables may stabilize. Depositary firms will offer packages of financial services, easily accessed through EFTS, including discount brokerage, credit, and insurance services. Therefore, transactions demands may more closely relate to broader measures such as total wealth, favored by Simpson and Parkinson, rather than to narrower measures such as liquid assets. The consensus in the literature is that permanent income (specified along rational expectations lines) and total wealth are becoming more appropriate scale variables for use in transactions demand relations.

On the other hand, as the principal motive for holding transactions balances is settling transactions, aggregate income or wealth may not be appropriate scale variables (scalars). This is especially true when changes in expenditures are satisfied by inventory adjustments rather than changes in aggregate output (GNP), when the ratio of exports or imports to GNP changes the demand for domestic deposits without affecting GNP or when the composition of GNP changes between sectors with different transactions-per-dollar-of-final-expenditures. In these cases, the demand for transactions balances will change but aggregate income will remain unaltered. In addition a secular reduction in asset conversion costs will increase the number of financial transactions per dollar of GNP, and a steady decrease in the vertical integration of business firms will raise the number of real transactions per dollar of GNP. Thus, with continued innovation, as indicated by Kimball, the ratio of transactions balances to income or wealth may become erratically smaller relative to the total number of financial and intermediate transactions. A superior scale variable may be a measure of the level of total (financial, intermediate, and final) transactions, as envisioned by Irving Fisher and the early Neoclassical macroeconomists and exposited by Havrilesky and Boorman.

Transactions Accounts as Precautionary and Speculative Balances

A number of researchers, such as Goldfeld and Simpson and Parkinson, raise the concern that transactions balances may become a savings vehicle as they begin to pay competitive explicit rates of return, especially when the yield curve is downward sloping and depositary institutions promote transactions accounts over term CDs, as pointed out by Kopcke. These concerns give rise to pleas by Goldfeld and Hamburger for the inclusion of long-term interest rates and dividend ratios in the transactions demand relation. They also generate fears, on the part of Judd and Scadding and Simpson and Porter, associated with aggregating across conceptually distinct (transactions and savings) balances in the same accounts. (This problem plagues the stability of the relation of income to the higher order monetary aggregates.) Finally, these worries evoke in Simpson the ancient Keynesian specter of "unstable and shifting" speculative preferences.

Reflection on the innovation process discussed in section II should ease these concerns. New financial claims and new delivery systems developed by protected depositary institutions will not disappear. Investments in the physical capital and human (learning) capital associated with new transactions technologies are irreversible. Moreover, consumer surveys indicate little mixing of transactions and savings accounts. Cook and Rowe report that the size, turnover, debit, and seasonal characteristics of checkable deposit accounts and savings accounts are simply very different. We may tentatively conclude that in a world of low conversion costs and a positive spread between short-term market rates and own rates on transactions balances only the most perversely sloped yield curve could induce substitution between transactions accounts and savings accounts.

Nonmonetary Effects

Household resources of time and wealth freed by new payments technology, as well as the reduction in household debt burdens brought about by the replacement of credit cards by debit cards, will have the obvious effect of increasing the demand for leisure and consumer goods and services. Shrinkage in the cash and current asset inventories of business firms and reduction in credit risks associated with the check-clearing process free up circulating capital, increase the rate of return to fixed capital, and thereby boost economic growth. These benefits are likely to occur incrementally and to be difficult to measure. They present an interesting challenge for future research.

In credit (loanable funds) markets several, somewhat more palpable, effects should transpire. Improved access to packages of financial services and explicit pricing of these services for households will likely increase the interest sensitivity of saving. Moreover, because the cost of funds to intermediaries will be more interest sensitive, there will be less nonprice rationing of credit; and the measured interest elasticity of investment expenditures, especially mortgage investment, and saving should rise. These effects would reduce the impact of spending shocks and increase the impact of monetary shocks and supply shocks on the level of aggregate real income. They would also reduce the inflationary impact of aggregate supply and spending shocks but increase the inflationary impact of monetary shocks.

IV. Monetary Policy Targeting in a World of Ongoing Financial Innovation

The preceding analyses of the demand for money and macroeconomic behavior in our evolving financial environment may help to clarify many of the continually raging controversies surrounding monetary policy targeting. We then evaluate suggested targets for monetary policy in light of this analysis.

Where real income can be affected by unanticipated inflation, it has been demonstrated that discretionary policy (the absence of a fully specified feedback rule) provides the policymaker with a glowing incentive for short-run surprises. Kydland and Prescott have shown that discretion in this sense will lead to a world of unnecessarily high inflation with no long-run effect on real income. In such a world, intermediate targeting of nominal aggregates is intuitively preferable to unconstrained discretion. The looseness of the targeting procedure will vary directly with the (political) incentives for the Fed to attempt to manipulate real income and interest rates in the short run and inversely with the disincentives associated with the resulting loss of Federal Reserve credibility.

Tight intermediate targeting, however, is not tantamount to a complete feedback rule because targeted variables are not precisely controllable. After decades of controversy the intermediate-targets problem is still not clearly understood by some of the economists who choose to engage in the debate. In realistically specified, stochastic macroeconomic models that include the parameter uncertainties envisioned in the preceding section, Havrilesky (1977) indicates that the policymaker has a very very small set of endogenous variables that are capable of being targeted.

Nominal Income

The magnitude of stochastic (structural) and information-gathering error in realistically specified models is simply too great to include nominal income in the set of feasible target variables. (Of course, aggregate *real* income is just about everyone's policy *objective*.) If unknowable and uncontrollable shocks bombard the economy, a feedback rule from GNP to the policy instrument would be unfeasible. In addition, observed changes in the growth of nominal income would bring pressure on the Fed to react to those changes. Nominal income has no role to play as a *target* in the control-theoretic sense.

Interest Rates

Like aggregate real income, certain interest rates may be favored *objectives* of monetary policy for some interest groups, depending on the financial regulatory regime discussed in section II. Thus, political pressures may affect the target choice problem. The practice of using models with inflexible nominal wages and prices and/or severely limited stochastic properties to model the control problem and thereby to recommend an interest rate *target* is, at best, extremely misleading. Like the concept of nonmonetary inflation, the concept of interest targeting makes no sense in mainstream general-equilibrium macroeconomic models (both ignore the resulting excess supply of or demand for money). A long line of economists, beginning at least with Wicksell, has demonstrated that the targeting of an interest rate at a level different from the market-clearing rate leads to explosive or implosive price and aggregate nominal income movements, unless, of course, the target is linked to a market-clearing nominal income or price level.

Broader Monetary Aggregates

The simple-sum monetary hybrids generate an enormous loss of information in aggregation. They lump together transactions and savings deposit accounts. They aggregate across financial assets that are not close substitutes. Shifts within private nonbank portfolios between the near money claims issued by intermediaries and marketable securities distort the meaning of the broad aggregates. The transactions/savings role of broader aggregates in individual portfolios is simply not stable over time.

If their meaning can be communicated and if the own rate on currency can be measured, the Divisia monetary services aggregates are an interesting concept for certain purposes. However, they are not valuable *ex ante* as a target because their weights are quite unpredictable.

Nonbank Transactions Balances

As shown earlier in this chapter, nonbank transactions balances may be an endangered species. However, as discussed in section III and as suggested by Judd and Scadding, Simpson, and Goldfeld (1976, 1982), if the proper explanatory variables are considered and appropriately specified—for example, conversion costs, an after-tax nominal interest rate differential, and a meaningful scalar—and if theories of financial innovation, financial regulation, and monetary regimes are developed and incorporated into empirical work, movements in the demand for transactions balances and their velocity may become predictable.

Until these improvements are made there will be problems. There is evidence that the observed cyclical variation in the velocity of transactions balances follows from lagged responses of nominal income and interest rates to variations in money supply growth. For example, in an ordinary lease squares regression using quarterly data for the 1960 to 1985 period, velocity growth ($\dot{V}_t$) responds negatively to contemporaneous money growth ($\dot{M}_t$) and positively to lagged money growth ($\dot{M}_{t-1}$):

$$\underset{}{\dot{V}_t} = \underset{(4.850)}{0.0420} - \underset{(-6.131)}{0.7560\dot{M}_t} + \underset{(3.780)}{0.4618\dot{M}_{t-1}}$$

$$\bar{R}^2 = 0.29 \qquad \text{DFE} = 99$$

The *t*-statistics are in parentheses. To test further for causality two regressions were run using the same data set. First velocity growth was regressed against lagged velocity growth over an eight-quarter distributed lag. In the second regression money growth over the same eight-quarter distributed lag was added. Comparing the two equations, the Granger test statistic exceeded the *F*-statistic at the 0.01 level. This suggests that money growth is Granger-causal on velocity growth.

I am left with the impression that a reprogramming of the agenda for empirical research on the demand for transactions balances is warranted. Unfortunately, by the time the theories are developed, sufficient data points are available, the econometric issues are digested, and a pre-1973-style consensus originally recorded by Boorman is reached, there may be no nonbank transactions balances left to track.

In the meantime, a consensus is emerging among economists and political scientists, such as Beck, Wooley, Lombra and Moran, Laney and Willett, and Havrilesky (1986a), which rejects as mythic the belief that the Federal Reserve is an independent, politically neutral institution. This view suggests that Federal Reserve officials will continue to find it in their self-interest to obfuscate the optimal policy problem with whatever device is convenient—e.g., misspecified models; the current fashion in broad economic aggregates; the most recent financial innovation; and the latest financial crisis and related regulatory and monetary policy responses. The prospects for "emergency" measures arising from the insolvency crisis, discussed in section II, may afford the Federal Reserve bureaucracy an excellent opportunity not only to stake out new regulatory turf, as indicated in note 9, but "to muddy the (monetary policy) waters that they may appear deep."

The Monetary Base

In the presence of realistic degrees of stochastic structural and information-gathering error, the monetary base emerges as the only viable target for monetary policy. The concept of "the total monetary liabilities of government" plays an important role in all reasonably complete macroeconomic models. As indicated in section I there is reason to believe that the total monetary liabilities of government will continue to play an important role. Eventually, the monetary base may be the only predictable monetary aggregate. For years economists of all stripes, such as Brunner, Tobin (1980), and Berkman, have touted the monetary base as their first- or second-best lower-level aggregate. It closely relates to the only true tool of monetary policy, open-market operations. The deluge of aggregational/compositional, information-gathering, and monitoring problems associated with other potential nominal, monetary aggregate target variables makes it the minimax strategists' target par excellence.

Base velocity has historically proven quite stable compared to the stability of money growth, base growth, and M1 velocity. Over the 102 quarters from 1961 to mid-1985, the coefficients of variation of narrow-money growth, monetary-base growth, the velocity of money, and the velocity of the base were 47.7, 37.1, 20.6 and 13.7, respectively.

Of course, these statistics cover a 25-year span and do not reflect recent variability. In recent years base velocity has been steadily falling relative to trend. However, increases in the money multiplier since 1980 have meant that the decline in base velocity has been smaller than the decline in M1 velocity. These recent deviations may not be entirely explained by variations in base growth. In an ordinary-least-squares regression the deviation of base velocity from an exponential trend estimated from data for the 1961–1982 period was regressed, as a dependent variable, against deviations in base growth about a twelve-quarter moving average growth path. This equation was then used to generate quarterly predictions of base velocity for the 1983–1985 period. The out-of-sample error terms grew fairly steadily over the entire period. These results suggest that a monetary-base target should be adjusted for changing trends in base velocity.

A Policy Proposal

Socially optimal monetary policy calls for the preannouncing of a monetary-base target with a feedback rule for trends in base velocity. These trends would reflect secular movement in potential output and shifts in the demand for the base (discussed in section I).[11] Barro, Kydland and Prescott, Lucas, Sargent and Wallace, and Taylor have demonstrated that the absence of a credible preannounced base target has no desirable effects, in the sense that aggregate real income is unaltered; but both the mean and variance of inflation will be excessive. With a precommitment policy market participants will separate the systematic from the random elements in periodic monetary-base releases. As a consequence there will be no systematic policy surprises and hence no effect on real income. However, sustained swings in base growth will cause variations in inflation.

Socially optimal monetary policy also requires the daily release of all monetary estimates that the Federal Reserve possesses. If the Fed restricts access to information, then its adherence to optimal policy cannot be verified directly and, as shown by Canzoneri, it is more difficult to get it to agree to precommitment. Moreover, private investment in networks for obtaining restricted monetary information that could be released free is socially wasteful. Regardless of the signal-to-noise ratio, more free monetary information cannot be worse than less. I use the word "free" because the advent of EFTS reduces the Federal Reserve's variable cost of generating daily disclosure. Even if the standard error is enormous, why not leave to private-market participants the daily and seasonal adjustments that they are qualified to make, especially if they know Federal Reserve intentions? Private agents would utilize the Fed's monetary estimates until private benefits matched private costs.

Federal Reserve officials argue that the noise in the data could be misinterpreted as a signal of Fed intentions. Research, however—by Urich and Wachtel: Urich; Hardouvbelis; Hein; Pearce and Roley; and Nichols, Small, and Webster—suggests that market responses are appropriate. Moreover, market participants pay attention to Federal Reserve releases simply because they are not sure that a recent fluctuation does not portend a significantly prolonged departure from target. They know from experience that departures from target are often not quickly reversed by the Fed. Therefore, its short-run errors tend to be transmitted into long-run errors. Rather than restrict the flow of free information, the cure is for the Federal Reserve to make more credible its monetary-base growth intentions.

V. Concluding Comment

Debates concerning the stability of the demand for money and monetary policy targeting promise to careen endlessly about the halls of academe and, yes, down the corridors of power. This chapter attempts to constrain the bounds of this careening. It does so by proposing a macrotheoretic terminus to the ongoing process of financial innovation to which EFTS advances are linked. The terminus is a zero transactions balances world. In such a world it is shown that monetary policy will continue to operate along present-day lines, and the traditional properties of monetary economies, such as price determinacy and the quantity theory, will prevail.

The innovation process is propelled by the regulatory incentives for firms to circumvent regulatory barriers. Regulation has created an underconcentrated and overspecialized financial services industry. Such a massive misallocation of resources leaves one with the impression that financial regulatory policy is motivated less by the fear of total collapse of the nation's payments mechanism than it is by the desire to create an electorally optimal number of specialized financial services firms. With a superfluity of firms monetary policy surprises are used to ward off the adverse electoral consequences of the failure of a large number of depositary institutions.

Awareness of these factors makes clear the dilemma facing empirical money demand researchers. The failure to account empirically for switches in the monetary policy regime greatly diminishes the value of existing estimates of the coefficients of interest rate and scalar variables. Even if these factors were incorporated into empirical work, trends in asset conversion costs and the interest- and income-sensitivities of the demand for money will be exceptionally difficult to track because of other factors. These considerations combined with the measurement errors associated with employing higher-level monetary aggregates in empirical work, suggest a reprogramming of empirical money demand research.

Ironically the penumbra of uncertainty confounding empirical estimation of money and nonmonetary macrorelations casts the targeting problem into bold relief. In realistically specified stochastic macro models, the monetary base is the only plausible policy target. Thus, this chapter reaffirms the oft-heard plea for a preannounced base target, and I include an added embellishment: Since EFTS reduces the cost of generating daily release of all monetary estimates, why shouldn't the Federal Reserve release all monetary aggregate data on a daily basis? Regardless of error, more, essentially free, information is always better than less.

Notes

1. Nonbanks (households and business firms) settle in transactions accounts but hold virtually no stock of transactions balances because conversion costs are zero and conversion is guaranteed by banks (and deposit insurers). McCallum (1985) calls this an accounting system of exchange.

2. If there were no central bank it would be a simple matter for the Treasury to swap assets with these depositary institutions—Treasury open-market operations—or to nationalize one of them as the central bank, and have its liabilities serve as the reserves of the others and then allow it to swap assets—central bank open-market operations.

3. Patinkin and others have claimed that open-market operations are nonneutral. Many say this because after nominal prices have adjusted in proportion to the change in the quantity of money, there remains a change in the aggregate real value of money relative to the aggregate real value of bonds in private portfolios. This, they say, requires an adjustment of relative asset prices in order to restore the aggregate real value of money relative to aggregate real value of bonds in private hands. If individuals fully discount the future liability for interest payments on bonds, this view is not justified. Open-market operations simply move bonds from private portfolios to the vaults of the monetary authority and vice versa. Whether bonds are held privately, where they increase the interest income of their possessors, or are held by the monetary authority, where they reduce the future interest payment liability of taxpayers, makes no difference. Open-market operations are neutral. If open-market

operations did happen to change relative asset prices and interest rates, as long as future interest rate expectations are unchanged, market participants (financial intermediaries) will substitute between markets and restore relative asset prices and interest rates to their initial equilibrium values.

4. Jurg Niehans would disagree with my assertion that such a world is neutral. Niehans adopts the non-Ricardian view that government bonds are part of private wealth. He apparently takes the position that current government indebtedness is providing an intermediation service to those individuals who are constrained by some specified private-market failure from borrowing against future income. For these persons a bond-financed cut in current taxation encourages greater current consumption, even though it is followed by future taxation increases and consumption cuts. For a mature economy such as the U.S. economy, with broad, well-developed, private financial markets, I find it hard to believe that the government is more efficient (than the private market) at providing intermediation services in this oblique way.

5. Regulatory policy, like fiscal policy, may simply be another way for government to redistribute resources in order to increase its chances of reelection. As such, its connection to monetary policy may resemble the public-choice theoretic model of the linkage of fiscal to monetary policy developed by Havrilesky (1987). Electorally motivated transfers of resources are induced by regulatory policy—for example, prior to 1980 regulatory policy promoted transfers to homeowners and the housing industry. Such transfers require higher (implicit) taxes or barriers to entry, which are economically wasteful. Manifestations of this inefficiency—for example, crises of disintermediation—may motivate monetary surprises.

6. This view of financial markets strongly suggests the removal of those geographic and product-line restrictions that result in there being too many firms. In addition, the technology for providing transactions services in the next decade may be subject to increasing returns to scale. The resulting oligopolistic financial services industry should reduce the exit of firms and breach of contract that is associated with deposit implosion and will allow a natural coalescence of financial services firms. When this occurs, money and banking models can no longer be based on the purely competitive equilibrium paradigm.

Unfortunately, the path to a consolidated financial services industry is strewn with the wreckage of failed depositary institutions. Even though 100% of deposits are not insured, the drive to spread the regulatory umbrella over an expanding domain has induced government to act as guarantor not just of certain deposits but of the nation's entire depositary system. As bearer of risks assumed by depositary firms, government has inherited effective ownership of that wreckage.

7. Domain-maximizing bureaucratic regulators are eager to hold sway over new firms. This leads to further overspecialization and underconcentration in the financial services industry.

8. For example, as of June 30, 1985, 465 thrift institutions were insolvent by generally accepted accounting principles but were kept open even though they would cost the FSLIC $14 billion to liquidate. Hundreds of others are in the process of collapsing into FSLIC "consignment." In addition, the top ten U.S. banks are carrying about $55 billion of loans to Latin America, the true worth of which could be 20% to 40% of face value.

9. In recent years the Federal Reserve has proposed the following expansions of its powers after alleged "crises": monitoring risks in the Farm Credit System (the farm debt "crisis"); stepping up its supervision of government securities dealers (the Drysdale Securities "crisis"); extending its investigations of financial institutions that it does not supervise (the S&L "crisis"); applying its margin regulations to debt issued in leveraged takeovers (the junk bond "crisis"); and controlling nonbanking firms' access to the wire payments system (the ongoing "nonbank bank crisis").

These actions might be better understood as attempts by Federal Reserve bureaucrats to protect their regulatory domain rather than to protect the financial system. As barriers to geographic and product-line competition dissolve, financial services firms are diversifying beyond the Fed's regulatory grasp. The January 1986 Supreme Court decision to disallow Federal Reserve authority over "nonbank banks" without the imprimatur of Congress may have temporarily stalled the Fed's drive to stake out new regulatory turf.

10. If monetary surprises are the result of electorally motivated regulatory policy, this would effectively debunk the myth of an independent, politically neutral Federal Reserve. For further discussion, see Havrilesky (1986a and 1986c).

11. Such limited monetary feedback rules have been criticized in that they do not allow discretionary policy responses to private shocks. However, Havrilesky (1985) shows that the existence of variable policy responses creates aggregate-relative price confusion and exacerbates the inflationary impact of such shocks by increasing the price elasticity of aggregate supply and, perhaps, aggregate demand.

References

Barro, R.J. 1976. Rational Expectations and the Role of Monetary Policy. *Journal of Monetary Economics* 2(Jan.):1–32.

Baumol, W.J. 1952. The Transactions Demand for Cash: An Inventory Theoretic Approach. *Quarterly Journal of Economics* 66(Nov.):497–505.

Beck, N. 1948. Domestic Political Sources of American Monetary Policy: 1955–82. *The Journal of Politics* 46(Jan.):787–815.

Berkman, N.G. 1980. *Abandoning Monetary Aggregates*. Federal Reserve Bank of Boston.

Black, F. 1970. Banking and Interest Rates in a World without Money: The Effects of Uncontrolled Banking. *Journal of Bank Research* 1(Autumn): 8–20.

Boorman, J.T. 1985. A Survey of the Demand for Money: Theoretical Formulations and Pre-1973 Empirical Results. In T.M. Havrilesky, *Modern Concepts in Macroeconomics*. Arlington Heights, Harlan Davidson.

Brunner, K. 1980. The Control of Monetary Aggregates. *Controlling Monetary Aggregates III*. Federal Reserve Bank of Boston.

Canzoneri, M.B. 1985. Monetary Policy and the Role of Private Information, *American Economic Review* 75(Dec.):1056–1070.

Carr, J.I., and M.R. Darby. 1981. The Role of Money Supply Shocks in the Short-Run Demand for Money. *Journal of Monetary Economics* 8(Sept.):183–199.

Coats, W.L., Jr. 1982. Modeling the Short-Run Demand for Money with Exogenous Supply. *Economic Inquiry* 20(Apr.):222–239.

Cook, T.Q., and T.D. Rowe. 1985. Are NOW's Being Used as Savings Accounts. *Economic Review*. Federal Reserve Bank of Richmond (May/June):3–13.

Davis, R. 1982. Monetary Targeting in a Zero Balance World. *Interest Rate Deregulation and Monetary Policy*. Federal Reserve Bank of San Francisco.

Fama, E. 1980. Banking in the Theory of Finance. *Journal of Monetary Economics* 6(Jan.):39–57.

Flannery, M., and D. Jaffee. 1974. *Electronic Funds Transfer Systems*. New York,

D.C. Heath.

Frey, B., and F. Schneider. 1981. Central Bank Behavior: A Positive Empirical Analysis. *Journal of Monetary Economics* 7:291–315.

Goldfeld, S. 1976. The Case of the Missing Money. *Brookings Papers on Economic Activity* 3:683–670.

Goldfeld, S. 1982. Discussion. *Interest Rate Deregulation and Monetary Policy*. Federal Reserve Bank of San Francisco.

Greenbaum, S.I., and C.F. Haywood. 1971. Secular Change in the Financial Services Industry. *Journal of Money, Credit, and Banking* 3(May):571–589.

Gurley, J.G., and E.S. Shaw. 1960. *Money in a Theory of Finance*. Washington, Brookings Institution.

Hafer, R.W., and S.E. Hein. 1982. The Shift in Money Demand: What Really Happened? *Review*, Federal Reserve Bank of St. Louis (Feb.):11–16.

Hamburger, M.J. 1984. Financial Innovation and Monetary Targeting. *Financial Innovation*. (Federal Reserve Bank of St. Louis), Boston, Kluwer Nijhoff.

Hardoubelis, G.A. 1984. Market Perceptions of Federal Reserve Policy and the Weekly Monetary Announcements. *Journal of Monetary Economics* 10(Sept.): 225–240.

Havrilesky, T.M. 1977. The Optimal Reaction Function: Confluence of the Instrument Problem and the Target Problem. *Southern Economics Journal* 43(Jan.):1288–1297.

Havrilesky, T.M. 1985. Endogeneity of the Inflationary Impact of Aggregate Supply Shocks. Duke University Working Paper 85–08.

Havrilesky, T.M. 1986a. Monetary Policy Signaling from the Administration to the Federal Reserve. Duke University Working Paper 86–01.

Havrilesky, T.M. 1986b. Three Monetary and Fiscal Policy Myths. In Thomas Willett (ed.), *Political Business Cycle: The Economics and Politics of Stagflation*, San Francisco, Pacific Institute for Public Research.

Havrilesky, T.M. 1987. A Partisanship Theory of Fiscal and Monetary Policy Regimes. *Journal of Money Credit and Banking* (forthcoming).

Havrilesky, T.M. 1986c. The Effect of the Federal Reserve Reform Act on the Economic Affiliations of Directors of Federal Reserve Banks. *Social Science Quarterly* (March).

Havrilesky, T.M., and J.T. Boorman. 1982. *Money Supply, Money Demand, and Macroeconomic Models*, 2nd ed. Arlington Heights, Harlan Davidson.

Hein, S.E. 1985. The Response of Short-Term Interest Rates to Weekly Money Announcements: A Comment. *Journal of Money, Credit, and Banking* 17(May):264–271.

Hetzel, R.L. 1982. The October 1979 Regime of Monetary Control and the Behavior of the Money Supply in 1980. *Journal of Money, Credit and Banking* 14(May):234–251.

Hirschleifer, J. 1971. The Private and Social Value of Information and the Reward to Inventive Activity. *American Economic Review* 61(Sept.):561–574.

Holland, R.C. 1976. Speculation on Future Innovation. In *Financial Innovation*. William. L. Silber (ed.), Lexington, D.C. Heath.

Jordan, J. 1984. Financial Innovation and Monetary Policy. *Financial Innovation* (Federal Reserve Bank of St. Louis), Boston, Kluwer Nijhoff.

Judd, J.P., and J.L. Scadding. 1982a. The Search for a Stable Money Demand Function: A Survey of the Post-1973 Literature. *Journal of Economic Literature* 20(Sept.):993–1023, in Thomas Havrilesky *Modern Macroeconomic Concepts*. Arlington Heights, Harlan Davidson, 1985.

Judd, J.P., and J.L. Scadding. 1982b. Financial Change and Monetary Targeting in the United States. *Interest Rate Deregulation and Monetary Policy*. Federal Reserve Bank of San Francisco.

Kane, E.J. 1984. Microeconomic and Macroeconomic Origins of Financial Innovation. *Financial Innovation* (Federal Reserve Bank of St. Louis), Boston, Kluwer Nijhoff.

Kane, E.J. 1985. Appearance and Reality in Deposit Insurance: The Case for Reform. Working Paper Series 85–90, Ohio State University.

Kareken, J. 1984. Bank Regulation and the Effectiveness of Open Market Operations. *Brookings Papers on Economic Activity* 2:405–456.

Kimball, R.C. 1980. Wire Transfer and the Demand for Money. *New England Economic Review* (Mar./Apr.):5–22.

Kopcke, R.W. 1985. Bank Funding Strategy and the Money Stock. *New England Economic Review* (Jan./Feb.):5–14.

Kydland, F.E., and E.C. Prescott. 1977. Rules Rather than Discretion: The Inconsistency of Optimal Plans. *Journal of Political Economy* 85(June): 473–491.

Laney, L., and T.D. Willett. 1983. Presidential Politics, Budget Deficits and Monetary Policy in the United States: 1960–1976. *Public Choice* 40:53–69.

Lieberman, C. 1977. The Transactions Demand for Money and Technological Change. *Review of Economics and Statistics* 59(Aug.):307–317.

Lombra, R., and M. Moran. 1980. Policy Advice and Policymaking at the Federal Reserve. In K. Brunner and A. Meltzer, eds., *Carnegie-Rochester Series on Public Policy* 13:9–68.

Lucas, R.E. 1972. Expectations and the Neutrality of Money. *Journal of Economic Theory* 4(Apr.):103–124.

McCallum, B.T. 1985. Bank Deregulation, Accounting Systems of Exchange, and the Unit of Account: A Critical Review. *Carnegie-Rochester Series on Public Policy* 23(Autumn).

Miller, M., and D. Orr. 1966. A Model of the Demand for Money by Firms. *Quarterly Journal of Economics* 80:413–435.

Nichols, D.A., D.H. Small, and C.E. Webster, Jr. 1983. Why Interest Rates Rise When an Unexpectedly Large Money Stock Is Announced. *American Economic Review* 73(June):383–388.

Niehans, J. 1982. Innovations in Monetary Policy. *Journal of Banking and Finance* 6:9–28.

O'Driscoll, G. 1985. Money in a Deregulated Financial System. *Economic Review*. Federal Reserve Bank of Dallas (May):1–12.

Osborne, D.K. 1985. What Is Money Today? *Economic Review*. Federal Reserve

Bank of Dallas (January).
Patinkin, D. 1965. *Money Interest and Prices.* 2nd ed., New York, Harper & Row.
Pearce, D.K., and V.V. Roley. 1983. The Reaction of Stock Prices to Unanticipated Changes in Money: A Note. *Journal of Finance* 38(Sept.):1323–1333.
Peltzman, S. 1976. Toward a More General Theory of Regulation. *Journal of Law and Economics* 19(Spring):211–240.
Pesek, B.P., and T.R. Saving. 1967. *Money, Wealth and Economic Theory*, New York, Macmillan.
Posner, R. 1974. Theories of Economic Regulation. *Bell Journal of Economics and Management Science* 5(Autumn):335–357.
Roley, V.V. 1985. Money Demand Predictability. *Journal of Money, Credit and Banking* 17(Nov.):611–641.
Rose, A.K. 1986. Money Demand in the 1980s. Unpublished.
Sargent, T.J., and N. Wallace. 1985. Rational Expectations, the Optimal Monetary Instrument, and the Optimal Money Supply Rule. *Journal of Political Economy* 83(April):241–254.
Sargent, T.J., and N. Wallace. 1981. Some Unpleasant Monetarist Arithmetic. *Quarterly Review.* Federal Reserve Bank of Minneapolis.
Silber, W.L. 1976. Towards a Theory of Financial Innovation. In *Financial Innovation.* William L. Silber (ed.), Lexington, D.C. Heath.
Simpson, T.D. 1984. Changes in the Financial System: Implicatons for Monetary Policy. *Brookings Papers on Economic Activity* 1:249–272.
Simpson, T.D., and P.F. O'Brien. 1985. Implications of Electronic Funds Transfer for Monetary Policy. Board of Governors of Federal Reserve System.
Simpson, T.D., and P.M. Parkinson. 1984. Some Implications of Financial Innovations in United States. *Staff Studies.* Board of Governors of the Federal Reserve System, Sept., 139.
Simpson, T.D., and R.D. Porter. 1980. Some Issues Involving the Definition and Interpretation of the Monetary Aggregates. *Controlling Monetary Aggregates III.* Federal Reserve Bank of Boston.
Stigler, G. 1971. The Theory of Regulation. *Bell Journal of Economics and Management Science* 2(Spring):3–21.
Tatom, J. 1982. Recent Financial Innovations: Have They Distorted the Meaning of M1? *Review.* Federal Reserve Bank of St. Louis, Apr., 23–32.
Taylor, J. 1975. Monetary Policy During a Transition to Rational Expectations. *Journal of Political Economy* 83(Oct.):1009–1022.
Timberlake, R.H., Jr. 1984. The Central Banking Role of Clearinghouse Associations. *Journal of Money, Credit and Banking* 16(Feb.):1–15.
Tobin, J. 1956. The Interest Elasticity of the Transactions Demand for Cash. *Review of Economics and Statistics* 38(Aug.):241–247.
Tobin, J. 1980. Discussion. *Controlling Monetary Aggregates III.* Federal Reserve Bank of Boston.
Tucillo, J. 1977. Taxation by Regulation: The Case of Financial Intermediaries. *Bell Journal of Economics and Management Science* 8(Autumn):580–591.

Urich, T.J. 1982. The Information Content of Weekly Money Supply Announcements. *Journal of Monetary Economics* 8(July):73–88.

Urich, T.J., and P. Wachtel. 1981. Market Response to Weekly Money Supply Announcements in the 1970s. *Journal of Finance* 36(Dec.):1063–1072.

Wooley, J. 1984. *Monetary Politics: The Federal Reserve and the Politics of Monetary Policy*. New York, Cambridge University Press.

IV MICROECONOMIC ISSUES: BANKS AND CONSUMERS

The strength of competitive responses is a common theme in this volume. Financial markets have benefitted greatly from the new technology and the new competition it has spawned. Local monopoly markets are reduced in number, and the future deregulation which the next two authors expect and support will continue to eradicate any lingering "pockets of monopoly." Indeed, the whole thrust of the new competition and deregulation has been in the direction of opening up markets and financial industries to competition on all sides. In light of this competitive upsurge, the role of antitrust has moved to the sidelines. New updated prosecution standards are in process of development.

Professor Almarin Phillips, Hower Professor of Public Policy and Law at the University of Pennsylvania, addresses these issues in chapter 8. More than anyone else, Professor Phillips has participated actively in deregulation and pursuit of competition. His work includes publication of many influential scholarly books and articles; he was also co-Director and Public Member of three regulatory reform and electronic funds transfer commissions. This broad perspective and interest is developed for the reader in chapter 8. Phillips ties together the many historical, analytical, and public policy strands in the interesting story and provides the wisdom and insights for future directions in public policy.

After a careful background review of the law and public policy here, which places recent successes into better perspective, Phillips analyzes specific thorny questions which demand future resolution. For example, policy makers must deal with issues of access to existing or proposed ATM and POS systems. Economists and lawyers must resolve the still lingering questions and ambiguities about sharing, exclusive contracts, EFT services marketing arrangements, and system membership rules and interchange fees. Courts may face the burden of excess numbers of cases of predation or monopolization brought by those firms unable to make it in an innovative and competitive world. Courts and policy makers both must distinguish between true monopolization by financial supermarkets and the likely frequent private complaints without merit. It is therefore appropriate that the Antitrust Division continue to assess the whole arsenal of antitrust weapons in financial service markets, and certainly that it avoid the naive application of *per se* restraint of trade doctrines.

Finally, questions of joint venture legality are going to be especially important, in view of the large-scale economies noted by earlier authors. Professor Phillips provides an innovative analytical structure for their proper microeconomic evaluation.

Another common theme in this volume is the presence of hidden subsidies, past and future. The difficulty of eradicating subsidies once firmly implanted is also highlighted in most of the foregoing chapters. Payors using the paper check-writing modes of payments transfer (a debit scheme) have for many years enjoyed the benefits of float, a well-known subsidy. The discussion in chapter 9 develops this issue from the consumer viewpoint. In chapter 1, Henderson described the evolution of subsidy as part of the U.S. payments system's focus on the depositor. Banking and telecommunications deregulation removes many business subsidies, for example, the local operating company subsidy at the expense of long lines operations (see Geller's chapter 3). Private attempts to promote the new technology and generate new demand create still different consumer subsidies, which we do not yet fully comprehend. Many credit cardholders enjoy a "free float" period prior to payment, for which the annual credit card charge may not provide full compensation. Other groups in society pick up the difference—for example, merchants or bank vendors or other cardholders who either do not pay on time or pay cash. The dialogue between vendors and regulators on these issues has been intense since about the early eighties. Seldom, however, are the consumer issues debated publicly. Chapter 9 attempts in small part to remedy this lack. It focuses on the difficult consumer trade-offs and choices. I conclude that we may usefully devote more attention to a macro- as well as microeconomic view of the new technology, and the way in which society gets to divide up the more efficient and appetizing payments pie.

8 THE NEW MONEY AND THE OLD MONOPOLY PROBLEM

Almarin Phillips

Concern about the power and the proclivity of banks to do social harm is an important facet of the financial history of the United States. In 1819, John Adams wrote that "banks have done more injury to the religion, morality, tranquility, prosperity and even wealth of the nation than they can ever have done or ever will do good."[1] A few years later, Jackson's veto of the bill rechartering the Second Bank of the United States was motivated by the "exclusive privilege" given that organization and "the consequent increase in the value of the stock far above its par value, . . . a gratuity of many millions to the stockholders."[2]

The states of Arkansas, California, Florida, Illinois, Iowa, Texas, and Wisconsin, the organized territories of Minnesota and Oregon, and the District of Columbia had no incorporated banks in operation as late as 1852 (Hammond 1957, p. 605). Constitutional provisions to the effect that the legislatures "shall not have the power to establish or incorporate any bank, or banking company, or monied institution whatever" existed in some of these jurisdictions.[3] In Indiana and Missouri, banking was restricted to state-controlled monopolies due to fears of the consequences of privately owned banks.

Distrust of "paper money" and concerns about state-created private monopolies due to limited franchising were important elements in agrarian political doctrines. These, of course, were of particular importance in the western regions of the country. Even so, the spread of general incorporation statutes in eastern states in the post-1838 free-banking period was not without continued antipathy towards banks. While the incorporation of banks was largely unrestricted for qualified persons, the activities of banks in states that adopted statutes similar to the 1938 New York law were limited to the "business of banking." The latter, when defined, included receiving deposits, buying and selling exchange, coin and bullion, discounting and negotiating promissory notes, bills of exchange and other evidences of debt, loaning money on personal security, and issuing and circulating bank notes (Symons and White 1984, pp. 163–169). Other corporations were not permitted to engage in the business of banking and banks were not permitted to engage in other businesses. Then, even as now, there existed the view that the mingling of relatively narrowly defined banking activities with general commerce in a single organization was fraught with danger of injury to the public.

The National Bank Act continued this tradition. The Act said in effect that, if we must have banks, let there be many small ones with heavily circumscribed operating powers; no branching, no trust departments, no real estate loans, and no securities activities save those necessary for maintaining required reserves of government bonds against notes and deposits. Moreover, the national banks were to be regulated by the newly established Comptroller of the Currency.

The banking system moved in unanticipated directions shortly thereafter. State-chartered banks, rather than disappearing, flourished as the use of demand deposits spread. Through the end of the nineteenth century and into the twentieth, chartering rivalry between successive Comptrollers of the Currency and state regulatory agencies heightened. In the process, the operating powers of state banks were broadened. The permissable activities varied widely among the states, but often included trust departments, real estate lending, limited branching, and the underwriting and brokering of securities.

National banks were given trust powers by the Federal Reserve Act in 1913; they were granted branching powers reasonably equivalent to state banks by the McFadden Act in 1927. National banks also operated securities affiliates and, indeed, by 1930 these bank affiliate securities organizations had become major factors in investment banking (Symons and White 1984, p. 54).

All of this was stopped abruptly in the period 1933–1935. The Banking Act of 1933, particularly in its Glass-Steagall provisions and in the sections creating controls and prohibitions on payment of interest on deposits, effectively prevented intra- and interindustry competition. At the same time, other legislation and regulatory changes limited competition among the thrift institutions and encouraged the private cartelization of investment banking and the securities markets.[4] This essentially noncompetitive and anticompetitive situation was unchallenged for roughly two decades.

The Emergence of New Market Forces

By the early 1950s, the regulatory framework designed twenty years earlier began to show its fragility. Behavior that was overtly competitive—at least from the view of the market participants—began to emerge.[5] One aspect of this was an accelerating branching movement, as shown in table 8-1. The geographic distribution of the branching was heavily influenced by

Table 8-1. Number of Commercial Banks and Branches—1950–1985

Year	*Number of Banks*	*Number of Branches* (not including head offices)
1950	14,583	4,761
⋮	⋮	⋮
1955	14,280	6,574
⋮	⋮	⋮
1960	13,329	9,753
⋮	⋮	⋮
1965	13,599	14,564
⋮	⋮	⋮
1970	13,515	19,964
1971	13,595	21,364
1972	13,716	22,711
1973	13,882	24,230
1974	13,962	25,110
1975	14,354	27,428
1976	14,387	28,487
1977	14,420	29,408
1978	14,387	30,654
1979	14,353	31,205
1980	14,402	33,045
1981	14,395	34,262
1982	14,392	35,512
1983	14,402	36,376
1984	14,301	36,918
1985	14,278	37,495

Source: *Polk's World Banks Directory.*

differences in state laws. So too was the extent to which branching occurred through the acquisition of existing banks rather than as *de novo* facilities. In many local and regional markets, however, existing banks were exposed to competiton from new entrants and some regulators, legislators, and bankers expressed fears concerning rising concentration.

Another early manifestation of breakdown in the regulatory framework was increased use of the bank holding company form of enterprise. This device was used at first primarily as a substitute for branching in states that inhibited general branching but nonetheless permitted holding companies. After 1965, "one-bank holding companies" (OBHCs) were widely used to expand both the geographic areas banks could reach and the range of services bank organizations could provide. Table 8-2 indicates the

Table 8-2. Percent of Total Bank Assets Held by Bank Holding Company Banks (Insured Banks)—1950–1984

Year	*Percent of Total Assets Held by Holding Company Banks*
1950[a]	12.0%
⋮	⋮
1965[a]	17.0
⋮	⋮
1970[a]	57.0
⋮	⋮
1972	63.2
1973	67.4
1974	69.6
1975	68.5
1976	67.9
1977	68.2
1978	68.7
1979	70.6
1980	74.1
1981	77.3
1982	82.2
1983	85.9
1984	88.1

[a] Percentage of total deposits.

Sources: Fischer, *American Banking Structure* (New York: Columbia University Press, 1968), p. 97; *Federal Reserve Bulletin*, vol. 58 (December 1972), pp. 999–1008; Board of Governors of the Federal Reserve Bulletin (unpublished data).

enormous growth in commercial bank assets held by holding company banks during this period. The advantages of the OBHCs disappeared after enactment of the Bank Holding Company Act of 1970. The amendments of that year nonetheless provided limited "grandfathering" of the expanded activities of the OBHCs and, more importantly, created a mechanism for gradually relaxing the constraints imposed on holding company activities by the Federal Reserve's Regulation Y. Table 8-3 shows the activities permitted subsidiaries of BHCs as of late 1984. Again, many observers saw competitive dangers inherent in these changes.

Two other recent phenomena have potentially far-reaching effects on the structure of banking. The first is the rapid adoption by many states of laws permitting interstate banking. Thus, in addition to 16 bank holding companies with over 1400 interstate offices of subsidiary banks that were grandfathered by the Bank Holding Company Act (and its amendments), and in addition to more than 250 interstate offices controlled by foreign banking organizations, there were at the end of 1984, 22 states that permitted some form of interstate branching and/or holding company banks.[6] Not surprisingly, most of these state laws prohibit or restrict *de novo* entry, favoring instead acquisitions of or mergers with incumbent banks. Controversy has surrounded the patterns of regional compacts arising under these state laws. Some money center banks would strongly prefer federal preemption of the emerging state geographic restrictions through repeal of the McFadden Act and the Douglas Amendment.[7] Those interested in preventing the growth of large, interstate banking organizations oppose both that kind of preemption and the new, permissive state actions.

Of at least equal importance to the future shape of banking is the rise of the so-called "nonbank banks" and other special-purpose banks. The former are more accurately labeled "non-Bank Holding Company Act banks," that is, banks with state or national charters that provide for either commercial lending or the acceptance of demand deposits, but not both. So organized, these institutions are exempt from the Bank Holding Company Act restrictions on interstate acquisitions and, indeed, on that Act's restrictions on the product-line activities of other subsidiaries of the same parent. Thus, many nonbank holding companies—Sears, J.C. Penny, and Merrill Lynch, for examples—have organized *de novo* or acquired nonbank banks. Since good substitutes for demand deposits and/or commercial lending exist for most bank customers, the nonbank banks are in many cases effectively full-service banks not subject to the Bank Holding Company Act.[8]

Further interstate expansion has come from limited-purpose banks

Table 8-3. Domestic Nonbank Activities Approved and Denied by the Board of Governors (as of February 1, 1984)

Activities Approved by Regulation

1. Extensions of credit
   - Mortgage banking
   - Finance companies: consumer, sales, and commercial
   - Credit cards
   - Factoring
2. Industrial bank, Morris Plan bank, industrial loan company
3. Servicing loans and other extensions of credit
4. Trust company
5. Investment or financial advising
6. Full-payout leasing of personal or real property
7. Investments in community welfare projects
8. Providing bookkeeping or data processing services
9. Acting as insurance agent or broker primarily in connection with credit extensions.
10. Underwriting credit life and credit accident and health insurance related to consumer loans
11. Providing courier services
12. Management consulting to all depository institutions
13. Sale and issuance of money orders with a face value of not more than $1,000, and travelers checks, and retailing of savings bonds
14. Performing appraisals of real estate
15. Discount brokerage firm
16. Underwriting and dealing in certain federal, state, and municipal securities.
17. Acting as a futures commission merchant regarding foreign exchange, U.S. government securities, certain money market instruments, and options on those instruments.
18. Arranging equity financing with institutional lenders for commercial and industrial income-producing properties.
19. Offering informational, advisory, and transactional foreign exchange services.

Activities Approved by Order

1. Operating a "pool reserve plan" for loss reserves of banks for loans to small businesses
2. Operating a thrift institution in Rhode Island
3. Buying and selling gold and silver bullion and silver coin
4. Operating a guaranty savings bank in New Hampshire
5. Operating an Article XII New York investment company
6. Acting as a futures commission merchant to cover gold and silver bullion and coins.
7. Retail check authorization and check guarantee
8. Providing consumer-oriented financial management courses

9. Executing unsolicited purchases and sales of securities as agent for the customer (limited securities brokerage)
10. Engaging in commercial banking activities through branches located in Nassau and Luxembourg of a limited-purpose Delaware bank
11. Operating a distressed S&L in the same state
12. Acquiring a distressed S&L in another state

Activities Denied by the Board

1. Insurance premium funding ("equity funding")—combined sales of mutual funds and insurance
2. Underwriting general life insurance not related to credit extension
3. Real estate brokerage
4. Land investment and development
5. Real estate syndication
6. General management consulting
7. Property management services generally
8. Armored car services
9. Sale of level-term credit life insurance
10. Underwriting mortgage guaranty insurance
11. Computer output microfilm services
12. Operating a travel agency
13. Operating a savings and loan association (except in certain states or unless the S&L is distressed)
14. Underwriting property and casualty insurance
15. Underwriting home loan life insurance
16. Real estate advisory activities.
17. Offering investment notes with transactional features

Source: Savage (1985).

permitted by special actions of state legislatures. By 1985, six states had acted to allow various aspects of wholesale banking or credit card operations. Taken in the context of other developments, some professing concern with what they see as tendencies toward the creation of monopolies have been opposed to the growth of limited-purpose banks.

A number of other changes have occurred that have been seen by some to raise antitrust issues. One of these is the complex joint venturing entailed in bank credit card systems. In their early history, the rules of one of the two major systems limited banks to membership in only one system; antitrust considerations led to the abandonment of such exclusivity.[9] There have also been complaints that the setting of the interchange fees for clearing obligations of issuing banks to merchant banks constitutes illegal price fixing.[10]

Another facet of joint venturing with antitrust implications concerns the recent spread of local, regional, and national systems of automated teller machines (ATMs). As is true of the bank card systems, the ATM ventures include agreements with respect to cost sharing and user fees. When the customer of one institution uses an ATM deployed by another, contractually fixed reimbursement fees are involved. To date, none of these arrangements has been found to constitute unlawful price fixing. But again as with the bank cards, questions relating to exclusivity and sharing have been addressed.[11]

Rules governing access to an existing or proposed ATM joint venture come within the "essential facilities doctrine" of antitrust policy.[12] Thus, if duplication of facilities by potential entrants is prohibitively costly and if their entry would not interfere unreasonably with the activities of the incumbents, access on reasonable terms by the newcomers may be required. Some states have mandated sharing to overcome possible weaknesses of using antitrust, but there are disadvantages of this approach as well.[13]

Other forms of joint venturing among financial institutions could raise similar antitrust issues. Point-of-sale (POS) systems are much akin to ATM arrangements. The rules governing participation in automated clearing houses (ACHs), like those of their predecessor organizations, could include aspects of price and/or nonprice behavior that exceed standards of reasonableness. Further, as the use of franchising expands as a means for marketing financial services, the reasonableness of vertical restraints, including tying arrangements and price restraints, may require examination.[14]

For completeness, it should be noted that worries have appeared about the possibilities of monopolization by so-called "financial supermarkets" (see Phillips 1985). If indeed some combination of size and multiproduct operations could conceivably succeed in conferring monopoly power on such firms, monopolization would become a major concern.

The Arsenal of Antitrust Weapons in Financial Service Markets

Not surprisingly, the long-running allegations about monopolistic market structures and anticompetitive behavior in financial markets have as counterparts a host of statutes designed to prevent such phenomena. The bank mergers of the 1950s brought forth the Bank Merger Act of 1960, a curious amalgom of competitive criteria and "banking factors" to be considered in each bank merger application.[15] What probably were fears among bankers that the Department of Justice would not properly understand the unique characteristics of bank markets led not only to the inclusion of the banking factors but as well to a division of primary enforcement responsibilities among the federal bank regulatory authorities.

The wave of strict enforcement of the amended section 7 of the Clayton Act[16] during the 1960s included the famous *Philadelphia National Bank* case,[17] holding *inter alia* that Clayton Act standards alone—without consideration of banking factors—could be used in merger cases brought by the Department of Justice. In the Lexington Bank case,[18] brought under the Sherman Act prior to Justice's becoming aware that the Clayton Act could be used, it was held in effect that Sherman Act standards for mergers were essentially the same as those of the Clayton Act and, once more, that the banking factors need not be considered.[19]

These decisions, augmented by the bank regulatory agencies' distress about the ambiguity of the law with respect to the weight to be given the banking factors, resulted in the 1966 amendments to the Bank Merger Act. Under the new provisions, cases brought by Justice under the Clayton Act were to employ the standards of the Bank Merger Act; such cases also had to be brought within 30 days of the decisions of the relevant regulatory agency. The competitive test—that the effect of the merger "may be substantially to lessen competition"—was the primary criterion. While banking factors adverse to the merger could alone or combined with the competitive test be used to deny merger applications, they could be used to negate the probable anticompetitive effects only if contributions to the convenience and needs of the community were so important as to "clearly outweight" the likely lessening of competition. No modifications were made in the Sherman Act standards as applied to bank mergers.

The Banking Act of 1933 required the registration of bank holding companies but contained no antitrust provisions with respect to such organizations. The Bank Holding Company Act of 1956 has substantive provisions but, as suggested above, provides a spectacular history of evasion.[20] The act contains the same sort of antitrust and banking factor tests as does the subsequent Bank Merger Act. A bank holding company was defined, however, in terms of owning or controlling two or more banks; and a bank was defined as "any national banking institution or any state bank, savings bank or trust company." The so-called "Douglas amendment," in parallel with the amended 1927 McFadden Act, prohibits bank holding companies from interstate acquisitions except as permitted by state laws.[21]

The definition of a bank was changed in 1966 to "any institution that accepts deposits that the depositor has a legal right to withdraw on demand." Certain nonprofit organizations were brought into the classification of holding companies. The one-bank holding company movement was underway at the time, but the Congress did not immediately close the loophole created by the "two or more banks" phraseology. The amendments of 1970 did close this loophole and redefined a bank with the conjunctive additional requirement "and engages in the business of making commercial loans." Thus, the "nonbank bank" loophole was born. Holding companies are unconstrained in owning organizations that are in every way banks save for their not offering one or the other of demand deposits and commercial loans. And, of course, nonbank banks have proliferated to become one of the most important vehicle for product-line and geographic market expansion.[22]

The Bank Holding Company Act permits BHCs to own or control subsidiaries the activities of which are "so closely related to banking ... as to be a proper incident thereto," with the broad consequences indicated in table 8-3. Companion provisions prevent tie-ins and exclusive dealing, making it illegal to "extend credit, lease or sell property of any kind, or furnish any service, or fix or vary the consideration for any of the foregoing, on the condition or requirement ... that the customer shall obtain some additional property or service from such bank [or other subsidiary] other than a loan, discount, deposit, or trust service."[23]

The 1978 change in Bank Control Act requires notification and approval where control of a bank is gained by an individual.[24] This act reaches "chain banking" and "group banking", noncorporate forms of de facto branching that in the United States are nearly as old as commercial banking itself (see Fischer 1968). The Depository Institutions Management Interlocks Act gives bank regulatory agencies power to prevent anticompetitive interlocking directorates and, notably, affirms the power of the Department of Justice to enforce its provisions.[25]

Aside from these antitrust-like provisions of laws relating specifically to banking, the sanctions of the venerable Sherman Act and—with some limitations beyond those imposed by the Bank Merger Act—the Clayton Act apply to banking markets.[26] Thus, private suits and enforcement actions by the Antitrust Division are possible for offenses relating to horizontal price fixing, division of markets, customer allocations, conspiracies to eliminate competitors, covenants not to compete, vertical price fixing, territorial restrictions, exclusive distributorships, tying, reciprocal dealing, refusals to deal, monopolization, predation, conglomerate acquisitions, or price discrimination.[27]

The Use of Antitrust Weapons: Is Monoply in Financial Markets a Major Problem?

A proper appreciation of the competitive consequences of recent and foreseeable changes in financial service markets requires a historical perspective beyond that presented thus far. The simple truth of the matter is that until the decades of the 1960s and 1970s, the public regulation of financial markets, combined with "customary" and "privately enforced" restraints of trade, rendered banking markets quite monopolistic in character.[28] Restrictions governing chartering and branching, product line restrictions separating classes of institutions, public regulation of interest rates, clearing house rules, and other means for assuring "united action on problems affecting the common welfare of ... banks" had pervasive effects (Horbett 1941; see also Fischer 1968, pp. 238–275). As late as 1970, Lane Kirkland, then Secretary-Treasurer of the AFL-CIO, was fond of saying, "Having a bank charter is like having a license to steal."[29]

What we have recently been witnessing are, in general, changes in structure and behavior that imply more, not less, competition. Since the early 1960s, the Department of Justice has shown no reluctance to bring Sherman Act cases where price fixing or other unreasonable restraints of trade are suspected.[30] Similarly, the regulatory agencies—often with the Department of Justice actively looking over their decisions—routinely prohibit mergers and holding company acquisitions the effects of which may be substantially to lessen competition. The affected geographic markets have been primarily defined in local, regional, or statewide terms, but the reality of this is that except in such terms there is no apparent tendency toward higher concentration. And, indeed, the occasional higher concentration found at these levels may not be competitively meaningful. Entry is easier, not only by institutions of the same historic classification but also through the product expansion of other institutions that now can provide good substitutes.[31]

It is true that Justice has not succeeded in convincing the courts of the economic validity of the potential-competition/toehold (or foothold) theory in either bank or general merger cases.[32] For banks, this has meant that efforts to stem what some regard as trends toward statewide competition have not been successful. Few dispute that maintaining free entry—or, if you will, having some potential competitors "standing in the wings"—is particularly important when markets are highly concentrated. Determining whether a particular firm, not in the market prior to merger, was having tempering effects on incumbents and, save for a merger, would have entered de novo or by toehold merger is another matter, however. Some see such an exercise as approaching the metaphysical even while supporting the application of contestability and potential competition concepts in merger cases.

On this score, the culprit in banking markets has traditionally been the regulatory milieu. State laws governing chartering, mergers, and holding company acquisitions have served to protect existing banks from the full force of potential competition. This is true—although perhaps to a lesser extent—even in states permitting statewide branching. Details of state regulation regarding branching and holding company acquisitions almost universally favor the banks already in a particular market over those seeking to enter.

Recent manifestations of this protection are seen in the interstate banking laws currently being fashioned. These laws usually limit the interstate moves to those made by acquisition, assuring the incumbents of the present value of future earnings. Such restrictions have much in common with the marketing of taxi medallions so far as public welfare is concerned. It should be noted, however, that the growing availability of bank-like services from nonbanks threatens the future value of the "bank medallions"; a good many incumbents may see the new interstate banking laws as "chances to get out while the getting is good."

If one or a few of the new, more enterprising groups of financial institutions actually succeeds in causing lower profits or losses in market shares or, indeed, the failures of some existing banks, it is to be expected that monopolization charges will be levied. The recent directions of the Antitrust Division indicate that suits by the government are unlikely unless it is clear that the injuries are caused by the abuse of market power, not by the superior efficiencies or preferred services of the successful firms. Nonetheless, the banks suffering losses care little about the distinctions between abuse of market power and improved efficiency; they see themselves as targetted losers whatever the underlying reasons. They will sue and the courts may be burdened with a good many predation cases that they are ill-equipped to handle.[33] Congress could be pressed to pass new protective legislation. The transition to more competition and a more efficient financial structure will not be without antitrust strains.

To this must be added the likelihood of antitrust cases relating to joint ventures created to bring new technologies into the marketplace. On the one hand, it is clear that technologically feasible new services are not being developed precisely because there are no existing interfirm organizations that can effectively internalize the costs and benefits of the development. On the other hand, efforts at the kinds of interfirm coalescence needed in order to achieve attractive cost-benefit internalization may be attacked on what are ostensibly antitrust grounds. Naive application of per se restraint of trade doctrines could conceivably arise in even today's Antitrust Division; more significantly, courts will have these doctrines pressed by existing firms adversely affected by the innovations and by other innovating firms that, for one reason or another, did not make it.

Joint ventures have been important in the past—important, for example, in the rise of the check system, credit card systems, and ATM/POS systems. They will be of increasing importance as the "new money" and the new monetary system come into being. Covenents that restrict the behavior of the participants and, particularly, covenents that define the interfirm sharing of costs and revenues are necessary if technologically feasible innovations are to become economically attractive. When, for example, the BankAmericard was provided only by branches of Bank of America, no interbank sharing of costs and revenues was needed. But so restricted, the system was not viable. As National BankAmericard, Incorporated (and the InterBank Card Association) were formed as joint ventures among banks, formal means for collecting revenues and sharing costs among issuing banks, merchant banks, merchants, and cardholders became essential (see Baxter 1983). And the systems could then generate revenues adequate to cover costs. Today, with varying degrees of commonality required among international bank card systems (credit and debit); travel and entertainment cards; proprietary cards of diverse issuers; and local, regional, national, and international ATM and POS networks, just the technical character of the intersections among the parties to financial transactions becomes mindboggling. When to this is added the complexities of joint venturing in videotext with myriad nonfinancial services, the matrix of contractually arranged commonalities is virtually of unlimited dimensions.

That there can be abuses within and among these systems can hardly be gainsaid. In the context of a rapidly changing technology, however, much of the relevance of static concepts of monopoly disappears. So too does the relevance of archaic notions that cast automatic suspicion on interfirm organizational ventures of this kind (see Phillips 1985).

Conclusions

The century and a half since Jackson prevented renewal of the charter of the Second Bank of the United States have not brought with them a great revolution in the public attitude toward banks. Banks and bankers—as a group if not individually—continue to be distrusted and disliked. We now have a central bank, and all of the states permit banks to operate; but many of the general public would not strongly dissent from the flavor of Jackson's 1832 remarks.

It is difficult to determine the extent to which these attitudes are peculiarly American—vestiges of the Agrarian and Populists movements—in contrast to being rational reactions to the ways banks have indeed treated the public. There certainly are still echos of agrarianism and populism in the themes being used on the political scene. In many cases, however, it is the banks (or some of the banks), not the public, that use those themes. And with very little probing, it becomes clear that the purpose is to protect the older structural forms and noncompetitive behavior from the inroads of new competitors.

Financial markets, to be sure, have many problems. One great one is that the basic structures of those markets are still the structures that arose when chartering was free and other regulations simultaneously prevented competition. As competition is now entering those markets—inevitably entering them—those basic structures can no longer be fully protected. There will be changes, with concomitant mergers, acquisitions, and—of course—bank failures. Some new ventures will succeed and others will not.

It would be foolish to assert that no conventional antitrust problems could appear in this situation. They can. It would be a larger mistake, however, to see the changing structures as evidence of a consolidation movement with severe anticompetitive implications. The basic cause-and-effect relationships are not those with which antitrust policy should be concerned. The new structures are not properly seen as sources of monopoly power. Rather, they are the vehicles for and results of a decline in monopoly power. Increased competition is forcing major changes in what has been an inefficient, protected financial structure. Those favoring more competition should applaud the process.

Notes

1. Cited by Hammond (1957), p. 36.
2. Veto message by President Andrew Jackson, July 10, 1882.
3. Hammond (1957), p. 606, quoting Article XI. Section 1 of the Constitution of Oregon.
4. For detail, see Committee on Banking and Currency (1963).
5. The underlying reasons for the structural changes after 1950 lie in changing technology and higher rates of interest, both juxtaposed against a regulatory system fashioned to fit radically different conditions. For detail, see Phillips (1979).

6. See Whitehead (1985) for details, including data on loan production offices and Edge Act subsidiaries.

7. "Citicorp's Different View" *Washington Post* (October 9, 1984), p. D1:1.

8. See *Board of Governors of the Federal Reserve System v. Dimension Financial Corp.* 46 CCH S. Ct. Bull. P. B757 (January 22, 1986) for the legal posture of nonbank banks in the absence of legislative change. For one proposal to limit nonbank banking, see H.R. 20, the proposed "Financial Institutions Equity Act of 1985," in which the definition of a "bank" would include "an insured bank as defined in ... the Federal Deposit Insurance Act."

9. In *Worthen Bank & Trust Co. v. National BankAmericard, Inc.* 345 F. Supp. 1309 (1972), the District Court found that this exclusive arrangement was a per se violation of antitrust laws. On appeal, this decision was reversed and remanded for retrial. 485 F. 2d 119 (1973). A redrafting of the membership rule was subsequently submitted to the Department of Justice. After receiving in October 1975 an opinion from the Department suggesting that the exclusivity rule might be challenged, dual membership was permitted. See Bernard (1980) for more detail.

10. *National Bancard Corporation v. Visa, U.S.A., Inc.*, 779 F.2d 592 (11th Cir., 1986). The trial court there held that the per se rule need not apply and, further, that the agreements involved in setting the interexchange fees were reasonable. 596 F. Supp. 1231 (1984). For an earlier decision based on a similar rationale, see *U.S. v. Morgan*, 118 F. Supp. 621 (S.D.N.Y. 1954). An excellent economic analysis appears in Baxter (1983). Phillips (1985) looks at joint ventures in the context of technological change. See also *Broadcast Music, Inc. v. Columbia Broadcasting System*, 441 U.S. 1 (1979) and *Arizona v. Maricopa County Medical Society*, 457 U.S. 332 (1982).

11. Letter from Assistant Attorney General Donald I. Baker to William S. Brandt (March 7, 1977) (on file at the Department of Justice). This letter pertains to the plan of the Nebraska Electronic Terminal System for a network of POS and ATM terminals in which all Nebraska commercial banks were encouraged to participate but which excluded thrift institutions and out-of-state banks. See Baker (1979) and Bernard (1980) for discussion.

12. The seminal case is *U.S. v. Terminal Railroad Association*, 224 U.S. 383 (1912). See also *Associated Press v. U.S.*, 326 U.S. 1 (1945) and *Hecht v. Pro Football*, 444 F.2d 931 (D.C. Cir. 1971) cert. denied, 404 U.S. 1047 (1972).

13. For a discussion, see Chen and Jacobs (1984), *EFT in the United States: Policy Recommendations and the Public Interest*, Final Report of the National Commission of Electronic Funds Transfer (1977), and Bernard (1980).

14. See Eickhoff (1985) for a provocative discussion of the use of franchising in marketing financial services. The subject is treated in Phillips (1985), as well. *The Antitrust Bulletin* (Spring 1985) contains a general symposium on vertical restraints of trade.

15. 12 U.S.C.A. Section 1828 (c).

16. 15 U.S.C.A. Sections 12–27.

17. *U.S. v. Philadelphia National Bank*, 374 U.S. 321 (1963).

18. *U.S. v. First National Bank & Trust Co. of Lexington*, 376 U.S. 665 (1964).

19. The questionable applicability of the Clayton Act to bank mergers arose because section 7 of that Act is ostensibly restricted to persons "subject to the jurisdiction of the Federal Trade Commission" and because section 11 stipulates that "enforcement ... is vested in the ... Federal Reserve Board where applicable to banks, banking associations, and trust companies." Excellent discussion of the history and the current status of the law can be found in Solomon (1985) and Loevinger (1985).

20. 12 U.S.C.A. Sections 1841–1850.

21. 12 U.S.C.A. Section 1842 (d).

22. *Board of Governors of the Federal Reserve System v. Dimension Financial Corp.* 46 CCH S. Ct. Bull. P. B757 (January 22, 1986).

23. 12 U.S.C.A. Section 1972.

24. 12 U.S.C.A. Section 1817 (j).

25. 12 U.S.C Sections 3201–3207 (1982).

26. It was not long ago, however, that banking was regarded as a industry so pervasively regulated as to be exempt in large measure from the antitrust laws. See Kaysen and Turner (1959), pp. 42–43, 291, and more generally, Berle (1949). The restricted applicability of the Clayton Act arises because section 3 pertains only to "goods, wares, merchandise, machinery, supplies and other commodities," not to services. In all likelihood, however, differences between Clayton Act and Sherman Act tests for tying would disappear in any case in which serious anticompetitive consequences were demonstrable. Note, however, that section 331 of the Garn-St. Germain Depository Institutions Act of 1982 (12 U.S.C. 1462 (a)) prohibits tying arrangements by thrift institutions except those reasonable "to assure the soundness of credit."

27. The applicability of Section 2 of the Clayton Act—the Robinson-Patman provisions—is perhaps happily limited to "commodities of like grade and quality" (15 U.S.C. Section 13 (a) (1982)).

28. For an evaluation of noncompetitive aspects of banking markets into the 1960s, see Phillips (1963).

29. Unrecorded comments from meetings of the Hunt Commission, quoted from the author's memory and with the permission of Mr. Kirkland.

30. See Williams (1964) and *U.S. v. Northwestern National Bank of Minneapolis*, 1964 *Trade Cases* para. 71,020; *U.S. v. First National Bank of St. Paul*, 1964 *Trade Cases* para. 71,022; *U.S. v. Bank of Virginia*, 1966 *Trade Cases* para. 71,947.

31. While The Supreme Court has not as yet defined product markets in ways that combine the historic institutional boundaries, both the Department of Justice and the regulatory agencies consider the full range of substitute services in assessing probable anticompetitive effects. See also *U.S. v. Connecticut National Bank*, 418 U.S. 656 (1974).

32. For example, *U.S. v. Marine Bancorporation*, 418 U.S. 602 (1974); *U.S. v. Falstaff Brewing Corp*, 410 U.S. 526 (1973); BOC International v. FTC, 557 F.2d 24 (2d Cir. 1977).

33. Could the nation stand 1000 cases like *Utah Pie v. Continental Baking Co.*, 386 U.S. 685 (1967) or *William Inglis and Sons Baking Co. v. ITT Continental Baking Co.*, 461 F. Supp. 410 (N.D. Cal. 1978)?

References

Baker, D.J. 1979. Bank Card Systems Are Not Immune to Antitrust. *American Banker* (vol. 164, no. 192, October 4), 5.

Baxter, W. 1983. Interchange of Transactional Paper: Legal and Economic Perspectives. *Journal of Law and Economics* (vol. 26).

Berle, A.A. 1949. Banking Under the Antitrust Laws. *Columbia Law Review* (vol. 49).

Bernard, J. 1980. New Directions in Bankcard Competition. *Catholic University Law Review* (vol. 30).

Chen, M., and S. Jacobs. 1984. A Look at Shared EFT Systems. Unpublished, available by request.

Committee on Banking and Currency (1963), *Comparative Regulation of Financial Institutions*. Washington, D.C.: Subcommittee on Domestic Finance, House of Representatives.

Eickhoff, G. 1985. Going Interstate by Franchise or Networks. *Economic Review*. Federal Reserve Bank of Atlanta (January).

Fischer, G.C. 1968. *American Banking Structure: Economic and Legal Analysis*. Cambridge, Mass.: Harvard University Press.

Hammond, B. 1957. *Banks and Politics in America from the Revolution to the Civil War*. Princeton, N.J.: Princeton University Press.

Horbett, J.E. 1941. Banking Structure of the United States. In *Banking Studies*. Washington, D.C.: Board of Governors of the Federal Reserve System.

Kaysen, C., and D.F. Turner (1959), *Antitrust Policy: An Economic and Legal Analysis*. Cambridge, Mass.: Harvard University Press.

Loevinger, L. 1985. Antitrust, Banking, and Competition. *Antitrust Bulletin* (vol. 30, no. 3, Fall).

Phillips, A. 1963. Competition, Confusion and Commercial Banking. *Journal of Finance* (vol. 19, March).

Phillips, A. 1979. The Metamorphosis of Markets: Commercial and Investment Banking. *Journal of Comparative Corporate Law and Securities Regulation* (vol. 1)

Phillips, A. 1985. Changing Technology and Future Financial Activity. In Aspinwall, R.C. and Eisenbeis, R.A. Handbook for Banking Strategy. New York: John Wiley & Sons.

Savage, D.T. 1985. Depository Financial Institutions. In R.C. Aspinwall and R.A. Eisenbeis. *Handbook for Banking Strategy*. New York: John Wiley & Sons.

Solomon, E.H. 1985. The Dynamics of Banking Antitrust: The New Technology, the Product Alignment. *Antitrust Bulletin* (vol. 30, no. 3, Fall).

Symons, E.L., Jr. and J.J. White. 1984. *Banking Law* (2d ed.). St. Paul Minnesota: West Publishing Company.

Whitehead, D.B. 1985. Interstate Banking: Probability or Reality? *Economic Review*. Federal Reserve Bank of Atlanta (March).

Williams, L. 1964. Banking and the Antitrust Laws. *The Banking Law Journal* (May).

9 EFT: A CONSUMER'S VIEW

Elinor Harris Solomon

The ultimate recipient of benefits from the new technology should be, of course, the consumer. The retail user will have available exotic new money forms which provide greater utility and convenience than ever before at comparable or lower real cost levels. However, a number of important questions are beginning to be asked about the extent to which consumers will promptly receive the promised benefits or whether some are available only at the cost of offsetting trade-offs.

Consumer Benefits and Concerns

The Benefits

Consumers benefit from convenience and banking location. Not only brick and mortar offices but also automated teller machines (ATMs) and home terminals become places from where consumers can make payments, receive loans, and present deposits. Predictably the transactions costs of "buying" banking services will decline; these may include information and

---

The author is indebted to Stephen Rhoades, John Kwoka, David Humphrey, Steven Felgran, Michael Bradley, Spencer Nilson, and Lisa Pittman for suggestions and help.

service costs, time and waiting aggravation, or measurable travel costs such as gasoline. Some consumers will also include under their aggregate enhanced utility the perceived greater safety of credit or debit card use as compared with the risks of holding large quantities of cash as a medium of exchange.[1] Checks can accomplish this, but it is often easier and faster to use a credit card than a personal check where one is not known by the vendor.

In addition, the consumer may need to keep a smaller inventory of cash at any one time because he knows he can cheaply and easily convert time deposits into cash from the ATM when needed. As shown by Tobin and Havrilesky in chapters 6 and 7, a larger proportion of paychecks can be salted away in interest-earning forms until actually needed for future expenditures. Both the rise in nominal interest rates and the reduction in cash conversion costs via the medium of EFT serve as economic incentives to reduce the noninterest-earning portion of consumer transactions money—that is, money needed for eventual spending purposes. Proliferation of the many new interest-yielding forms of electronic near-monies will provide easily convertible substitutes for the low or zero-return cash inventories of consumers in the mainstream economy. The government will, in the process, lose to consumers a large percentage of the present large seigniorage benefits, or income stream from issue of noninterest-bearing forms of money.

The high-speed electronic links between depository institutions (DIs) and the money and capital markets aid the investment of these surplus funds released from use as a direct medium of exchange. The consumer/investor has some subjective preferences as between earnings and risk on assets overall but is constrained by available investment opportunities. Electronic communications improve the availability of data about these market opportunities. The generally faster speed of executing market orders permits the attainment of higher individual and hence aggregate social utility in portfolio decision making and execution.[2]

But probably the greatest consumer benefit from the new technology is an enhanced payments system efficiency (Walker 1978, 1980). Consumers and vendors jointly will determine the system ultimately used; and as shown by Henderson and Moore (chapters 1 and 2) the eventual mix of paper, tape, and electronics will depend upon specific advantages to user groups. However, whatever the ultimate mix, we are likely to see in the future further major social-cost advantages over the old fully paper based system. While different econometric procedures yield different results, there is general agreement that the EFT technology yields substantial and potentially rising efficiencies as payments transfer volume rises along a declining cost curve (Humphrey 1984). Moreover, the push to future new technologies suggests further major social gains. For cosumers, the efficiencies inherent in the new payments mode will translate into better and faster services and higher interest return, given lower conversion costs and a money mix away from cash.

The Consumer Concerns

Among the most serious concerns for consumers, although few may now be aware of them, are the payments system risks on large dollar transfers already discussed by Dr. Humphrey in chapter 4. Consumers almost never use these wholesale wire transfer nets. However, they may pay for any Fedwire losses; they may lose deposits or dividends, even capital, in the event of private-wire settlement losses. In addition, the legal rights and liabilities regarding most electronic payments are not yet clearly defined. Individuals may have privacy concerns if an easily accessible "big brother" type of electronic network charts financial life histories and provides instant playback on command.[3]

White-collar crimes such as computer embezzlement have received widespread attention in the press. More subtle types of concerns relate to possible market failures at any one of a number of points in the chain of money distribution to final buyer at retail. These are serious concerns for business and interbank users first and, again indirectly, to consumers. If market failure or market power exists somewhere along the line, the new technology efficiencies may fail fully to be reflected in the lower costs and prices that our ideal vision for the future will otherwise predict.

Market concerns have appeared to run as follows:

1. Consumers may find retail point-of-sale (POS), or other payments systems for which they feel unprepared, prematurely embedded in the payments mechanisms.
2. Consumers may wind up with systems they do want, but with fewer options or at higher cost due to private-market power and control.
3. Consumers may lose subsidies such as free float, perceived as rightful system advantages, and presently enjoyed under both the paper and credit card systems.
4. Some consumers may get left out of the new payments system altogether, for example through private-supplier "cream skimming" that targets the affluent user and leaves by the wayside the poorer and higher-cost, higher-risk groups.

5. The efficiencies created by the new technology may not get fully passed on to retail, because market power persists somewhere up the line and vendors can extract monopoly profits at the retail user's eventual expense.
6. Or, finally, the government may so fully control the new payments system that private innovation and a private system of optimal efficiency is discouraged by the govenment scrambling of normal market incentives.

The Historical Story: The Changing Market Focus

The T and E card era: The sixties

While consumers have realized novel new payments modes, concerns of this nature have proven so far not to be warranted.[4] But the systems did originally target the affluent few while only recently seeping down to the bulk of consumer users. The story of the EFT forerunner, the credit-based card, begins in about the mid-sixties. Then, American Express, Carte Blanche, and Diners Club developed the "proprietary" (or single-ownership) travel and entertainment (T and E) credit cards for use by frequent travelers who needed a readily acceptable means of charging for high-ticket items away from home. The T and E systems signed up as many cardholders as possible, to whom an annual fee was charged for membership; and at the same time they persuaded merchants to agree to accept the card as payment for the ticketed item, say, the meal. If the diner used the American Express (AmEx) card, the American Express merchant member would transfer the credit slip to his local AmEx office.

In return for an interest charge (the merchant discount, or percentage deduction from face value), AmEx provided funds to the merchant's bank account. AmEx later billed the cardholder who in effect received a short-term loan until the account was settled in full. As more merchant establishments joined one or more of the three major T and E systems, each card became still more useful to cardholders. Quite clearly, synergy was operative between numbers of merchant members and breadth of cardholder base.

The Bank Credit Card: The Seventies

Somewhat later, in the late 1960s, the all-purpose bank credit card was born. The delay probably reflected both the large scale needed for general-purpose card entry and the recognition of advantages of joint as compared with proprietary system operation. The bank credit card systems, Visa and MasterCard, started as local joint ventures between member banks. Generally nonprofit, they operated under specific rules and regulations designed to lower costs and unnecessary duplication, and help eliminate fraud and misuse.

In order to achieve greater acceptability, a prime ingredient for any medium of exchange, the local and then regional bank card systems merged. They thereby formed stronger national card systems with still broader merchant and cardholder bases, and with acceptability not only in the United States but also abroad. Around the world a new credit-based payments medium based on the so-called "plastic money" was born. About 1970 two competing national bank systems emerged to promote the all-purpose cards, National BankAmericard (with a later name switch to VISA), and Master Charge/Interbank (later MasterCard).

In the National BankAmericard joint venture each card-issuing member bank was a principal (Class A) member. Agent (Class B) system members dealt through their principal (Class A) banks, often their correspondents. NBI's competitor, the Master Charge/Interbank system, developed in similar fashion from local bank card systems, the California Bank Card Association and Marine Midland Bank system. Electronic delivery and interchange became prevalent within systems. Both NBI and Master Charge/Interbank developed outside the Federal Reserve clearance process, each now utilizing electronics extensively.

These systems generally did and still do work as follows. Bank credit cards are offered to depositors or other credit-worthy individuals. The bank members of the credit card system agree to provide a line of credit to the cardholder at the member retail establishment. Merchants pay a merchant discount, or percentage of gross, for the privilege of turning the charge paper over to the member bank agent of the bank card company for prompt bank account credit. The merchant's bank, then, clears or "interchanges" that paper with the cardholder's bank, again for a charge (the interchange fee). The cardholder's bank, finally, collects from the cardholder.

We show the bank credit card clearing process in figure 9-1. The transaction proceeds in the following step-by-step fashion:

1. Assume that the consumer charges a $1 purchase and receives merchandise valued at $1.
2. The merchant submits the paper to its agent bank B, and B discounts the paper by crediting the merchant's account for $0.96 at an assumed merchant discount of, say, 4%.

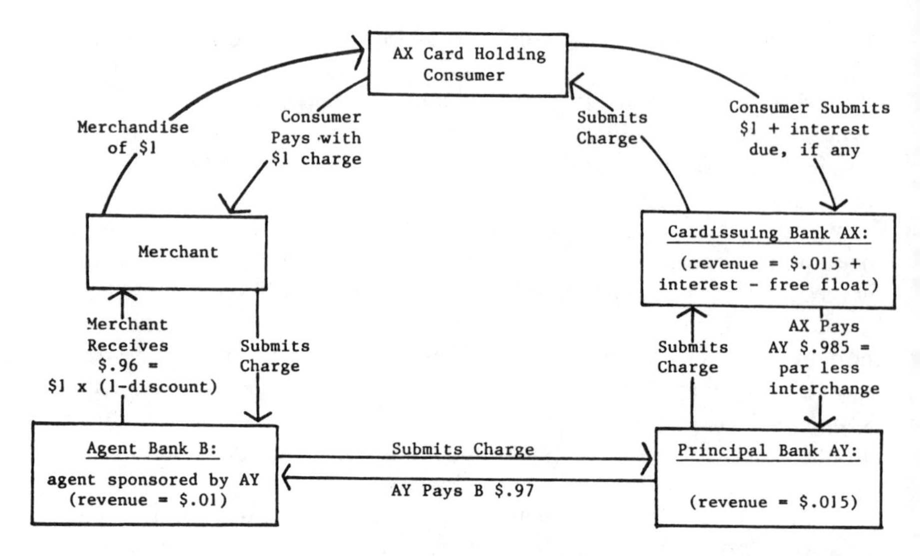

Figure 9-1. Bank Credit Card Network Interchange. We assume the purchase transaction value is $1.00, the merchant discount is 4%, and the interchange (clearing) fee is $1\frac{1}{2}$%.

3. Bank B submits the paper to the principal merchant bank AY, and AY credits B for $0.97. B's revenue (not profit—we have considered neither costs nor other benefits to B such as interest income on loans made possible by the merchant's demand deposit account) is $0.01. Agent bank B has paid the merchant $0.96 and received $0.97 from principal merchant bank AY. The net revenue of the agent bank is or should be a market-determined price; we have assumed it is $0.01.
4. Principal merchant bank AY submits (interchanges) the merchant paper to bank AX, the cardholder bank that issued the credit card. In the interbank clearing process AX discounts the paper by, let us assume, 1.5% (the "interchange fee"), and pays merchant bank AY $0.985. Merchant Bank AY's revenue (not profit) is $0.985 – $0.970, or $0.015.
5. Card-issuing bank AX now bills the cardholder the full $1, plus any interest due on revolving accounts. AX's revenue (not profit) is $0.015 plus interest, if any. From its gross revenue AX must deduct transactions and fraud costs plus opportunity costs of the interest-free loans to card users who pay within the free-float period.

In the beginning, the credit-worthy cardholder was enticed into the bank card system by mailings and incentives; he normally did not pay any annual fee nor incur any interest charge until a free-float period, then normally three to four weeks, was over. Late payors, of course, did incur interest charges on outstanding revolving credit balances. For system members, the main revenue, and profit, came largely from two classes of system users: the merchants who paid the merchant discounts as a percent of gross and the late-paying cardholders who paid interest charges on loans supplied by the cardholder's bank.

Early on, too, competitive questions surfaced. The ultimate fear was that the two bank card systems might merge either legally or *de facto*; were this to occur, it was thought, the consumer would be severely limited in his choice of national systems. AmEx could be the sole remaining effective competition for the merged BankAmericard/MasterCard. The relatively rigid nature of the interchange fee, which was for a time the same for both card systems, was the subject of Antitrust Division inquiry. Specific antitrust questions about user access and rules within systems were also left for Antitrust Division resolution (Penney and Baker, 1980). For example, the 1974–1975 bank card "duality" antitrust Business Review addressed the question of whether NBI could prohibit dual-system membership; NBI's rule would deny its members the opportunity to join any other competing bank card system, such as MasterCard. The Division refused clearance; it feared that this bylaw could effectively freeze out potential system newcomers from the credit card market, and hence limit buyer options generally.[5]

Card users often had other complaints. Even when market interest rates were relatively low, the bank card rates all generally hovered around the state statutory usury ceilings of 18%. Meanwhile, merchants often expressed dissatisfaction with high levels of the merchant discount rate, which most retail users found embedded eventually in price.

The Debit Card: The Eighties

But the market made corrections. Burgeoning intersystem rivalry has been the story of the eighties. The Monetary Control Act of 1980 (MCA 1980) legitimized the deployment of ATMs across state lines. Consumers called ATM cards "debit" cards because they provided cash through immediate electronic debit, or deduction, from bank balances. MCA 1980 also permitted thrift institution participation in both debit and credit card systems. Banks and thrifts both were now depository institutions (DIs).

(For the sake of simplicity, however, we shall continue to refer to all DIs merely as "banks.") Banks realized that they could better serve consumers hence compete for deposits more effectively, if they formed joint-venture ATM systems within an area. With a joint venture such as CIRRUS or PLUS, depositors can get cash not only from ATMs of their own banks but also from ATMs of other member banks. The system's marketing attraction rises. The acceptability of the card also rises.

At the same time, the ATM card has expanded the scope of its services. ATM debit cards increasingly can do some of the same things as a bank credit card, not only offering cash and account balance information to customers but also extending short-term loans. These new debit cards reach down into very broad consumer sectors cutting across all income groups. Potentially, both ATM and credit cards can be converted to point-of-sale (POS) cards, which deduct instantaneously (on-line) the cost of purchase from the customer's bank deposit balance at the point-of-sale at the merchant's store.[6] A number of nationwide systems including ATM, T and E, and bank credit cards now compete head-on. Consumers have considerable choice of systems.

Innovation and EFT cost reductions continue. Much new nonbank entry has developed. Merchant discounts can range from as low as 1–4% depending on merchant system automation and ticket size, or administrative cost. More competition for the cardholder's business intrasystem (that is, between local banks offering cards of the same system) has also been obvious in recent years. This rivalry between members for consumer business shows up as differing terms of the contract and quality of the overall service package. Consumers do not perceive all available MasterCard or VISA cards in their area to be the same; they shop around in response to competitive offers from bankers outside their local or regional areas.[7]

New system entry also is coming from originally unexpected quarters such as J.C. Penney and Sears, which use their already broadly based terminal and merchant outlets all over the country to tap new consumer business. New types of consumers can thus be wooed. Merchant-based systems offer consumers very different kinds of electronic payments services and pricing schemes. Emphasis is placed on signing up mass retailers such as Trailways Corp., F.W. Woolworth, or Budget Rent-a-Car—or on tapping previously neglected retail segments (perhaps through the Sears or J.C Penney's retail base). Use of the cheaper technologies involving magnetic tape rather than on-line systems has cut costs and prices including merchant discounts.

The Sears "Discover" card now competes with Citicorp's CHOICE or

Carte Blanche to serve the family-oriented consumer and middle-America traveler throughout the country. New to the competitive arena, too, are the "no frills" debit card readers positioned strategically in high-volume low-ticket business outlets, such as gasoline stations and supermarkets. In order to cut cost, and lower retail price, they employ the somewhat cheaper automated clearing house (ACH) off-line next-day processing capability.[8]

The Present Retail Scene

The new plastic technology thus has gradually blanketed a larger group of consumers, starting with a narrow base but now extending into gasoline stations and middle America. In each of the last three decades there has been a shifting EFT focus on successive new consumer markets. The T and E systems targeted the elitist high-ticket retail outlets, in well-travelled coast and other major metropolitan markets. Upper middle-income consumers, next, benefitted through the bank card inauguration.[9] Both now compete with ATM systems and the newly proliferating debit card systems with their broad and nonselective retail base: the gas stations and supermarkets. Of the original T and E cards only American Express remains as a separate entity; Citicorp around 1980 purchased the then floundering Carte Blanche and Diners Club companies with the cards retained as a specialty card of a general Citicorp mix of services.

The recently formed nationwide CIRRUS and PLUS ATM systems now vie in transactions volume with VISA and MasterCard; but the major regional ATM bank systems, led by Pulse, Exchange (Northwest), Honor, Avail, and ITS, now lead in transaction volume (Nilson 1985–1986). The ATM consumer base is both very broad and egalitarian, since the member bank dispenses these debit cards to virtually all its depositors. Credit overlines accessed by the ATM card may often follow. Automatic bank credit card membership is frequent, given multiple system interlinks.

ATM nets reach widely into the retail electronic market. About 9000 banks, along with uncounted numbers of thrifts and credit unions, participate in at least one of the 175 regional shared ATM networks. Many of these institutions are also members of one or more of the eight national shared ATM networks (Felgran 1985). They also generally belong to one or both of the two major bank credit systems, VISA and MasterCard.

Given the links established through shared networks, electronic payment at the retail point-of-sale (POS) becomes feasible. Some few pilot programs already are operational. A POS network interchange system among banks is shown in figure 9-2. A merchant's POS terminals can be accessed both by customers who hold debit cards issued by the merchant's bank and by customers of other banks belonging to all the connected networks. Whenever a POS terminal is used, the processor of the merchant's bank will determine whether the customer has an account with that bank. The processor directs "on-us" transactions to the bank's computer, but sends "on-other" transactions to its network switch. This switch then routes the transactions to the customer's institution either directly or through another switch, depending on network arrangements.

The terms of POS terminal ownership, services, and prices are negotiated between merchants and their member banks. Network interchange fees are usually lower for POS than for ATM or credit card transactions, because POS systems are less expensive to operate and maintain (Felgran 1985). In order to reduce cost further, many partial (processing) or outright system consolidations, too, are on the drawing board. These planned system links and mergers, designed to provide cheaper and universal service, in turn raise new questions and trade-offs down the line for consumer users.

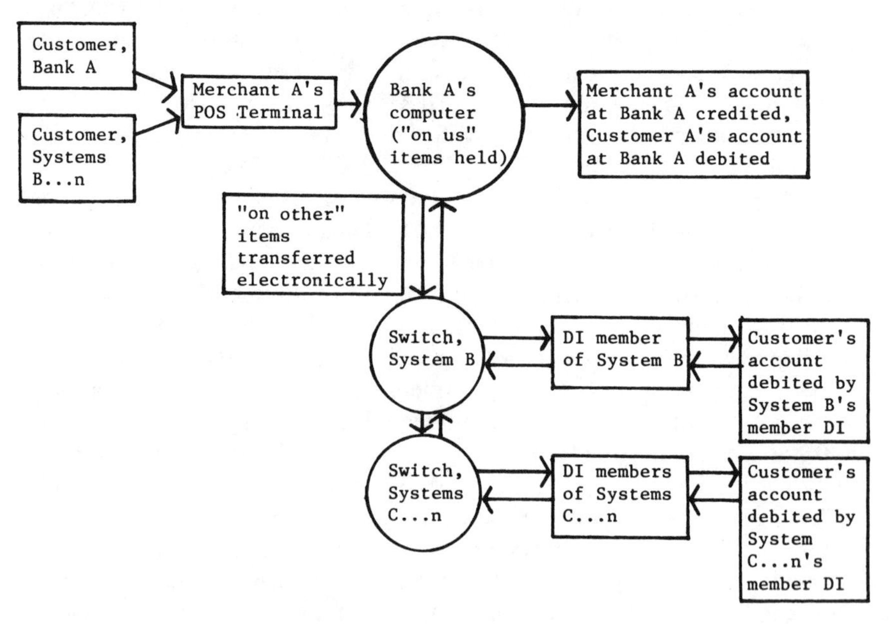

Figure 9-2. Funds Flows in Point-of-Sale (POS) Systems

The Trade-offs

The Consumer Conflicts

Trade-offs for the retail user of the new payments technology can best be grouped according to four main issues: market (allocative) efficiency, distributive efficiency, competition, and payments systems risk.

Allocative Efficiency (#1). Of major interest to the retail user, first, is the development of improved and major new payments technologies. Private investment, risk taking and innovation raise the level of systems technology; consumers will not realize the promised benefits without them. A second separate question is how best to achieve maximum-scale efficiencies for any given technology. Again, consumers can not have optimal efficiency unless they are somehow induced to use the new technology. A lot of discussion thus far centers on the necessary pricing inducements to raise the volume of EFT payments modes, in order to achieve optimal volume along the long-run cost curve.

In order to discuss incentive pricing, we refer to figure 9-3. Arguments for incentive pricing are based on the belief that early declining firm cost curves are U-shaped. Short-run average cost is represented at a given fixed technology as SAC; long-run cost here is thought to be lower (LAC). D_1 represents the present nascent market demand giving rise at firm equilibrium A to excess capacity in this differentiated new technology product. At normal firm pricing (P_n) consumers will only buy the limited quantity Q_n. Consumers will buy the larger quantity Q_s at the subsidized price P_s (equilibrium B). Vendors hope that the temporary subsidy price may shift out demand more quickly toward D_2 and optimal output Q^* (equilibrium Z). Price then can rise from the bargain P_s, with its firm losses,to the higher P^* which fully covers costs and a normal rate of return.

It may be, therefore, that the firm does not seek short-run profit maximization but rather wants to build up market share by some lower "promotional" pricing. The manager's best strategy depends on the expected magnitude of demand shifts over time. The "real" economic/marketing problem is then a dynamic optimization problem. The trajectory of prices over time is chosen so as to maximize the present value of a future profits stream, subject to projected cost curves and demand shift patterns. Prices may start out low so as to build volume early, since part of the pay-back to such low prices now is lower costs later. But recent payments systems controversies note the possible uneven cutting edge of these subsidies in the interim, prior to their eventual removal (Felgran, 1985).

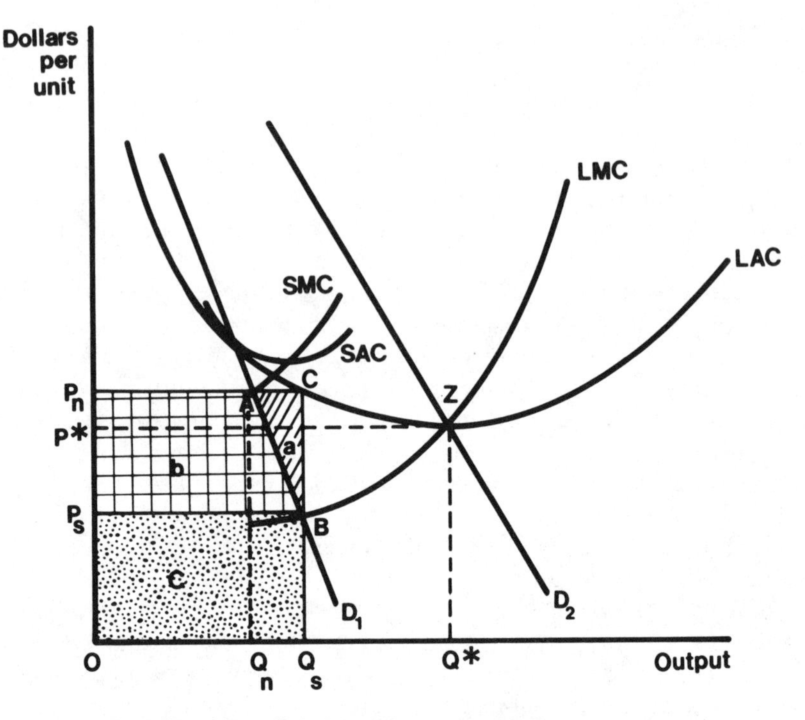

Figure 9-3. The Short-Run Subsidy: Microeconomic Issues

Distributive Efficiencies (#2). For example, the short-run or temporary Federal Reserve System subsidy to the Fed-run automated clearing houses (ACHs) was designed to achieve rising volume and optimal scale efficiencies. That form of incentive pricing also was an early focus of controversy between the Federal Reserve and private potential suppliers of these same services. Private vendors, along with the Antitrust Division, suggested the Fed was offering unfair ACH competition hence discouraging new private entry and innovation. Fed subsidies, they said, would benefit consumers in the short but not long run because more efficient private payments technologies would be discouraged.[11]

The temporary Fed subsidy was removed in 1986, but the same arguments show up with regard to new temporary merchant or bank subsidies designed to build up ATM volume (hence raise long-term profits). One important present question is who pays, who charges, when terminals doing banking business are placed on merchant premises (Felgran 1985). Those banks that provide multiple ATMs for frequent depositor use for a time may bear disproportionately the costs for developing the technology and hardware in competition for consumer deposits and market shares (Berger 1985).[12] That is, as was often the case in early pre-1980 credit card markets, some major innovative banks may choose to supply electronic services at a loss and below short-run marginal costs for that particular banking function. The idea of supplying this "loss leader" generally is to build up national recognition and prestige along with long-run market share within consumer financial markets. Citicorp, for example, turned earlier credit card losses into broader consumer banking profits at a time when less diversified money center banks were hardest hit by energy-related loan losses.

Let's take another example. Because initially they did not charge any annual customer membership fees, the bank card systems more quickly built up consumer user base and achieved scale efficiencies. Through this strategy they also more rapidly achieved nationwide acceptability of the bank credit card. Merchant members facing elastic demand curves who could not pass on the costs to consumer credit card users in the form of higher prices often absorbed the merchant discount costs. Luckier merchants who sold a differentiated product (faced more inelastic demand curves) managed to pass on these costs at retail; cash-paying customers paid the higher prices along with customers who charged their dinner.

If some consumers prefer cards, and others prefer to pay with cash, then one can logically make the argument, on microeconomic terms, that this is just a matter of revealed customer preferences. True, some customers may be hurt for a time but that does not imply the system is 'unfair" in any normative welfare sense. Consumers formerly cut out of the credit-debit card world now find themselves wooed by Sears' Discover card on TV football prime time. If they cannot charge at Lutèce's or Maxim's, they can use a new card to dine, instead, at Denny's. Meanwhile, prompt-paying cardholders benefitting from free float now pay annual fees and increasingly may find the free float grace periods shrunken in time. The changed pricing methods will pave the way for consumer acceptance, eventually, of POS, which eliminates float.

This process fulfills our microeconomic expectations and, happily, reduces the role of antitrust. Is that all there is to consider in the story though? The normal antitrust emphasis is microeconomic, or allocative efficiency of social resource use; the macroeconomic concept of distributive efficiency is generally not a primary antitrust concern.[13] However, the notion of consumer equity and base-level payments services is embedded in the original Federal Reserve legislation of 1913 and the Monetary Control Act of 1980, and some macroeconomic and income distribution questions inevitably filter into the antitrust focus. For example, implicit under equity is an adequate compensation to investors for risk, innovation, and entrepreneurial skills, through charges necessary to deal with the "free rider" problems of vendors who are granted access to the essential facilities developed by others. There is also the question of fair profits distribution and incentives between entrepreneur-sellers in a joint venture.[14]

Professor Phillips, in chapter 8, has just considered analytically the joint-venture issues. System members must struggle with the proper costing of services provided by principal (investment-supplying) to agent (middleman) banks. Merchants are embroiled in controversy with their banks about who should bear the costs of ATM or POS terminals at merchant locations. As the outcome of these deliberations filters down to retail, sellers and consumers get to divide between themselves the rewards of EFT scale economics. We saw that some innovative DIs deliberately have absorbed short-run losses of credit card deployment, for long-run gains as in any new technology; but in other cases the subsidy may be unintentional and longer range.[15] Given that rising use of the new technology is becoming a reality, with all the attendant cost advantages, how are the slices of the bigger or more attractive pie going to be passed around and divided as between consumer markets? What are the time lags, the frictions in the competitive process? Which consumer groups, if any, eventually provide a subsidy, and which consumers gain special pricing benefits? Are these subsidies merely a needed short-run spur to development, or likely rather to become permanently embedded in the pricing structure of the new technology?

Market Competition (#3). The market assumes still a third role here, that is, to assure that efficiencies from the new technology are passed on fully to retail users. Even if they are not, of course, normal welfare criteria as assessed under microeconomic theory may indicate a net gain to society as measured by the sum of consumer surplus and producer profit. The question is whether the optimal consumer gain is fully realized or gets thwarted by the presence of market power down the line.

Note that some of the same issues under allocative efficiency get turned around here. That is, some devices designed to raise technology levels and increase its use (#1) also raise the potential for reduced retail competition (#3), for example the joint-venture format or other consolidation techniques. The new technologies often require common standards for rules and encryption, along with sharing of systems use and costs. Those rules and standards for joint venture use "upstream"—that is, where productive processes originate—can theoretically impact "downstream" to retail.

Competition filters down through many stages of the financial "productive process" from the handful of upstream initial payments providers (Fedwire or CHIPS) to the millions of final retail EFT buyers downstream.

The concept of financial markets interaction thus embraces an image which starts with the first wholesale or clearing function of DIs (discussed earlier, in chapters 2 and 4), then fans downward to consumer DI services. Efficiencies from the new technology, and the cost saving, are passed down from one level in the payments production process to the next. A buyer at one level is seller at the next level, in competition with many other bank and nonbank sellers. The number of such potential bank and nonbank sellers rises as we move downstream. In the process of successive market interactions consumers eventually reap the cost benefits, assuming no "clog" to competitive pass-through exists.

However, while joint ventures permit innovation and are often necessary in provision of universal service by new wholesale payments systems upstream, they can also potentially reduce retail competition downstream. For example, cooperation at the top joint-venture level may inhibit competition for consumer financial business downstream if the joint-venture rules contain unneeded or restrictive clauses about entry, access, and resale pricing. Restrictive technical specifications can also present problems; it will take engineering as well as banking skills to differentiate the necessary from the unneeded.[16] The Antitrust Division plans to monitor these joint-venture developments, including scrutinizing unneeded rules leading to possible horizontal pricing or exclusionary effects in retail markets (Rule 1985).[17] But too close an antitrust involvement is resented by private suppliers as inhibiting investment and rising technology improvements, and there can be pressure on the authorities to relax restraints or enhance defenses.

The Antitrust Division analyzes the possible anticompetitive effects of mergers according to the new Merger Guidelines (U.S. Department of Justice 1984). Its present complex and criticized approach to markets delineation is intended to take into account the new broader market realities (see Blecher and Pollack 1985). This new approach to economic decision making also has to an increasing extent changed the role of the Antitrust Division from prosecutor to *de facto* regulator of industry conduct ("We will not sue to stop the merger or venture if you do X, Y and Z.") while at the same time increasing the costs and potentially deterring private antitrust litigation.[18]

Risk (#4). Unfortunately, the new technology can increase retail payment risk in a number of ways at the same time that it improves payments systems efficiency and the quality of consumer services (Humphrey and Moore, chapters 4 and 2). While most competitive questions have been successfully resolved by the market thus far, the risk questions have proved more worrisome in practice than earlier anticipated. Indeed, deregulation and the ensuing rise in competition may have contributed to unacceptable risk taking by some DIs and the greater present short-run chances of payments systems failure. These questions and the recent Fed presence as lender and settlement agent of last resort are vividly described by Dr. Humphrey in this volume. Any private-system settlement failure is borne by the DIs first but later, especially given the specter of an ultimate unwind, the cost is assumed by the consumer/depositor or consumer/taxpayer, depending upon the extent of Fed and regulatory agency "bailout."

The Consumer Balancing Act

It seems clear, therefore, that consumers cannot attain all four goals simultaneously without giving a bit on some. The question is, which goals are consumers willing to sacrifice, or perhaps put on the back burner for a while?

For example, an overly zealous push to achieve scale efficiencies (#1) before the market is fully ready, or the evidence of their existence is solid, is likely to alter the fairness balance for some consumers in the present payments system (#2). The reason is that someone is going to have to provide the subsidy or pricing incentive to assure the retail acceptance of the new technology before its time has come, as it were. That someone is going to lose chips, temporarily at least, to the favored user group in society, depending on the speed of market adjustment and the temporal bargaining process.

One short-run strategy may be calculated deliberately to generate longer-run card system profits, and perhaps bank deposits too, at the cost of temporary short-term credit card losses. It has been highly successful for a limited few major money center banks and through them for their customers also. In other cases, some market participants may be unaware that they are paying higher prices as a result of benefits gleaned by others—for example, consumers who pay for cash at fancy retail outlets where credit card costs are embedded directly in the general price structure. Once aware of major cost and price differentials, customers may buy goods not in Bloomingdales but in the cheaper noncredit-card-oriented Loehmanns of the world. But a plastic-inspired retail segregation can present social questions.

The arguments at wholesale are of a different order. Some merchants may believe they bear disproportionate costs of new ATM or POS hardware installations. They perceive the terminals rented from banks as building up deposits volume for the bank while using retail clerks and space in a manner disproportionate to direct consumer benefits such as greater safety and check-out speed. Again, some merchants' response has been to rent or buy their own terminals, then sell authorization services to user banks to their customers' advantage (J.C. Penney).

The retail consumer is also indirectly impacted by the debate on the present role for an embattled Federal Reserve System. Although some would argue with this premise, the push to eliminate a government presence in the payments mechanism, to assure maximum innovation and private risk taking (#1), may at the same time increase the risks to retail users (#4). The Federal Reserve by statute is supposed to protect the payments systems, free from political pressures. Recent DI failures and difficulties are likely to reinforce that view. Elimination of the Federal Reserve as guardian of the payments mechanism could shift some benefits from retail customers and middle-tier solvent banks and thrifts to innovators and risk takers at the other end of the spectrum, affecting income distribution or distributive efficiency (#2). The consumer slice of the efficiencies gain may be smaller. The following argument can also be made. If the Fed does not perform its traditional lender-of-last-resort function at time of payments crisis, and an unwind were actually to occur, then everyone would be loser.

Let us provide another example of built-in conflict. The private sector's attempt to suppress Fed competition in the payments mechanism helps raise technology levels and encourages entry by the most capable private innovators (helps achieve goal #1). At the same time, elimination of the Fed's costing advantage and subsidy in the production of ACH services has increased the short-run costs to respondent retail bank buyers of payments who formerly enjoyed the benefits of that Fed subsidy. The higher electronic clearing costs have been more than fully passed on in the form of higher price of clearing services for resale at retail. Hence consumer prices and costs are arguably raised in the short-run period before the ACH payments product can be successfully developed and marketed by private vendors so as to achieve full-scale efficiencies. That is, for long-run gains the present short-run advantage is shifted to the innovating upstream correspondent and nonbank vendors, to the temporary disadvantage of the (formerly subsidized) respondent bank buyers of these services and their retail customers. This process affects the macroeconomic distribution of technical gains (#2) as between consumer users. Predictably, each group in the early eighties questioned whether the Fed strategy was appropriate.

The more drastic strategy of eliminating the Fed System as provider of base-line services would certainly shift the balance between help for one group, generally the most impoverished retail users, in favor of the innovators (#1 vs. #2). Presumably the market in the long run again would correct inequities through provision of no-frills payments services for low-income groups otherwise forced out of the payments system altogether. But short-run hardships could be severe. The question is whether tax-payers in the interim might better assume the cost of subsidy than the DIs in today's deregulated and competitive environment.

Finally, the attempt to achieve maximum scale efficiencies (#1) may lead not only to sharing and joint ventures but also consolidations, hence to a different and less locally oriented financial system. Consider the effect on the depositor who used to buy most financial and payments services from his local bank. Now he deals, indirectly, with the joint-venture seller upstream through his local bank or DI. In order to enjoy the new technology, more retail services over time will likely be switched from the old-style format of specialized local financial "boutique" to the upstream joint-venture seller. The local DI then becomes for some electronic banking services the local franchisee, akin to the McDonald's local fast food outlet. There is nothing in the record to suggest this may not work out well. Again, provided seller pricing options or quality at retail are not squelched by system rules or cooperation upstream, there is probably no loss to competition (#3), but potentially great gains from efficiency (#1). But, again, it behooves the consumer user to be aware of exactly what is going on so he can pinpoint prospective difficulties, especially in the transition.

This discussion of shifting costs and benefits for different retail consumers is of course sketchy. Of considerable use to everyone will be a fairly systematic evaluation of who bears the costs, both direct and indirect, and also shares the benefits, under different new EFT pricing systems. In a credit, debit, or POS card evaluation some finer breakdowns still will be valuable: large- and small-ticket spender, card users who pay on time but acquire free float, those that permit their balances to revolve. Pricing effects on the consumer who holds no or limited-use cards also merit attention. Merchants also enjoy variable impact depending upon volume, ticket size, and their ability (or inability) to pass on costs in the form of higher prices. This also affects consumers in differential ways.

For debit card systems there are complex questions of variable short- and long-term cost sharing between banks, merchants, and cardholders (thoughtfully discussed by Felgran 1985). Private marketing strategies consider already these costing questions and will of course do so more fully in the future as further complex sharing questions evolve. Consumers have taken enthusiastically to retail discounting at gas stations designed to promote the no-frills debit card service, and that bodes well for broad-based entry and dissemination of the new technology.

The Public Policy Issues

All in all, therefore, things have gone well for most retail consumers in the EFT world. From the consumer's viewpoint why, then, alter the balance between government and market forces at all? Again, multiple trade-offs present themselves. There are some who argue government should occupy a less important role than now (scenario 1 below); while others feel threatened by greater private-monopoly dominance (scenario 3 below). Let us examine some hypothetical future market stories for their insights into potentially serious questions, ranging the gamut, which eventually can affect retail payments users of the new technology.

Unregulated Competition (Scenario 1)

A system of completely market-determined payments modes is of course the consumer's dream. In this ideal vision of the future technology, the switch or central processing unit (CPU) is analogous to the (jointly run) clearing house of a paper-based system. It is inefficient for every bank to clear paper separately with every other, and the centralization of clearing operations through a central processing unit (CPU) eliminates endless numbers of bilateral paper (or electronic funds) transfers.

In our market ideal, private firms will run switching centers to interface between the numerous networks. The combinations of switching center (CPU) and telecommunications lines will depend on the market's evaluation of relative costs. Sellers of EFT will seek the lowest-cost (i.e., optimal) computer network configuration, in this ideal world we are now sketching. Vendor access is available to the essential telecommunications links and to any "bottleneck" facilities, so that entry is open consistent with market opportunties. Consumers at retail will have the greatest possible number of payments possibilities.

These systems, moreover, will be very flexible and provide a rapid phasing-in for consumer use of any new improvements. The optimal system configuration will change as technology in the telecommunications and data processing industries is altered. The big-city correspondents, or other sellers that can put together the best and most flexible package at lowest cost, may capture a rising market share. It seems realistic to assume that some form of joint-venture solution will often be required. But here the joint venture at wholesale interferes not at all with head-on retail competition between the DIs. We see a retail EFT system and clearing house analogy in terms of clearing joint efficiencies. Bank and other DI members of the system join together at the wholesale level of clearing because the joint venture format is mandated by scale efficiencies; but system rules do not interfere, as between bank members, with the day-to-day competition intrasystem for the retail consumer's business.

The retail consumer has the best of all possible worlds. He enjoys the EFT cost benefits of sharing at one level, because these system savings are passed fully down the line to him; he also enjoys full bank-to-bank competition at retail between even members of the same wholesale (clearing) system. There is little for the Antitrust Division to do in this best of all possible worlds except conduct research activities and provide moral support.

Figure 9-4 shows one possible configuration of such a nonregulated shared system. User banks and thrift institutions of the system are in some cases owners as well (e.g., DIs A . . . n). Or, small DIs (e.g., respondent banks D and E in figure 9-4) can choose to "buy" EFT services indirectly via correspondent/owner banks or nonbanks, depending upon relative quality and cost. These banks then all sell to retail users, consumers, merchants, and so on, as shown in the box on the left.[19] There may develop also private "superswitches," or clearing systems analogous to quasi-central banks. They hold reserves for smaller institutions for which they also maintain clearing arrangements, and make short-term loans, as needed. But the functions of the superswitch are strictly limited to settlement or wholesale clearing requirements and never spill over in any undesired way into retail DI markets. The consumer gleans fully the benefits of EFT with few if any of the risks or competitive or equity costs.

Competitive Solution with Government Safeguards (Scenario 2)

Perhaps a more realistic scenario for the future is one with a more than minimal government presence, both antitrust and Federal Reserve. That is how things have worked out thus far in practice. Some safeguards have been necessary to protect entry and competition, along with full consumer access to the payments mechanism. The Fed monitors some settlement

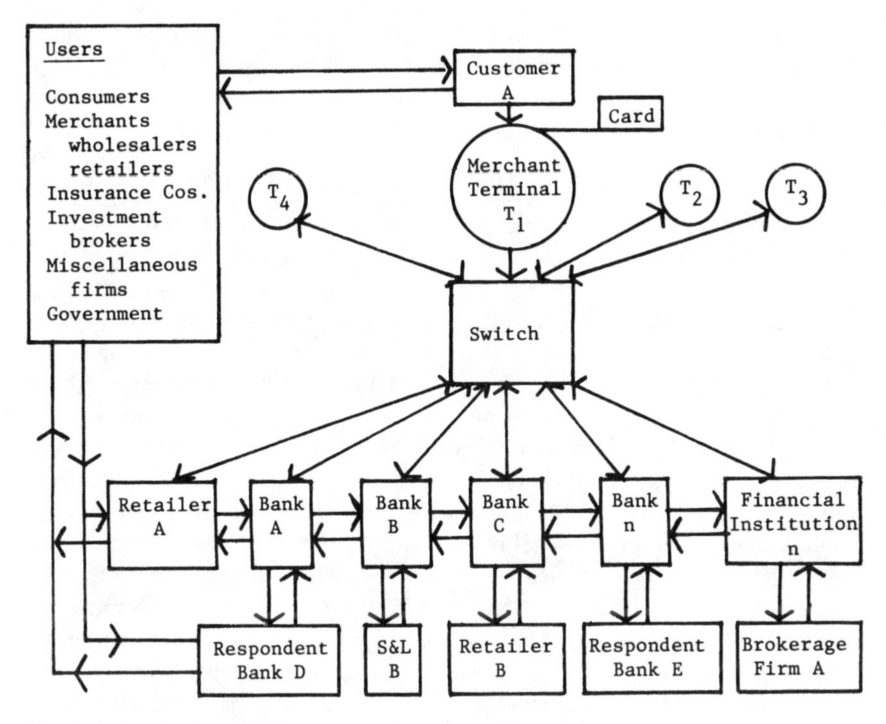

Figure 9-4. A Shared Electronic System Configuration

activities of payments systems and establishes rules to minimize risk, such as setting caps on private interbank daylight overdrafts (Humphrey 1984). The Antitrust Division has assured open access to any essential "bottleneck" facility. The Division has also enjoined any "reverse boycott" that would foreclose the individual correspondent banking route for those DIs that opt to stay out. The agent (respondent) banks, and their consumer users at retail, then, have ready system access. They retain the option of whether to join the local system, and "buy" EFT services directly for use or resale (the first tier of users in figure 9-4) or whether to stay out of the system and buy services indirectly, from principal (or correspondent) system investing banks at a negotiated and competitive price (our second tier of users in figure 9-4).

Recent Assistant Attorney Generals of Antitrust say they remain vigilant about enjoining any explicit joint-venture horizontal pricing rules, at retail (merchant/cardholder) levels (Rule 1984). They will still guard the consumers' option of purchase of EFT services of varying quality and price from other systems, and from nonbanks. This intermediate scenario regards market circumstances as close to optimal, requiring only occasional antitrust monitoring and court intervention to correct interim difficulties.[20]

A Monolithic or Regulated Scenario (Scenario 3)

But consumers may consider also the worst possible case of EFT development, in order to avoid it. Undesired, centralized direction of the payments system is the other extreme, which would restrict consumer options and quality probably no matter who exercised the control. There are numerous variations including private as well as public control.

Control might be exercised privately by oligopoly proprietary or joint-venture systems, rather than the market. In an Antitrust Division horror story, these systems might maintain explicit rules governing franchising, membership, or terms of retail resale by members. Implicit rules could be just as bad, only more difficult to prosecute. The rationale for restricting retail pricing or quality options would be to keep the system from inefficient operations or general instability, but at the possible competitive expense of nonmembers and consumer users. Other rules such as those governing intrasystem advertising might be tacit, but nonetheless restrictive in terms of inhibiting head-on retail competition. In the unacceptable scenario, we see system rules directly (or indirectly) prohibiting bank-to-bank price or service competition for the consumer retail payments dollar, based on some bogus efficiency justification.

In a second variant, the central clearing system is entirely run by the Federal Reserve, or other government agency. This variant takes regulation of the monetary system well beyond that presently employed in the United States, or most other developed countries, which normally provide private clearing alternatives. Even in this model, provided access is open and provided to all on a nondiscriminatory basis, competition can develop at retail as between the various retail sellers of EFT financial services. The impact on private incentives at the wholesale systems level can, however, prove disastrous and thwart technological progress and the attainment by consumers of optimal efficiencies at lowest cost.

The final option, of which there are also a number of gradations, involves direct regulation of banking prices, comparable for example, to regulation of natural gas prices. Sweeping legislative and institutional changes producing inefficiencies and deterioration in quality might occur. More direct regulation might come about if banking structural changes were rapid and financial institutions unable to adapt, bank failures were severe, or private owners developed monopoly power which was used to keep out new entry.[21] A public utility solution, which gets into direct rate regulation, may develop where a "natural monopoly" is shown to exist and certain classes of customers have no other alternative or equitable means of payments system access. If personal-privacy questions fail to be protected, there will also be a clamor for more government control of payments mechanisms. One can argue that risk and privacy are non-economic issues, hence not the proper concern of economists, but in the end the way the future electronic system comes to look may be a direct result of any market failures in these often nebulous areas of concern to all.

Policy Conclusions

In simplest terms, the trade-offs for consumers may be as follows. On the one hand, premature government interference in the development of the new technology can cut off private options and dampen the retail introduction of the most efficient and lowest-cost private EFT configurations. On the other hand, lack of an adequate government antitrust or bank regulatory presence behind the scenes can leave the way open to greater payment risks or private restraints on competition. Payments risks and repeated DI failures in turn can raise the specter of reregulation, or in the extreme, even two parallel consolidated private and government nationalized financial sectors (Havrilesky, in chapter 7).

Thus while competitive abuses have receded, at least in short-run public focus, the risk and DI failure questions have quickly come to the forefront. So also have questions of continued provision of base-line consumer payments services to those unable to afford all banking services including the new EFT. Less easily recognizable are the more subtle forms of payments benefits and shifts implicit in the new technology. The incentive pricing plans commonly designed to build up volume and achieve scale efficiencies are peculiarly difficult to assess from the retail point of view. Pricing issues such as these merit careful systematic analysis for their possible uneven impact upon various segments of the retail user markets.

The role of antitrust, now downgraded, will likely assume new importance if, as seems likely, future joint-venture systems come to supply progressively more of financial services needs. System rules particularly bear close continued scrutiny for their effects on DI buying costs at wholesale as well as consumer retail market prices, which reflect the upstream costs. A pressure for system consolidations also may upset the present positive competitive balance. Here, as elsewhere, for consumer users, trade-offs and their careful evaluation are the name of the game.

Notes

1. A "credit card" permits the holder to access a previously agreed "line of credit," or loan, in order to make a purchase while a "debit card" supplies cash or payments out of the holder's bank account directly. (See Geller, chapter 3 above, pp. 71–73.) Benston (1984) and Arthur D. Little, (1982) present a concise and well-reasoned analysis of benefits from EFT for all the diverse groups including consumers. The Office of Technology Assessment (1984) describes in detail the retail financial services and their benefits (ch. 4, pp. 97–133); and discusses possible transition problems such as privacy and security (ch. 7, pp. 167–187). For consumer rights and related legal consumer issues, see Penney and Baker (1980, 10.1–16.1).

2. These theories based on the work of Tobin and Baumol have been developed in the EFT setting by Simpson and Porter, Goldfeld, and Havrilesky, and are analyzed in greater detail in this volume by Havrilesky (chapter 7) and Tobin (chapter 6).

3. See Weston (1979) for early expression of these consumer concerns. Seminal work on all the consumer issues was also provided by A. Phillips and the Federal Reserve Bank of Boston (Phillips 1974), and by Flannery and Jaffe (1973); Penney and Baker (1980, 15.1–15.7). treat privacy and security questions in detail.

4. Any new technologies that affect wholesale payments transfers will of course affect the quality and price of consumer services. Solomon (1984, 1985) discusses the impact on consumer retail markets of the introduction of new technologies upstream. We focus here, however, on the advent and rise of credit, debit, and ATM cards through which consumers can directly access the new payments mode at retail stores and the DIs. As shown above by Humphrey (chapter 4), the dollar value of these small retail systems payments still is small; value processed totals less than one percent of that for checks. However, for consumers these amounts loom large as a percentage of total and future retail payments to vendors, and will grow markedly when merchant point-of-sale (POS) systems become established reality.

5. The Division's refusal to grant clearance was based primarily on the grounds that sufficient information was not yet available to determine whether the bylaw would prove pro- or anticompetitive. See letter from Thomas E. Kauper to Francis Kirkham and Allan N. Littman, Business Review Clearance for NBI Membership Rules (Oct. 7, 1975). Penney and Baker (1980, at 20.1–20.16) provide comprehensive analysis of specific Department actions and court decisions on these and other EFT matters.

6. See Whitehead (1984). Zimmer (1985) provides detailed information and analysis of ATM use and deployment today. The use of POS still is limited in this country, given the kind of resistance Dr. Henderson describes (chapter 1). New incentives to retail use of ACH systems may build up POS volume, however. See Nilson, Issue 385, 1986.

7. The continued "stickiness" of cardholder loan rates on revolving balances, however, has prompted sentiment to legislate interest rate caps tied to market rates such as the Treasury bill rate. U.S. Senator Alfonse D'Amato is introducing federal legislation to cap credit card interest rates at eight percentage points above the one-year yield on Treasury securities (*Washington Post*, August 28, 1986).

8. An innovative economic analysis of the pricing and sharing issues is presented by Felgran (1984, 1985), who discusses vividly the new competition and its impact. See also Nilson (1985–1986).

9. But given differing credit risk, DI market targeting understandably is somewhat selective. Potential as well as present income-earning capability of credit card users is important. For example, American Express and the bank credit cards solicit graduating seniors of well-known colleges, while Mellon Bank seeks out the business of still-younger college students reportedly on the basis of brokerage account lists and subject to parental credit guarantees (Nilson, Issue 368, 1985).

10. Triangle a in figure 9-3 represents short-run deadweight loss at equilibrium B. Area b is rent transfer from subsidizing banks (or others) to users; rectangle c is bank revenue. This dynamic strategy of short-run subsidy seeks to trade off short-run a and b losses to eliminate the higher unit costs at outputs less than optimal Q^*.

An output Q^* at the higher price P^* realizes full-scale economies and normal profit margins given the existing long-run technology. Output Q^* achieves lowest average cost given available technology; at that point, average costs = marginal costs. In a static pricing model, private entry can occur at price P^*, which fully covers production costs including a reasonable rate of return.

11. See, for example, the panel at the Federal Reserve Bank of Chicago's Bank Conference on Structure and Competition (Reichert *et. al.* 1981), where vendors, the Fed, and consumer spokesmen presented different points of view on this issue.

12. Berger (1985) presents careful retail cost estimates and comparisons between EFT and paper systems not elsewhere available.

13. In an innovative mathematical model, Schmallansee (1981) suggests that these equity issues may properly become more directly integrated into antitrust welfare analysis of price discrimination.

14. The joint-venture and sharing issues were treated first by the National Commission for Electronic Funds Transfer (1977). Felgran (1984, 1985) looks carefully at the economic competitive questions some years later. Kwoka (1985) analyzes the joint-venture issues and trade-offs in an innovative mathematical model.

15. Berger (1985) suggests that banks are subsidizing the consumer often through providing ATM services below cost. For comprehensive analysis of pricing and cost issues, see Humphrey (1984) and Berger and Humphrey (1986). In early 1986 banks are, however, beginning to charge a per item fee for ATM use, which can eliminate the consumer surplus and original subsidy, or loss-leader ATM pricing technique.

16. See chapter 1 (Henderson). The four major credit card systems met with the American Bankers Association (ABA) to work on technical specifications, encryption, and other standards necessary to assure universal access and systems compatibility. But the excluded regional systems have already met, too, to determine standards on their own (Nilson, Issue 373, 1985).

17. For legal analysis of special antitrust problems of joint ventures along with the series of factural balancing tests, see Penney and Baker (1980, 18.1–18.29).

18. The divergent issues are discussed from vendor, central banker, and consumer perspectives by Reichert and the Federal Reserve Bank of Chicago Panel (1981). The trade-offs also look different depending upon whether equity (or income distribution) considerations are included in the model. Substantive differences between the modern Chicago School of antitrust analysis and its theoretical foundations, in this regard, are cogently discussed by Rhoades (1985) and Schmallansee (1981).

19. See the seminal work of Flannery and Jaffee (1973) and Phillips (1974 and 1979).

20. The Acting Assistant Attorney General Charles Rule discusses (1984) the Antitrust Division's present approach to joint ventures. The lucid analysis of Warren-Boulton (McGrath and Warren-Boulton 1985) explains the economist's role.

21. Phillips (1979 and 1974) and Stevens (1976) first presented a story of the possible role of hypothetical private mini central banks and described the potential risks and benefits posed for money and the payments system.

References

Arthur D. Little, Inc. 1982. *Report on the Payments System*. Washinton, D.C.: Association of Reserve City Bankers.

Benston, George J. 1984. "Off-Bank" Retail Payments Systems: The Economic Issues. Federal Reserve Bank of Atlanta. *Economic Review* 69(July/August): 6–12.

Berger, Allen N. 1985. Electronic Payments Technology—Can Banks Profit from It? Federal Reserve Board of Governors, October 2.

Berger, Allen N., and D.B. Humphrey. 1986. The Role of Interstate Banking in the Diffusion of Electronic Payments Technology. In C. Lawrence and R. Shay (eds.), *Technological Innovation, Regulation, and the Monetary Economy*. Cambridge, MA: Ballinger.

Blecher, Maxwell M., and Earl E. Pollack. 1985. The "New Antitrust":Implications for the Practitioner. *Antitrust Law Journal* 54:43–55.

Federal Reserve Bank of Atlanta. 1984. The Revolution in Retail Payments. *Economic Review* 69(July/August):4–55.

Felgran, Steven D. 1984. Shared ATM Networks: Market Structure and Public Policy. *New England Economc Review* (January/February).

Felgran, Steven D. 1985. From ATM to POS Networks: Branching, Access, and Pricing. *New England Economic Review* (May/June).

Flannery Mark J., and Dwight M. Jaffee. 1973. *The Economic Implications of an Electronic Monetary Transfer System*. Lexington, MA: Lexington Books.

Humphrey, David B. 1984. *The U.S. Payments System: Costs, Pricing, Competition and Risk*. Salomon Brothers Center for the Study of Financial Institutions Monograph 1984–1/2, New York: New York University.

Kwoka, J. 1985. *Market Power from Horizontal Mergers and Joint Ventures*. Unpublished Manuscript, November.

McGrath, J.P., and F.R. Warren-Boulton. 1985. Report from Official Washington *Antitrust Law Journal*. 54:129–152, 109–115.

National Commission on Electronic Funds Transfers. 1977. *EFT in the United States Final Report*. Washington, D.C.: GPO, October.

Nilson, H. Spencer. *The Nilson Report*. Feb. 1985–Aug. 1986, issues 350–385.

Office of Technology Assessment. 1984. *Effects of Information Technology on Financial Service Systems*. Washington, D.C.: U.S. Congress, OTA-CIT-202, September.

Penney, N., and D. Baker. 1980. *The Law of Electronic Fund Transfer Systems*. Boston: Gorham Lamont Publishing.

Phillips, Almarin. 1974. Discussion: *The Economics of a National Electronic Funds*

Transfer System. Federal Reserve Bank of Boston, Conference Series #13.

Phillips, Almarin. 1979. Implications of the New Payments Technology for Monetary Policy. In *Issues in Financial Regulation*. F.R. Edwards (ed.), New York: McGraw-Hill, 269–286.

Reichert, Alan, et al. 1981. Workshop on New Trends in Pricing and Product Development of Correspondent Financial Services. *Proceedings of a Conference on Bank Structure and Competition*. Chicago: Federal Reserve Bank of Chicago, 221–258.

Rhoades, Stephen A. 1985. Interstate Banking and Product Line Expansion. *Loyola Law Review* 18, 1115.

Rule, Charles F. 1984. Antitrust Analysis of Joint Ventures in the Banking Industry: Evaluating Shared ATMs. Remarks before the Federal Bar Association, Washington, D.C., May.

Schmallansee, Richard. 1981. Output and Welfare Implications of Monopolistic Third Degree Price Discrimination. *American Economic Review* 71.

Solomon, Elinor H. 1984. Bank Product Deregulation: Some Antitrust Tradeoffs. *Economic Review*. Federal Reserve Bank of Atlanta 69(May):22–27.

Solomon, Elinor H. 1985. The Dynamics of Banking Antitrust: The New Technology, the Product Realignment. *The Antitrust Bulletin* 30(Fall):537–581.

Solomon, Elinor, H. 1985. EFT and Money Supply. *The Bankers Magazine* 168(July–August):77–81.

Stevens, E.J. 1976. The Impact of EFT on the Sources and Uses of Member Bank Reserves. Report Prepared for the National Commission on Electronic Fund Transfers, Washington, D.C., November.

U.S. Department of Justice, 1984. 1984 Merger Guidelines. 1, 46 *Antitrust & Trade Reg. Rep.* (BNA) No. 1169, special supp. June 14.

Walker, David A. 1978. Economies of Scale in Electronic Funds Transfer Systems. *Journal of Banking and Finance* 2(June):65–78.

Walker, David A. 1980. Electronic Funds Transfer Cost Models and Pricing Strategies. *Journal of Economics and Business*. 33(Fall):61–65.

Westin, Alan F. 1979. Privacy Aspects in EFT Systems. *Issues in Financial Regulation*. In F.R. Edwards (ed.), New York: McGraw-Hill, 300–314.

Whitehead, David, 1984. Firms Involved in ATM, POS, and Home Banking: A Survey. Federal Reserve Bank of Atlanta, *Economic Review* 69(July/August): 4–5, 13–19.

Zimmer, Linda F. 1985. ATMs 1984. *The Magazine of Bank Administration* (May):20–22.

Index